THE
INDIAN WARS

BATTLES, BLOODSHED, AND THE FIGHT FOR FREEDOM
ON THE AMERICAN FRONTIER

ANTON TREUER

NATIONAL GEOGRAPHIC

WASHINGTON, D.C.

CONTENTS

112

156

222

FIGHTING OUT OF THE CAULDRON:
WARS FOR SURVIVAL

For my son, Robert Treuer, a living embodiment of tribal resilience.
It is in making the peace rather than winning the war that real men are made.

PREVIOUS PAGES: The Indian wars called upon all the military skills tribes could muster:
sophisticated communication systems (as seen in the smoke signal shown in the painting, inside cover);
incredible horsemanship (like the Comanche, painting on title page); and military alliances
(like those developed by Curley, a Crow scout, pictured across from Contents page).

INDIAN SLAVES De Soto was quick to enslave war captives for labor,
food production, and the sexual gratification of his troops.

invisible pathogen proved the most deadly part of the de Soto expedition, and it killed more people than every military campaign against Indians since then.

WATER BURIAL De Soto was secretly buried at night in the Mississippi River in 1542, as the surviving Spanish forces desperately tried to avoid any signal of their declining strength.

BATTLE OF MABILA

De Soto brought his entourage deep into present-day Alabama and encountered more large and powerful Muskogean villages. In Alabama, tribal diplomacy, which had been effective in some large Coosa towns, eventually failed. When the Spanish tried to take what the tribes would not give away, a major battle broke out in the fortified Indian town at Mabila.

The chiefs tried to parley with Spanish officers, but de Soto attacked. Chief Tuskaloosa led the tribal defense. The Indians knew they were fighting for their lives. Caught by surprise and unarmed, some even grabbed Spanish swords and lances by the blade. Women fought by the side of male warriors.

Spanish soldiers eventually breached the outer wall of the village with axes; mounted troops drove the people into their houses, where they could avoid being trampled or lanced. Then the Spanish lit the buildings on fire. The warriors were numerous and put up a spirited defense, but between the fires, the metal weapons, and the horses, they suffered tremendous casualties and eventually were overcome.

The battle lasted nine hours. Eighty-two Spanish soldiers and officers were killed. Another 250 were wounded, making the casualty rate nearly 100 percent in de Soto's force. Over a quarter of his horses died. But the Indians fared far worse. Estimates varied from 2,000 to 11,000 Indians killed, making it one of the bloodiest Indian battles ever fought in North America. After the killing, one Indian hung himself by his own bowstring rather than be left as the sole survivor from his family.

and new British settlements at Henricus and Wolstenholme Towne were annihilated. Then the British mounted a fearsome counterattack. For the next 10 years, British settlers sustained a brutal campaign against the Powhatan, continually raiding smaller Indian villages, stealing corn, burning buildings, and killing the inhabitants. Powhatan warriors had to be full-time providers and also full-time warriors. That stressed the tribal economy, social, and political structure in the midst of large-scale loss of life. The British continued to receive reinforcements and supplies from England. They strengthened defenses, palisaded the towns, built a six-mile protective wall, and pressed the attack. The Powhatan defenses imploded. Greatly debilitated, they agreed to a peace in 1632. The British knew they could no longer count on exploiting Indians for all their food supplies and labor needs, and moved to develop a new labor strategy for the colonial economy. In 1619, Portuguese slavers brought the first 50 African slaves to America and sold them to the British at James Fort. The addition of African slaves helped prompt a renaming of the settlement as James Towne. Slavery was formalized in America in 1640, just eight years after the 1632 Powhatan peace agreement. Most of the new slaves brought to Virginia initially worked the English tobacco plantations throughout the former Powhatan homeland.

JAMES TOWNE Jamestown, founded as James Fort in 1607, was the first permanent British settlement in North America and the focal point of the Anglo-Powhatan Wars in the early 1600s.

DEATH THROES OF THE POWHATAN

In 1644, Opechancanough was very advanced in years. He could see British towns encroaching on the Powhatan tribes all around him. The British demanded tribute every year, and the tribes had to pay to avoid what would have been crushing military attacks. Opechancanough was certain that between British diseases and guns, his people would be exterminated. The only hope was to inflict a blow on the invaders potent enough to encourage them to leave. He rallied the tribes in one last effort to punish the British. His coalition was impressive and caught the British unaware. The attack was initially effective, killing 500 British settlers. The British, however, were now far more numerous than in 1622, so the effect was less pronounced. The British fought back, intent on protecting the communities and punishing the Indians. By 1646, the Powhatan were on the defensive. Their villages were looted and burned. Casualty rates were high. Opechancanough was captured and shot in the back while in captivity. He was 92 years old. With their survival at stake, the Powhatan signed treaties confining their tribes to reservations and paying annual tribute to the British. The Pamunkey and Mattaponi communities survived the British and American periods and live on today, although many of the other Powhatan tribes were annihilated or sought refuge and merged with other tribal groups. ∎

POCAHONTAS

Pocahontas remains a legend in native and nonnative circles today, but her story is tragically misunderstood. She lived through unbelievable adversity and disempowerment, rather than unrequited love and peaceful cultural exchange. Immediately after the establishment of Jamestown, Opechancanough, half brother to the principal Powhatan chief, Wahunsunacawh, captured Captain John Smith. Pocahontas, Wahunsunacawh's daughter, helped Smith escape in an effort to avoid conflict between her tribe and the English. She had no romantic involvement with Smith. Smith wrote about his captivity in 1608, 1612, and 1624, embellishing the story with each telling, eventually giving the impression that he was involved with Pocahontas. In 1614, the English captured Pocahontas and held her for ransom. Wahunsunacawh agreed to peace in exchange for the return of his daughter, but the English did not honor their bargain. Pocahontas, still just a teenager, was baptized and married to English planter John Rolfe (not John Smith), even though she was promised to and may have already married a Powhatan man. She was never allowed to exercise her own free will, and felt deeply conflicted over her obligations to her tribe, family, and Powhatan husband on the one hand, and a sense of obligation to her English husband on the other. She accompanied Rolfe to England, where her beauty made her a great curiosity, but she died before she could return home. Her son, Thomas Rolfe, survived and returned to Virginia, and many Virginians today trace their lineage to him.

PEQUOT WAR
GENOCIDE IN NEW ENGLAND

Trouble was brewing in New England in 1634. The Pequot, who were allied with the Niantic and in occasional intense conflict with the Mohegan and Narragansett, were in a diplomatic standoff with English colonists. They had accommodated white settlers and embraced trade with the Dutch and later the English. But the balance of power between enemy tribes and the new English arrivals was tenuous and strained. Dutch traders captured a Pequot chief named Tatobem and held him for ransom, but murdered him after the tribe paid the ransom. Pequot warriors were furious, but not sure who to hold responsible. In retaliation, they attacked a small group of British colonists, killing several. Then, in a separate incident, John Stone, a British smuggler, was killed. The primary Pequot chief, Sassacus, reached out to protect the eroding peace and offered compensation to aggrieved parties. The offer seemed sufficient to make and keep peace until another British settler, John Oldham, was killed in 1636. The Pequot denied any hand in Oldham's death, but the English held them responsible.

ENDECOTT ATTACKS

John Endecott gathered a militia and brought a force of 70 to attack Indian villages at Block Island. They made an amphibious assault and quickly descended on two villages. These were Niantic villages, rather than Pequot. Endecott then left the island and moved inland, attacking a Pequot village. The primary Pequot chief was Sassacus, an influential man who was proud almost to a fault. He rallied Pequot warriors and some Niantic allies to besiege Endecott's force at Fort Saybrook in the spring of 1637. Then he started raiding English settlements throughout modern-day Connecticut. The Pequot inflicted few casualties, but succeeded in inflaming the entire English settler population.

White settlers rallied a local militia at Hartford under the leadership of Captain John Mason. Mason wisely reached out to the Mohegan and Narragansett to ally with him. Sensing

MYSTIC MASSACRE Hundreds of Pequot were killed and captured in 1637, when colonial forces converged on the Pequot village at Mystic River while most warriors were gone. It was the seminal battle in the Pequot War.

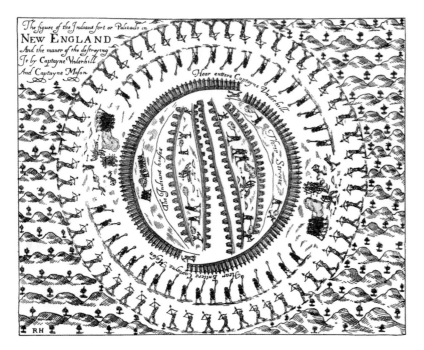

OUTMATCHED Captain John Mason recruited Mohegan and Narragansett warriors, pictured here with colonial militia, to help attack the Pequot.

an opportunity, the tribes turned out in droves. Mason had 400 militia and an untold number of Indian allies when he reached the primary Pequot village on the Mystic River. Sassacus was raiding Hartford with 150 warriors when Mason attacked. The village was poorly defended. With overwhelming numbers, Mason and his allies rained down musket fire on the villagers, who were primarily women, children, and elders. The palisade was breached and the buildings set afire. The English set upon the terrified Pequot with zeal, causing their Narragansett allies to recoil at their joy in killing children. Around 700 Indians were killed. A handful were taken as prisoners, and another small number survived. Mason said that God "laughed his Enemies and the Enemies of his People to scorn making [the Pequot] as a fiery Oven . . . Thus did the Lord judge among the Heathen, filling [Mystic] with dead Bodies."

THE GREAT SWAMP FIGHT

Pequot survivors from Mystic and surrounding communities fled, and Sassacus tried to regroup his people, reaching out to allies and unrelated groups for refuge as they abandoned their villages and ran for their lives. The tribes at Long Island refused to take them in. Some joined the Shawnee and other groups as the tribal population scattered. John Mason led 160 soldiers in a punitive expedition with 60 Mohegan scouts. He caught Sassacus near Fairfield, Connecticut, pinning the

Pequot against a vast swamp in what was later called the Great Swamp Fight. Sassacus refused to surrender. About 80 Pequot escaped with him through the swamp, but another nearly 200 were captured. Mason hunted down as many more Pequot as he could, taking another 200 as captives and selling them into slavery in Bermuda and the West Indies or distributing them among their Indian enemies. The Mohegan and Narragansett, who had no tradition of slavery, molded their customs to the European tradition and took the Pequot slaves as property.

At its height, the Pequot had a population of around 16,000. They were reduced to around 500 during the Pequot War, and those survivors were dispersed as slaves or refugees among other tribes. The Pequot ceased to exist as an independent political and cultural group. It was genocide. At the Treaty of Hartford in 1638, the Mohegan and Narragansett divided Pequot lands and slaves between them. The Mohegan and Narragansett victory was short-lived, as they would not keep the land for long. The English soon turned on their Indian allies from the Pequot War, too, and the cycle of division and conquest continued. ■

INDIAN SLAVE TRADE

Indian tribes frequently took war captives, sometimes adopting them into tribes as equals. The extent to which Europeans used slaves as an oppressed labor force was new to most tribes, but some quickly adopted the European practice. The Cherokee, for instance, integrated slavery wholesale. Others, such as the Mohegan, kept Pequot war captives as part of a subjugation plan for former enemies.

Even more commonly, many tribes, especially on the Atlantic coast and Southeast, started to raid their neighbors and sell captives to their European allies. The Spanish, French, and British all embraced Indian slavery. They just had no idea that Indians would be so susceptible to European diseases. To maintain numbers, they continued slave raiding in Indian communities or asked native allies to do so. At the time of the U.S. Civil War, 15 percent of America's slaves were still Native American. The number was even higher in the Spanish Empire, including in California and the American Southwest.

Europeans embraced slavery not just because Indians were an available supply of labor, cheaper to access than African slaves, even if they did not live as long. They did so also to remove native enemies as obstacles in their colonial ambitions. In short, slavery was both a labor plan and a military tactic.

DECLARATION OF WAR The Pequot delivered red arrows to colonists at the
outbreak of the war, declaring hostilities rather than making a surprise attack.

NEW AMSTERDAM The Dutch founded New York City as New Amsterdam,
shown at the time of settlement. Manhattan had been home to natives for 10,000 years.

PEACH TREE WAR
SUSQUEHANNOCK VICTORY ON THE HUDSON

In the 1600s, the Dutch and British Empires vied for trade territory and colonies in present-day New York. Even where Indians had ceded no land, Europeans laid competing claims to ownership of the land, its resources, and the human beings who lived there. The Dutch had a friendly relationship with the powerful Iroquois Confederacy, trading with them and selling them guns, which they used to raid the neighboring Susquehannocks. The Dutch also directly fought the Susquehannock, Raritan, and Wappinger peoples. In 1643, Governor Willem Kieft flexed Dutch muscle with the Indians and enforced heavy taxes, viewed as glorified tribute, on the Raritans, thus further increasing tribal resentment of the Dutch. Kieft then accused the Raritans of killing Dutch pigs and used that as a pretext for a major military campaign. The Raritans denied the charge but there was no way to avoid the Dutch militia's attack. The Dutch even secured their British trade rivals as allies in subjugating the Indians. The British and Dutch were at odds over trade and colonial rights but united in wanting to push the Indians away from the coast to open land for more colonies.

As the conflict escalated, the Dutch made a point of exercising incredible brutality to shock the tribes into capitulating. At one point, Dutch troops decapitated Raritans and used their heads in a ball game. Dutch settler David de Vries reported, "Infants were torn from their mothers' breasts, and hacked to pieces in the presence of their parents, and pieces thrown into the fire and in the water, and other sucklings, being bound to small boards, were cut, stuck, and pierced, and miserably massacred in a manner to move a heart of stone." The tribes had to defend themselves.

Thousands of Indians from several coast tribes were killed during the Kieft's War. The Dutch reported killing 500 Indians in Long Island and 700 in Stamford. The Dutch also killed 1,600 Wappinger and 1,000 Metoacs. Long Island's Native

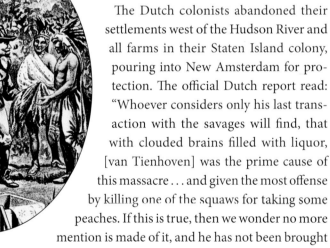

DUTCH TRADE Natives welcomed Dutch traders to the Hudson River Valley. The Susquehannock had no patience with Dutch subjugation, though, and their 1655 conflict permanently weakened the Dutch Empire in America.

American population, as high as 10,000 in the year 1600, was reduced to 500 by 1659. Dutch colonies swelled from 2,000 to 10,000 during the same time. The surviving tribes had to accommodate the Dutch to avoid conflict in the face of rapid white settlement and new disease pandemics in Indian country.

KILLING FOR PEACHES
In 1655, Dutch settler Cornelis van Tienhoven killed a Wappinger woman for stealing a peach. Peter Stuyvesant, who had replaced Kieft as governor, was away with most of the Dutch garrison from New Amsterdam, dealing with a potential conflict with a Swedish settlement nearby when the Indians attacked Hoboken, Pavonia, and Staten Island. More than 600 Susquehannock and allied Indian warriors landed in New Amsterdam and attacked farms in Manhattan. They took 150 hostages, and killed more than 100 Dutch settlers.

The Dutch colonists abandoned their settlements west of the Hudson River and all farms in their Staten Island colony, pouring into New Amsterdam for protection. The official Dutch report read: "Whoever considers only his last transaction with the savages will find, that with clouded brains filled with liquor, [van Tienhoven] was the prime cause of this massacre . . . and given the most offense by killing one of the squaws for taking some peaches. If this is true, then we wonder no more mention is made of it, and he has not been brought to justice as a murderer." In spite of that, van Tienhoven was never tried for killing the Wappinger woman. The conflict dealt the Dutch a heavy blow; they realized that their guns, trade position, and forts were not sufficient to allow them to brutalize the tribes with impunity. The Susquehannock ransomed their hostages for peace and agreed to sell settlement rights to the Dutch for the west Hudson River settlements, although Staten Island was never reopened for Dutch settlement. ∎

The Indian Fort SASQUESAHANOK

BACON'S REBELLION
VIRGINIA FRONTIER IN FLAMES

In 1676, Nathaniel Bacon led English colonists in Virginia in a major revolt against British authority. In many ways his rebellion foreshadowed the issues burning in settler minds when the American Revolutionary War erupted a century later. But the issues of class, race, and Indian policy converged in Bacon's time to fan the flames of hatred with special, devastating effect.

Bacon was a white Virginia frontier farmer. He was a hard worker, a heavy drinker, and a devout Indian hater. Bacon believed that the colonial government in Jamestown, led by Governor William Berkeley, was out of touch

SUSQUEHANNOCK INDIAN FORT
The Susquehannock often built palisades and earthworks around their villages for defense. Nathaniel Bacon overwhelmed their defenses with a large militia and powerful Indian allies.

with frontier settler needs. He wanted lower taxes and more armies. The Susquehannock still occupied a vast territory west of the English farms and he felt that the local militia should forcibly take their land and subjugate them to enable further English expansion. Many settlers wanted more Indian land and wished to see the local tribesmen killed off or driven out. They often squatted on Indian land, and when the Indians retaliated or even scared white settlers, altercations broke out. Bacon and other settlers were quick to use such moments to campaign for military action against the tribes.

Berkeley was resistant to Bacon's pleas for

a tougher Indian policy and an active militia to push the Susquehannock out. Bacon drafted a declaration, which among other things chastised the Virginia government, "For having protected, favored, and emboldened the Indians against his Majesty's loyal subjects, never contriving, requiring, or appointing any due or proper means of satisfaction for their many invasions, robberies, and murders committed upon us." After meeting fellow frontiersmen over a fifth of brandy, he was elected leader of a new movement, and took matters into his own hands.

BLOODLETTING IN VIRGINIA

Bacon disliked Indians of all kinds, but the Susquehannock most of all. To bring about a more dramatic result, he reached out to the Occaneechi tribe for alliance. Then he marched his English followers and Indian allies on the nearest Susquehannock village. They stormed the palisades, routed the inhabitants, and destroyed the village. Bacon brought a posse of 500 English frontiersmen to Jamestown to demand a formal commission to raise a militia and destroy the Susquehannock. Berkeley refused, citing the need for peace to trade, farm, and protect white civilians. Berkeley even bared his chest and dared Bacon to shoot him. Bacon then threatened other local officials until he received a commission.

While Bacon was in Jamestown getting his commission, the Indians killed eight settlers. Bacon raised a militia of 1,000 to suppress the tribes. They set out to attack the Indians, but had to deal with Berkeley first. He labeled Bacon a rebel and sent word for a British royal troop deployment to put down the rebellion. Bacon then marched his militia on Jamestown. Bacon burned most of Jamestown to the ground, including Berkeley's personal residence and several government buildings. Berkeley retreated, and Bacon's force engaged British regulars and Berkeley's militia in a series of battles. British merchant ships and royal forces were used to suppress the rebellion. Berkeley launched a series of amphibious assaults against Bacon's strongholds.

> "WE MUST DEFEND OURSELVES AGAINST ALL INDIANS, FOR THEY WERE OUR ENEMIES."
>
> NATHANIEL BACON

Bacon died of dysentery in late 1676, and many of his militiamen went home, although much of his force fought on. Thomas Grantham, the admiral who led the British maritime force, promised pardons for rebels and disarmed a major rebel garrison. Eventually Berkeley and Grantham overcame the rebels.

Berkeley's retribution came fast and hard. He tried and hanged 20 rebels. Afterward, Charles II removed him from the governorship and recalled him to England. The king said of Berkeley, "That old fool has put to death more people in that naked country than I did here for the murder of my father." British elites were shaken by the rebellion. To preserve order and appease frontier settlers, they passed stronger property requirements to vote, lowered taxes, and established a far more aggressive Indian policy. Through the course of the rebellion, many white and black indentured servants and freed slaves joined Bacon. The thought of poor folk rising up against elites was especially scary for the British establishment. They countered the threat with appeasement of white frontiersmen, but also with much stronger racial rules for slavery. The Virginia Slaves Codes of 1705 clearly segregated black slaves from white indentured servants and reduced the chances that the two groups would ever cooperate in resistance to the government again. ■

CALL FOR KILLING Nathaniel Bacon presented a declaration to the Virginia council in 1676 in an attempt to gain political support for a genocidal war.

KING PHILIP'S WAR

NEW ENGLAND TORN APART

The British who settled at Plymouth, Massachusetts, in 1620, a group of religious dissenters known as the Pilgrims, had cordial relationships with the native Wampanoag people, led by Massasoit. For four decades, Massasoit's influence over his Pilgrim neighbors and his own people was so strong that peace was never a quest or a question, but simply the culture of the region. The peaceful relationship deteriorated after Massasoit died in 1661. Pilgrim elders who knew they owed the survival of their colony to Wampanoag friendship had largely died off, and younger Pilgrims and new arrivals disdained their Indian neighbors. They recruited Wampanoag to work as laborers and servants but not as equals. They established praying towns, in a coercive effort to convert all the Wampanoag to Christianity. The peace deteriorated further in the 1670s, as the colonists enforced the Puritan code of conduct on the neighboring Wampanoag. People who entered non-Christian marriages or hunted on the Sabbath were sometimes put to death.

Massasoit's son Wamsutta (Alexander) was named chief after Massasoit's death. Wamsutta died immediately after his first parley with the English as chief, during which he drank a potion, and some Wampanoag suspected he had been poisoned. The colonists outlawed direct commerce with the Wampanoag, and Wamsutta had just sold a piece of property. His death was likely a homicide, and certainly was seen that way by many Wampanoag. Wamsutta's brother Metacom (Philip) became chief in 1662 at age 24. King Philip, as the colonists called him, maintained the peace for another 13

BATTLE OF BLOODY BROOK In 1675, Nipmuck Indians ambushed a British supply train at Bloody Brook, killing 40 militiamen and 17 teamsters. Five percent of New England's white population died in King Philip's War.

DEATH OF KING PHILIP King Philip's death signaled the end of the conflict, but animosities continued for generations.

My father was then sachem. He relieved their distresses in the most kind and hospitable manner. He gave them land to plant and build upon . . . They flourished and increased . . . By various means they got possessed of a great part of his territory. But he still remained their friend till he died. My elder brother became sachem. They pretended to suspect him of evil designs against them. He was seized and confined and thereby thrown into illness and died. Soon after I became sachem, they disarmed all my people . . . Their lands were taken . . . But a small part of the dominion of my ancestors remains. I am determined not to live until I have no country."

The relationship disintegrated even further in 1675, when the English hanged three Wampanoag men for a murder they did not commit. The Wampanoag now felt that their religion, lifeways, and very lives were under assault. King Philip had had enough. He rallied the Wampanoag for a forceful response. There were fewer than 1,000 Wampanoag in the main cluster of villages. King Philip reached out to other tribes and a confederation of 10,000 Indians from tribes that once battled each other offered the English formidable resistance. King Philip's War was on.

BATTLE FOR NEW ENGLAND

King Philip planned a brilliant series of attacks on British towns and fortifications. Of the 90 English settlements in New England, his alliance destroyed 12 English towns and burned parts of 40 more, including Swansea, Freetown, Middleborough, Dartmouth, Mendon, Brookfield, Lancaster, Deerfield, Hadley, and Northfield. At both Swansea and Brookfield, Nipmuck and other tribal forces laid siege to the towns. Colonial militias were in shock and unable to effectively counter

years, but conditions never improved. In 1671, the colonists insisted that King Philip sign a treaty that required the Wampanoag to surrender their guns. He signed to keep the peace, but felt humiliated and distrustful afterward.

The chief said, "The English who came first to this country were but a handful of people, forlorn, poor and distressed.

THANKSGIVING

In 1614, Spanish slave raiders captured a Patuxet Indian named Tisquantum, often known as Squanto today. Squanto spent five years as a slave in Spain, but was eventually freed and made his way to England, and then back to America. In 1619, he returned to his ancestral village to find it completely depopulated from outbreaks of smallpox and other diseases. Squanto was the last surviving member of his village. He sought refuge with the neighboring Wampanoag, who were also suffering from debilitating diseases brought by

Europeans. To the surprise of Squanto and his Wampanoag hosts, English colonists settled at Squanto's home village site in late 1620. By spring, half the English had starved to death.

Squanto traveled with the Wampanoag chief Massasoit to the struggling Plymouth colony to meet the Pilgrims. The chief offered a treaty of mutual protection and friendship. The Pilgrims gladly accepted, and Squanto stayed at Plymouth, teaching them how to farm in the tribal tradition by rotating crops to maintain soil fertility and raising corn,

beans, and squash in the same plots to maintain nitrate levels without reducing yields. The first clear evidence of a tribal–white harvest celebration appears after the Pequot War in 1637, rather than as part of the Wampanoag efforts to teach Puritans to survive. New England natives did have a tradition of giving thanks and they shared it with the English. That much of the Thanksgiving lore is true, although goodwill shattered with the outbreak of King Philip's War in 1675.

BATTLE OF BROOKFIELD Nipmuck warriors laid siege to Brookfield and Swansea at the height of King Philip's War. Terrified residents took refuge in blockhouses as the Indians burned many of the buildings.

the Indian attacks for several months. At Bloody Brook, the Nipmuck ambushed a well-guarded supply train loaded with the fall harvest from Deerfield and Hadley. They killed 40 Massachusetts militiamen and another 17 teamsters. The Indian alliance then turned to Springfield, Massachusetts, and routed the townsfolk. They took refuge in a nearby blockhouse, and the Indians burned every building in town to the ground.

In December 1675, the Wampanoag alliance suffered its first major defeat in the war at the Great Swamp Massacre. More than 1,000 colonial militiamen converged on a large camp of Narragansett. Many families escaped into the swamp, but hundreds were trapped in bark lodges, with no hope for escape. The colonists set the lodges on fire, burning the inhabitants alive, killing more than 300. By the summer of 1676, the tide of battle had turned against the Indians. The Wampanoag could not plant their spring crop, and food supplies were low. They fought on the run, with their families moving with them

to avoid another massacre like the one at Great Swamp. Indian casualties climbed rapidly. The colonists eventually caught King Philip's wife and nine-year-old son, selling them into slavery in Bermuda. Philip returned to his ancestral village and waited for the inevitable attack. When it came, he stood up until shot down by an Indian mercenary. The war was over. Five percent of the region's white population died in the conflict, as did 40 percent of the Indian population. The Wampanoag were reduced to only 400. King Philip was decapitated, drawn, and quartered, and his head was displayed on a pike in Plymouth for more than 20 years.

There were now close to 80,000 English colonists in New England. They rebuilt and fortified their towns. The British imposed heavy taxes to pay for military protection and continued punitive raids and campaigns against tribes from New York to Maine, including many that were never involved in King Philip's War. All groups touched by the conflict were forever changed. ∎

SECOND PUEBLO ENCOUNTERS
THE REVOLT OF 1680

Spanish conquistadors unwittingly united the Pueblos and Hopi against a common foe and inspired one of the most peaceful tribes in America to rise up against naked Spanish aggression. The Pueblo Revolt of 1680 killed a fifth of the Spanish population in the Southwest and drove the rest (more than 2,000) through Texas to Mexico. It took the Spanish 12 years to reassert a presence in Pueblo country.

The Pueblos knew the Spanish well. Juan de Oñate led the first Spanish colonization of the region in 1598. Oñate stated the Spanish rationale for colonization: "Another reason is the need for correcting and punishing the sins against nature and against humanity which exist among these bestial nations and which it behooves my King and Prince as a most powerful lord to correct and repress . . . Another reason is the great number of children born among these infidel people who neither recognize nor obey their true God and Father."

FROM FARMERS TO WARRIORS

The Pueblo population was more than 40,000 strong when Oñate arrived, although more than 15,000 died from European diseases to which the Pueblos had no natural immunity. The Spanish came to convert and sometimes enslave the native population, harvest resources, and settle. At Acoma, the Pueblos resisted, but after hundreds were killed, hundreds more enslaved, and many had their feet amputated, the resistance collapsed. Fighting seemed futile, so the people accommodated and survived. But even the Pueblos had limits.

By 1680, the Pueblos had made many accommodations, developed syncretic ceremonies, and carried on as much of

PUEBLOS RISING The Pueblo Revolt in 1680 killed or evicted all the Spanish from Hopi, Zuni, and Pueblo lands. It took 12 years for the Spanish to return. The revolt forever changed their empire in the Southwest.

their ancient lifeway as possible. The Spanish brought horses, sheep, chickens, peaches, watermelon, wheat, and metal plows, which the Pueblos incorporated into their economy. But the Spanish also suppressed Pueblo religion, and that was a constant source of resentment. Catholic priests confiscated masks, prayer sticks, and effigies, directly suppressing treasured ceremonies. Alonso de Posada outlawed kachina dances by the 1650s. More moderate Spanish rulers such as Nicolas de Aguilar were charged with heresy and subjected to a full Catholic inquisition when they advocated restraint. The Spanish accused Pueblo men of witchcraft and hanged many, selling many more into slavery, and imprisoning others, including Ohkay Owingeh (Popé), a San Juan Indian. The Pueblos from San Juan and some of the surrounding pueblos marched on Santa Fe and demanded that the prisoners be returned. The Spanish could see the broad discontent. It took a lot for the Pueblos to mobilize en masse. Most of the Spanish fighting force was away from Pueblo country, engaged in a campaign against the Apache. Spanish authorities released the prisoners, and life went on as it had for years. But the Pueblos had had enough of being oppressed.

Popé moved from San Juan to Taos and plotted resistance. He traveled secretly and tirelessly, eventually securing the alliance of 46 pueblos, plus the Hopi and Zuni. To coordinate timing, allies were given knotted rope and told to untie one knot each day and then commence attacking Spanish settlements and soldiers. The Spanish discovered his plan when they captured two Tesuque youth who had been entrusted with the message and knotted cords. They tortured the boys for information and mobilized

"THE WARRIOR, FOR US, IS ONE WHO SACRIFICES HIMSELF FOR THE GOOD OF OTHERS. HIS TASK IS TO TAKE CARE OF THE ELDERLY, THE DEFENSELESS, THOSE WHO CANNOT PROVIDE FOR THEMSELVES, AND ABOVE ALL, THE CHILDREN, THE FUTURE OF HUMANITY."

SITTING BULL

THE PALACE OF THE GOVERNORS Governor Antonio de Otermín was besieged in Santa Fe when the revolt began, but escaped, then was chased from New Mexico by Pueblo warriors.

WEDDING DAY This folding screen depicts an Indian celebration near Mexico City, with pre-Columbian games and dances. On the right, a newlywed Indian couple leaves the church, evidencing conversion of the natives.

troops against the Pueblos. Popé knew that he had to act immediately or he and many other Pueblos would simply be executed. Pueblo men dropped their farm tools and gathered weapons. Hundreds started to coalesce and move against the Spanish. There was no way to stop the Pueblo Revolt.

SPANISH DEFEAT

Three days after the Spanish discovered Popé's plan, the Pueblos besieged Santa Fe, the seat of Spanish authority.

Some of the remote pueblos and Hopi communities, following the original plan and not realizing the Spanish had discovered their intentions, commenced attacking the Spanish in their respective areas. Pueblo forces swept through the Rio Grande Valley and destroyed the Spanish settlements in the region. The Hopi and Zuni also rose up and chased Spanish troops out of their territories. Unable to call for reinforcements because of the simultaneous attacks, Spanish forces had no choice but to

priests, and there were no Spanish left in Pueblo, Zuni, or Hopi lands.

Otermín tried to return in 1681, attacking the pueblo of Isleta. Again the Pueblos repulsed him. For 12 years the Pueblos were free from Spanish rule. Popé unsuccessfully tried to persuade the Pueblos to cast aside all Spanish foods and tools. That did not happen, but the Pueblos were masters of their own land again.

In 1692, the Spanish returned again, under the leadership of Diego de Vargas, but with a diplomatic solution instead of a military one. They offered formal land grants to each Pueblo community and appointed a public defender to argue Indian cases in Spanish courts. According to Joe Romero, a former lieutenant governor of Cochiti Pueblo, "We taught them a lesson. We killed them and chased the rest all the way through Texas to Mexico. They came back years later, but they came with a little more respect."

The Spanish may have had more respect for Pueblo war tactics, but not for Pueblo religion or life. In 1693, Vargas executed 70 Pueblo warriors who blocked entry to Santa Fe. He sentenced their families to 10 years of servitude. The Spanish reasserted control over the Pueblos, but they had a much more cautious approach to their subjugation. ∎

POPÉ

Ohkay Owingeh, or Popé, was born in 1630 at San Juan pueblo, a Tewa community in New Mexico. Although not much is recorded about his early life, what has made it into history books suggests he was intense and deeply spiritual, picked at an early age to learn ancient rites and religious practices from his elders. He excelled, and by the age of 45 was a well-respected spiritual leader. When Juan Francisco Trevino arrested Popé and 46 other Pueblo spiritual leaders in 1675, the people rallied to their defense. At great risk, they marched on Santa Fe and successfully demanded the release of their spiritual leaders.

Popé then retreated to Taos and plotted a major military overthrow of the Spanish. His success in uniting dozens of pueblos speaking six different languages across a 400-mile stretch of territory was truly remarkable. The Pueblos had a common opposition to Spanish rule, but had never worked together politically before. More than 2,500 warriors rallied to his cause when the Pueblo Revolt began in 1680. He struggled, though, to unite the people in peace. Popé pushed the people to abandon Spanish tools, weapons, religion, and culture, with only modest impact. He did beat back a Spanish attempt to retake the Pueblos in 1681. He died in 1688, and the Spanish waited until he was gone before they tried again in 1692.

retreat. Spanish survivors fled to Santa Fe, or evacuated the region. Antonio de Otermín, the governor of Santa Fe, eventually staged a daring escape from the Palace of the Governors. As Otermín and other Spanish settlers and soldiers reeled from the ferocious and well-planned Pueblo attacks, they started a fighting retreat from New Mexico. The Pueblos pursued their oppressors, successfully chasing more than 2,000 to Socorro, and from there to El Paso. By the time the conflict ended, the Pueblos had killed more than 400 Spaniards, including most of the Franciscan

BATTLE OF DEERFIELD
WINTER SHOWDOWN IN MASSACHUSETTS

Deerfield, Massachusetts, was a focal point of conflict in New England for decades. In the 1670s, English settlers fought the Pocumtuck Indians, eventually forcing them out of their homeland with help from Mohawk allies. English settlers immediately moved to the Indian village site and renamed it Deerfield. When King Philip's War began in 1675, the Pocumtuck and related Algonquian groups raided Deerfield. Half the male English residents died fighting Indians that year. The village was abandoned, and tribal forces burned most of buildings. The English gained the upper hand in that conflict in 1676, though, and retook Deerfield after the nearby Battle of Turner's Falls. By 1704, the English had solid control over

BLOOD IN THE SNOW In a winter raid, French soldiers allied with Abenaki, Wyandot, Pocumtuck, and Pennacook Indians attacked a village in Deerfield, Massachusetts, killing 50 settlers and taking over 100 prisoners.

most of Massachusetts. The Pocumtuck, however, wanted to reclaim their burial and village sites. Queen Anne's War, which lasted from 1702 to 1713, was in full swing. It was really the second in a series of French and Indian wars against the British. When the Pocumtuck recruited French allies, eager to disrupt British encroachment on French colonies to the north, Deerfield was a ripe target.

Just before dawn on February 29, 1704, a force of 48 French and about 250 Abenaki, Wyandot, Pocumtuck, and Pennacook allies launched a daring raid on Deerfield. Jean-Baptiste Hertel de Rouville had the French command and brought four of his brothers in the force. The British settlements in New England were ready for trouble because there had been many minor skirmishes already in Queen Anne's War. The English, who were warned when de Rouville's force left Chambly, near Montreal, erected a large palisade around Deerfield. They kept a force of 20 professional militia under the leadership of Captain Jonathan Wells, in addition to the 50 fighting men living in the village. They posted a sentry every night. When the French and Indian force approached Deerfield, the attackers set a base camp 25 miles away, snuck up to the village, and then sent an advance force scampering over the snowbanks to breach the palisade and open the gates. Despite all the preparations, the sentry was surprised and overwhelmed.

French troops and Indian warriors stormed the houses. Forty-seven English were killed, and perhaps a dozen attackers. Of the village's 41 homes, 17 were burned, roughly 40 percent of the village. Reverend John Williams said that the Indians came "like a flood upon us." One hundred and twelve Deerfield men, women, and children were captured. Warriors quickly started to move the captives to their base camp before reinforcements arrived. Seeing the numerous fires, large numbers of English militiamen converged on Deerfield, and the attackers withdrew. Of the 291 residents of Deerfield, only 126 remained the next day. Because of the harsh winter conditions, the English militia did not pursue the raiders. Some families were annihilated. Mary Catlin saw her husband, two sons, and two daughters killed in the raid. According to one report, she "being held with the other prisoners in John Sheldon's house, gave a cup of water to a young French officer who was dying. He was perhaps a brother of Hertel de Rouville. May it not have been gratitude for this act that she was left behind when the order came to march? She died of grief a few weeks later."

THE DEERFIELD CAPTIVES

The captives endured a terrible ordeal. They were taken on a 300-mile forced march to Canada through cold and snow. Only 89 survived. Over the next two years the English tried to get the captives back. Sixty were ransomed and returned to Deerfield. The other 29 captives chose to stay in Canada, some in French towns, and most in

> ### "THEIR ANCESTORS ENSURED THE SURVIVAL OF THE PILGRIMS— AND LIVED TO REGRET IT."
>
> *WE STILL LIVE HERE: ÂS NUTAYUNEÂN*

native villages. Eunice Williams, the daughter of Reverend John Williams, was the subject of a famous captivity narrative. She was ultimately adopted by Catholic Mohawk Indians and renamed Marguerite Kanenstenhawi. She married Francois-Xavier Arosen as a young woman and changed her name to Marguerite Kanenstenhawi Arosen. She maintained contact with her Deerfield family, especially her father, her brother Stephan Williams, and uncle Samuel Williams, even visiting Deerfield in 1739 and 1741. She communicated with them through an interpreter, as she preferred to speak French or Mohawk. In spite of numerous attempts to persuade her to move back to Deerfield, she chose to stay in the Mohawk village at Kahnawake.

In 1704, when the drama of the Deerfield raid was over, Queen Anne's War was heating up. The Pocumtuck would never reclaim their homeland. For decades the English-French conflict engulfed the tribes, who often fought for the Europeans as allies and proxies. The English doubled the bounty on Indian scalps immediately after the Battle of Deerfield. In 1703, Reverend Solomon Stoddard urged the Northampton parishioners to use dogs to "hunt Indians as if they were bears." He told his congregation that Indians "act like wolves and are to be dealt with like wolves." ■

CAPTURED At Deerfield, 112 men, women, and children were captured, like those being taken to the Abenaki camp pictured here.

TUSCARORA WAR
TURMOIL IN NORTH CAROLINA

The Tuscarora, part of the Iroquoian language family, moved south to the Piedmont region of North Carolina long before Europeans arrived, fleeing intense intertribal conflict in the eastern Great Lakes. In 1653, the first permanent English colonies were established on the North Carolina coast. Many Tuscarora accommodated the new arrivals. When conflict with English settlers broke out in 1711, the two most well-known Tuscarora chiefs went by English names—Chief Hancock and Chief Tom Blount. For more than 50 years they preserved peace. The peaceful disposition of the Tuscarora made them a target for repeated slave raids by whites and their Indian neighbors. The southern frontier ran a brisk commerce in Indian slaves. Eventually, the Tuscarora were fed up.

In 1711, 60 Tuscarora hunters captured English settlers John Lawson and Christoph von Graffenried on the Neuse River. After a tribal council, the Tuscarora agreed to release them. Then Cor Tom, a chief from the neighboring Coree tribe, showed up, conducted his own hasty trial, and sentenced the two settlers to death. The Tuscarora told the Coree to release Graffenried, but allowed them to execute Lawson. The Tuscarora War had begun.

BLOODBATH ON THE NEUSE RIVER

The Tuscarora gathered 500 fighting men at Catechna. Warriors from many tribes soon joined them—Pamplico, Cothechney, Coree, Mattamuskeet, Matchepungo, Bay River, Machapunga, Neusiok, Coree, and Pampticough. They fanned out to attack the settlements on the Pamlico, Neuse, and Trent Rivers, and in Core Sound. Bath and New Bern swelled with English refugees. The Indians burned English towns with impunity for three days. Best estimates are that around 140 whites were killed and 30 captured.

Governor Edward Hyde called up the North Carolina militia and sent word to South Carolina for reinforcements. They marched to Bath, and joined forces with another militia group on the Neuse under the command of Captain William Brice. The militia swelled to more than 600. Soon reinforcements arrived from South Carolina, including 495 Cherokee and Yamasee allies. Captain John Barnwell of South Carolina assumed command. The Tuscarora assumed defensive positions in nine small forts. Barnwell immediately attacked the largest, overwhelming the defenders, killing 52 and taking 30 prisoners.

In February 1712, Barnwell marched on three Tuscarora villages on the Pamlico River. As the militia crossed the river, tribal forces ambushed them. Although they fought their way out of the river crossing, Barnwell's force was now down to 25 white men and 178 Indians. This was partially due to casualties, but also the length of the campaign. Both tribal allies and militiamen had to provide for

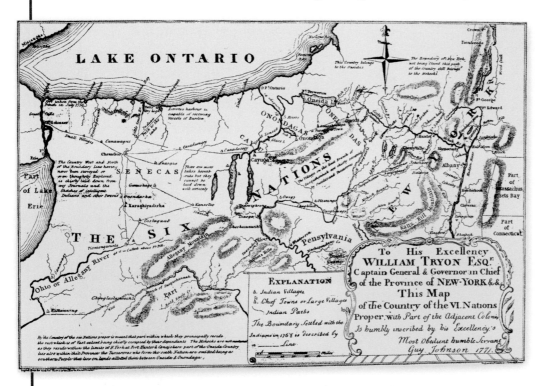

TUSCARORA SANCTUARY After the war, the Tuscarora sought refuge with their Iroquois cousins in New York, joining the Iroquois Confederacy, whose homeland is mapped here.

families and could not be in the field for many months without reprieve. Barnwell finally brought his troops to Chief Hancock's fort near Catechna on the Contentnea Creek on April 7, 1712. As they prepared for the inevitable British assault, the Tuscarora tortured their white captives. The local militiamen, who had captive family members inside, begged Barnwell to parley. The Tuscarora agreed to the surrender of Chief Hancock and three other leaders and amnesty for the remaining Tuscarora, plus the return of captives and cessation of hostilities. That was enough to make peace.

Many North Carolinians were furious that the Tuscarora were not dealt a decisive and punitive blow. The North Carolina government formally censured Barnwell. Breaking the peace he had negotiated with the Tuscarora, Barnwell seized many of the Tuscarora captives as slaves and retreated to South Carolina. Barnwell's violation of the surrender terms reignited the war. The betrayed Tuscarora resumed attacks along the Neuse and Pamlico. Governor Edward Hyde had to rally local militia himself. In the summer of 1712, he was

TRIBAL CONTROL For the first three days of the Tuscarora War, white settlers were refugees, bottled up in three main strongholds. The Tuscarora burned English settlements and hunted down stragglers.

struck down by yellow fever. The white response fizzled.

South Carolina militia again came to the rescue. They assembled a substantial force that again included many Indian allies—more than 900 Yamasee and Cherokee. Colonel James Moore assumed command and laid siege to the Tuscarora fort, which was reinforced with massive logs and earthworks. They stormed the fort on March 20, 1713. Moore's troops killed 392 Tuscarora. Over the next three days they killed or captured another 166 Tuscarora nearby. By the end of the campaign, more than 1,000 Tuscarora had been killed or captured and sold into slavery. The remaining Tuscarora abandoned their other strongholds. Most fled inland. Desperate for sanctuary, they reached out to their Iroquoian cousins in upstate New York and were welcomed as the sixth tribal nation of the Iroquois Confederacy. A small group of Tuscarora stayed in North Carolina where they endured punitive raids for three more years. In 1718, they signed a treaty by which they ceded most of their land and agreed to confinement on a reservation. ∎

YAMASEE WAR

INTRIGUE AND BETRAYAL IN SOUTH CAROLINA

The Yamasee, who lived along the Savannah River and Port Royal Sound, were allies of English colonists for the first 50 years of white settlement in South Carolina. They supplied most of the fighters for colonial militia during the Tuscarora War. When it became clear that English settlers wanted to enslave other human beings to work on their plantations, the idea was strange to the Yamasee, but they rose to the task, converting their war skills to slave raiding. They frequently attacked the Tuscarora and other neighboring tribes, selling captives to the British. They hunted deer as well, for food and the skins that formed the primary commodity in the other early Southern market—the deerskin trade.

By 1715, the Indian slave trade still dominated the southern labor market, but the susceptibility of Indian slaves to disease was leading the white settlers to rely more on African slaves. The deerskin trade was declining, and the South Carolina rice plantations were becoming more self-sufficient. The colonial Yamasee economy was in decline. Now white settlers wanted Yamasee land.

> "THE YAMASEE INDIANS WERE . . . KNOWN AFTERWARDS AS THE FIERCEST OF THE INDIAN TRIBES OF THE SOUTH."
>
> INDUSTRIAL COMMISSION ON AGRICULTURE, U.S. 57TH CONGRESS

FRACTURED ALLIANCE

Colonial politicians reached out to the Yamasee in 1715, hoping they would arbitrate tensions with the Creek. But the Yamasee saw the divide-and-conquer tactics at play and decided to make a stand. On April 15, 1715, Yamasee warriors killed four English diplomats. Then they gathered warriors and descended on Port Royal. Most of the settlers escaped onto ships. The Yamasee turned to isolated plantations and trading posts, killing more than 100 settlers and 90 out of the 100 English traders in the region.

Charles Craven, governor of South Carolina, called up the militia. With 240 men, he found the main body of Yamasee warriors and engaged them in an open field battle at Salkehatchie. Casualties were roughly equal, but the Yamasee retreated, and were on defense for most of the conflict afterward. Militia routed Yamasee warriors in two other major battles, killing roughly 150 warriors. The fate of the Yamasee looked grim, until the Catawba sent 400 warriors and the Cherokee another 70 to join them in attacks on English towns. Settlers abandoned their plantations and retreated to Charleston, which was besieged by warriors. Simultaneously, the Ochese Creek, who were nearly at the breaking point before the Yamasee rose up, also attacked white settlements in southern South Carolina, killing all the traders there.

EVERY KIND OF ENEMY

The Cherokee were deeply divided. The northern Cherokee towns had sent warriors to join the Yamasee. But the southern Cherokee had fought the Creek since time immemorial. Although some advocated neutrality, others wanted the entire Cherokee nation to pick a side. In January 1716, the Cherokee factions tried to parley with the Creek at Tugaloo, but hotheads prevailed, and some of the Cherokee killed a dozen Creeks. The Cherokee broke with the Yamasee and reforged their friendship with the English colonists. The Yamasee would have to fight without them.

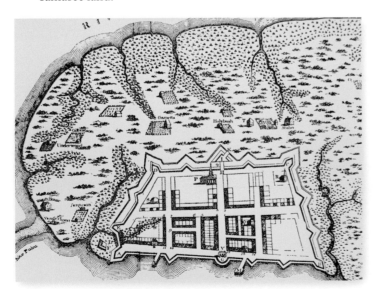

CHARLESTON A 1715 map of Charleston, South Carolina, where settlers sought refuge from the Yamasee attack.

The Creek and Cherokee slugged it out for two years, eventually settling at a standstill with equal losses. Although that conflict was not decisive on its own, it did mean that the Yamasee could not count on the Cherokee or the Creek for help. The Creek sent emissaries to the Iroquois in New York, who sent 20 delegates to South Carolina. Now truly terrified, the English brought a shipment of goods to buy goodwill from the Creek. The Yamasee and Catawba pulled back. The English did not press their advantage against the Yamasee. Their militia was depleted. Charleston was an isolated refugee center. Nearly 10 percent of their citizens were dead. The Yamasee had lost 25 percent of their people in the war, and they set up a new base of operations farther south, from which they raided English settlements through the 1720s. ∎

BATTLE OF COMBAHEE RIVER Governor Charles Craven leads
South Carolina militia against the Yamasee at the start of hostilities in 1715.

NATCHEZ WARS
DESTRUCTION OF THE PEOPLE OF THE SUN

The Natchez were a proud people, descendants of the ancient Mississippian mound builders who constructed Cahokia and other cities prior to European contact. They chased Hernando de Soto's expedition out of America, endured horrible disease pandemics, and then saw the French come to colonize their homeland. They were willing to accommodate the new arrivals, but the French had much to learn about how to speak to the Natchez in their cultural language.

In 1716, French officials passed over Natchez chiefs on a major diplomatic mission. It was a major offense to the hierarchical Natchez, who retaliated by killing four French traders. The French had their own notions of justice and offense. They staged a peace parley, ostensibly to address bad feelings, but instead captured a number of Natchez. Then the French ransomed them for the killers of the French traders, all of whom were summarily executed. The Natchez endured that insult to avoid widespread conflict, although the wrong was not forgotten.

The French began sending colonists among the Natchez communities, and a fragile peace lasted for nearly a decade. In 1723, some of the French colonists reported harassment

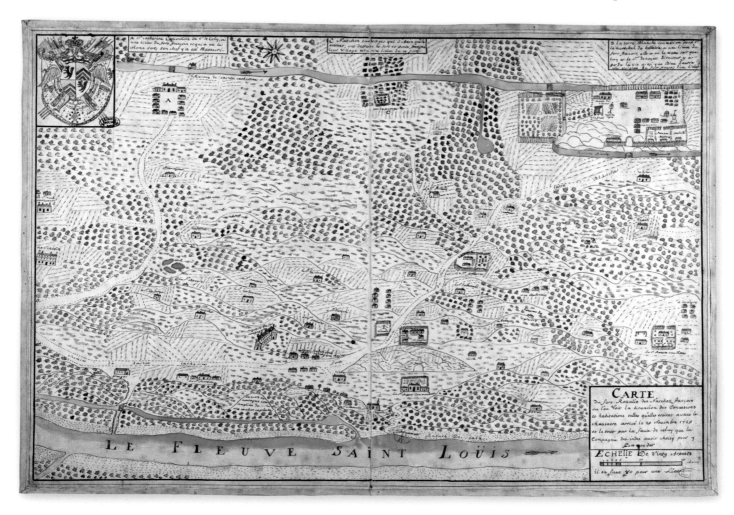

FORT ROSALIE When Fort Rosalie, mapped here, encroached on Natchez temples and burial grounds, the peaceful Natchez rose up against the French colonial government.

from the Natchez, and French troops razed the village at White Apple only to discover that they had been lied to about Natchez behavior. Conditions further deteriorated when a French colonist murdered the son of a prominent chief. The Natchez retaliated, killing the colonist. The French then sent a troop deployment from New Orleans. The Natchez surrendered and watched helplessly as the French executed their chief. The bitter Natchez avoided further retaliation, but their list of grievances was long and complicated.

The French were engaged in a decades-long battle with the British over colonial rights, trade, and territory. Both were operating trade networks and colonies in the Southeast. The French would have been wise to placate allies and peace-minded tribes rather than exercising a heavy hand. That error soon brought its own set of consequences.

THE ATTACK ON FORT ROSALIE

The French built Fort Rosalie adjacent to a major Natchez village near present-day Natchez, Mississippi, about 130 miles north of New Orleans. The colonists blundered into Natchez cultural protocol again in 1729 when, without negotiation or provocation, Sieur de Chépart, the commandant of the fort, announced the expansion of the fort into the primary Natchez temple site and burial ground at White Apple. The Natchez complained and sought diplomatic redress of their grievances as well as protection of their sacred sites, but Chépart dismissed them.

The Natchez seized French ships in the harbor to prevent French escape and commenced an all-out attack on Fort Rosalie. Their ferocity and organization surprised the French. The Natchez killed 150 colonists and soldiers at the fort; only 20 escaped. The Natchez pressed the attack. Chépart was captured and executed. The Natchez then hunted French colonists elsewhere in the region, eventually bringing the total number of French fatalities to 230. Fort Rosalie was in ashes.

The French, panicked with fear of a general Indian uprising, sent for reinforcements from New Orleans, and then massacred the innocent Chaouacha people, who had no involvement in the Natchez assault. Then they marched on the Natchez. Realizing that the resistance was isolated to that tribe, they reached out to the Choctaw for alliance and brought overwhelming force against the Natchez villages. All were

> "THIS NATION WAS ALWAYS CONSIDERABLY STRONG, BUT THEY NEVER HAD THE FOOLISH AMBITION OF CARRYING ON WARFARE WITH THEIR NEIGHBORS . . . THEY DO NOT RANK AMONG INDIANS AS A COURAGEOUS NATION."
>
> JEAN BAPTISTE LE MOYNE DE BIENVILLE, ON THE NATCHEZ

burned to the ground. They took more than 400 captives and sold most into slavery in the Caribbean, although some captives were publicly tortured in New Orleans. The Natchez were reeling, and sought refuge among the Chickasaw. That proved to be a temporary reprieve, as the French then attacked the Chickasaw between 1730 and 1731. The Natchez moved on, seeking refuge among Creek. Their population dispersed. By 1736, the Natchez were no longer a viable polity, and their remaining people were scattered across slave populations in the Indies or absorbed into the Creek peoples of the Southeast.

The French colonies along the Mississippi River were administered independently by the French West India Company prior to the Natchez War. The colonists, deeply affected by the events, petitioned to have the administration of the colony transferred back to the French crown. The governor of Louisiana, Étienne Périer, was recalled to Paris for the massacre of the Chaouacha and mismanagement of the formerly peaceful Natchez. ∎

RISE OF THE NATCHEZ

The Natchez were one of the largest and most powerful tribes in the southern reaches of the Mississippi River when Hernando de Soto encountered them in 1542. They were also distinct from all the neighboring tribes in several ways. Although most of the Muskogean people of the Southeast, including the Creek and Chickasaw, were descendants of the ancient Mississippian mound builders, the Natchez appeared to be the primary inheritors of their ancient religious beliefs and political structures. The ancient Mississippians built large earthen mounds at Cahokia and elsewhere throughout the Mississippi River Valley and Southeast. Their customs revolved around the power of the sun. Quigaltam, one of the primary Natchez chiefs in 1542, introduced himself as the son of the sun. He was born on a litter so his feet would never touch the ground. This kind of hierarchy, more common in Mayan and Aztec cities elsewhere in North America, was a unique part of Natchez political organization.

The Natchez, who had large villages and many people living near each other, suffered tremendously with the outbreak of European diseases. Their population fell to 4,000 people living in nine towns in 1682, when French explorer Robert de la Salle encountered them. Continued exposure to disease after French contact cut their numbers in half again by 1720.

FATHER RALE'S WAR
ANGLO-WABANAKI BATTLES IN ACADIA

In the early 1700s, the French and British sparred over territory, colonial rights, and economic dominance in the borderland between French Acadian colonies in Nova Scotia and British settlements in New England. Those lands were controlled and occupied by the Wabanaki Confederacy (Mi'kmaq, Maliseet, and Abenaki Indians), who had never ceded any of the disputed lands to either European power. Issues came to a head after the British conquest of Acadia in 1710. That pushed the edge of British settlement farther north. Queen Anne's War ended with the Treaty of Utrecht in 1713, an accord that drew new borders between French and British domains with no Indian consultation or permission. Some Wabanaki tribes signed the Treaty of Portsmouth that year to affirm peace and friendship, but they never consented to British rule or to new English colonies in their midst.

The French were happy to undermine British interests. In 1722, they sent Father Sébastien Rale to the Abenaki town of Norridgewock to set up a church. He was also authorized by the government of New France to supply the Indians with weapons and ammunition if they rose up against the British. As new British fishing towns and settlements encroached on Wabanaki lands, conflict seemed inevitable. English settlers pressed their claims while the British government built new forts in Maine, Massachusetts, and Vermont in anticipation of renewed conflict with the French and their Indian allies. They demanded that Father Rale be removed from Norridgewock, but the Wabanaki refused. The tribes delivered a written statement to the British, defining the territory and their willingness to defend it. The British responded by sending 300 troops to arrest Rale. Although Rale escaped, the British found letters confirming their suspicion that he was an agent of New France.

ACADIAN INDIAN Most Acadian Indians were members of the Wabanaki Confederacy (Mi'kmaq, Maliseet, and Abenaki), indigenous to northern New England and Nova Scotia.

THE RAIDS BEGIN

Preempting a British strike, the Abenaki raided Fort George and took 60 prisoners, who were later released. Now Chief Gray Lock, Chief Paugus, and Father Rale planned a series of escalating raids to force a British retreat from Wabanaki lands. Maliseet and Penobscot warriors raided British forts. British troops landed in New Brunswick and counterraided. Then Maliseet and Mi'kmaq warriors attacked Port Royal (Annapolis Royal), a major port in Nova Scotia. None of the raids resulted in significant casualties, but the British did not want to give the French time to maneuver or scheme. Two months after the raids started, they formally declared war against the Wabanaki tribes. Five hundred Wabanaki attacked Arrowsic, Maine, and nearby Fort Richmond. The British burned an abandoned Penobscot village. In total, 14 Wabanaki raids occurred in 1723, and there would be another 10 in 1724. They attacked British merchant vessels and fishing ships, slowly gaining advantage in a war of attrition. The British abandoned their blockhouses and consolidated their people at the forts.

Aiming for a decisive victory, they marched on the Abenaki stronghold in the Battle of Norridgewock on August 22, 1724. More than 200 British rangers descended on the tribal town. Father Rale was killed. The Wabanaki went on defense. The British sent scalp raids against the tribes, paying a bounty for Indians of any age or gender killed. Captain John Lovewell led three such parties, killing many Indians, including Chief Paugus; Lovewell died in the last of the three confrontations. Eventually all sides agreed to a cease-fire and then a peace agreement, but British domain was secure. The British, who had ignored tribal leaders and land interests in Acadia for decades, changed their policy and actively sought tribal permissions for new settlements to placate potential enemies and disrupt French influence and intrigue on the frontier. ∎

BIG ROCK The Abenaki stronghold was a hub of military activity in Father Rale's War, as Indians from Norridgewock traveled by canoe to get within striking distance of the British.

LORD DUNMORE'S WAR

SHAWNEE AND MINGO RESISTANCE

Tempers in the Ohio River Valley had reached the boiling point. In 1763, the French signed the Treaty of Paris, by which they abdicated colonial claims to North America. In 1768, the Iroquois Confederacy signed the Treaty of Fort Stanwix, in which they relinquished territorial claims on the Ohio River Valley to the British. English colonists flooded the frontier in what would become western Pennsylvania, Ohio, and Kentucky. The problem was that although the French and Iroquois claimed that territory, it was actually home to the Shawnee and Mingo Indians, and they had ceded no title or interest.

In 1773, English frontier settlers included Daniel Boone, who came to the Ohio with 50 emigrants. The area was still technically part of Virginia, and fell under the administrative oversight of governor John Murray, the Fourth Earl of Dunmore. The Shawnee captured and killed Daniel Boone's son, James Boone, and another boy, the first fatalities in what would become a major conflict. Their deaths were

> "FROM ALL QUARTERS WE RECEIVE SPEECHES . . . AND NO TWO ARE ALIKE. WE SUPPOSE THEY INTEND TO DECEIVE US."
>
> BLUE JACKET, SHAWNEE CHIEF

widely publicized and set the English colonists in an uproar. Shawnee, Delaware, and Cherokee residents, frustrated with the aggression of many colonists, increasingly detained and sometimes attacked white migrants, traders, and settlers.

Captain Michael Cresap, at the urging of many new white residents in the region, pulled together a militia, and they were spoiling for a fight. Cresap wrote to Captain John Connolly at Fort Pitt, who advised Cresap to attack the Shawnee. The Cresap militia ambushed the Shawnee at Pipe Creek. There were a few casualties on each side, but the biggest effect of the event was to ignite the Ohio tribes in a concerted military action against the colonists. Settlers fanned the flames of war when they attacked the peaceful Mingo, whose chief, Logan, had consistently signaled peaceful intentions. Several Mingo were lured into a trader house and butchered without resistance, including a pregnant Mingo woman who had children with a local white trader. The Mingo sprang into action beside the Shawnee in a formidable Indian alliance.

ELIZABETH RIVER BRIDGE Lord Dunmore brought a 2,500-man militia across the Elizabeth River to subjugate the Shawnee and Mingo in 1774.

LORD DUNMORE'S CAMPAIGN

Lord Dunmore, who still had diplomatic options available to him in dealing with the Shawnee and Mingo, was contending with other issues, too. He was a staunch British loyalist and could see the rifts opening between colonists and the British crown. Seeking to distract the frontiersmen from starting trouble with the British, while simultaneously expanding Virginia domain and his political appeal, he decided on a high-risk, high-reward strategy. Dunmore asked the Virginia House of Burgesses for a formal declaration of war against the natives. Then he called up militia throughout the sprawling Virginia colonies and personally led them into the field. His force was truly substantial—2,500 regular militia.

Dunmore divided his force and converged on the Shawnee towns at Scioto from two directions. One wing of his force was engaged by Shawnee warriors before they reached the Shawnee towns at the Battle of Point Pleasant. In an intense daylong fight, the Shawnee inflicted 215 English

RETREAT OF LORD DUNMORE Dunmore, a British noble and loyalist, found his war against the Indians insufficient to repair the mistrust the colonials held for him. As the American Revolution began, he fled Virginia.

casualties—75 killed and 140 wounded. The Shawnee lost 40 warriors, but their force was eventually flanked and forced to retreat. Nothing stood between the English colonial militia and the Shawnee towns. As Dunmore's force camped and prepared for a punitive assault on the Shawnee, most of the chiefs came to parley for peace. In the Treaty of Camp Charlotte, most Shawnee agreed to a cease-fire and relinquished their hunting grounds on the Ohio. Some Shawnee factions and the Mingo refused to attend the peace conference. Dunmore brutally annihilated the Mingo village nearby.

Dunmore pulled back the militia, thinking the peace was secure. Most Shawnee honored the agreement, but some Shawnee held out and soon attacked Daniel Boone's group in 1775. By then, the Revolutionary War had broken out and Dunmore had bigger problems. The disaffected tribes, still feeling mistreated by the colonists, sided with the British during the Revolution. ∎

CALIFORNIA MISSIONS
The Spanish missions
in California kept Indian
slaves. They changed to
a sharecropper system
during the transition to
Mexican independence.

ALLIANCE AND BETRAYAL

After the first waves of disease struck Indians in North America, entire tribes disappeared. When Spain, France, England, and Russia descended to conquer and colonize, other tribes folded or dispersed. When European empires collided, most of the tribes that survived the first wave of empire building were themselves large, formidable, well led, and militarily accomplished. All these European and native nations played one another, colluded, compromised, and collided. The fates of nations and empires were at stake, and outcomes hinged upon the power of alliance and leadership.

When so many powerful tribes and European nations competed for the land, resources, and people of early America, those who figured out the power of alliance usually fared the best. The English knew they would be fighting the French and Spanish for colonization rights, trade wealth, and land. In 1677, they latched onto the powerful Iroquois Confederacy to form a major political and military union called the Covenant Chain. Throughout numerous conflicts in the Northeast, Ohio River Valley, and ultimately the French and Indian War, that alliance preserved the British Empire in North America. For the Iroquois, it kept them well armed, better supplied than their native neighbors, and more often than not in control of major military campaigns against those neighbors.

The French could not fight the English and the Iroquois alone, so they reached out to the Huron and then to the Three Fires Confederacy (Ojibwe, Ottawa, and Potawatomi).

> ## "THE IMMEDIATE OBJECTIVES ARE THE TOTAL DESTRUCTION AND DEVASTATION OF THEIR SETTLEMENTS AND THE CAPTURE OF . . . PRISONERS."
>
> GEORGE WASHINGTON, 1779

Together they crushed common tribal enemies such as the Fox, and maintained the French Empire in North America, even when the British outnumbered them 20 to 1.

As the English, French, and then the Americans encroached on tribal lands, tribes forged alliances with one another. Miami chief Little Turtle and Shawnee chief Blue Jacket built a formidable coalition against American expansion in the Ohio River Valley, defeating General Arthur St. Clair at the Battle of the Wabash in a confrontation that killed more American soldiers than any other Indian battle in U.S. history. Pontiac rallied more than a dozen tribes to fight the British. Tecumseh had just as many in his alliance with the British against the Americans. Alliance was always key to strength.

When an alliance crumbled, disaster usually followed. The Wabanaki struggled against British aggression when their French allies pulled back. The Cherokee were divided and

1769–1835
Spanish missions dominate tribal life in coastal California, forcing Indians into slavery and conversion to Christianity.

1690–1733
Fox Wars threaten the French Empire as the tribe blocks trade and communication between the Great Lakes and Louisiana.

1754–1763
French and Indian War brings many powerful native nations into the conflict between France and England as proxies and allies.

1763
Ottawa chief Pontiac rallies a dozen tribes to resist English rule, burning down or besieging forts in the Great Lakes.

more easily conquered when their internal alliance was shaken. The Creek, once one of the most powerful tribes in the Southeast, imploded in civil war when they divided into factions and fought the Red Stick War. Tecumseh, a true military genius, was stranded and isolated on the battlefield when his British allies tepidly fled at the Battle of the Thames. It cost Tecumseh his life, his united tribes their coalition and land, and it likely cost the British the War of 1812.

The Ojibwe have an ancient game of luck and skill called the moccasin game. Players hide musket balls under moccasins, counting successful searches with sticks. Twenty sticks bundled together made one "soldier." Together, 20 sticks were strong, but separated and isolated they were easily broken. So too was it with warriors, soldiers, and nations.

GLOBAL WAR As Spain, Russia, France, and England fought incessantly in the 18th century, tribal allies and enemies were swept up in conflict. Painted here is the Battle of Fort Duquesne, 1758.

THE POWER OF LEADERSHIP

Strong alliances required strong leaders in both peace and war. Sometimes one human could be so electric that the fate of nations was decided in a moment. The Indian wars had many, many such moments. Every day was a referendum on leadership, often decided on the battlefield.

Ottawa chief Pontiac built a coalition and challenged British control of the Great Lakes in 1763, using a deft combination of subterfuge, trickery, diplomacy, and show of force. Some of the British forts surrendered without firing a shot. Others were besieged. At Mackinac, Pontiac staged a sprawling game of lacrosse in front of the British fort, gaining access in the middle of the game. Pontiac's force killed most of the garrison and burned the fort. Brilliant leadership and

1758–1776	1785–1795	1811–1813	1812–1813
Cherokee fight a devastating series of conflicts in the Southeast with English colonists and then the new U.S. government.	Little Turtle and Blue Jacket build major tribal coalition to stop encroachment of white settlers in the Old Northwest War.	Creek nation devolves into civil war in the Red Stick War, culminating in defeat at Horseshoe Bend and a Creek diaspora.	Tribes unite behind Shawnee chief Tecumseh to battle American expansion in the Ohio River Valley.

> "THIS UNFORTUNATE RACE, WHOM
> WE HAD BEEN TAKING SO MUCH PAINS
> TO SAVE AND TO CIVILIZE, HAVE BY
> THEIR UNEXPECTED DESERTION AND
> FEROCIOUS BARBARITIES JUSTIFIED
> EXTERMINATION AND NOW AWAIT OUR
> DECISION ON THEIR FATE."
>
> THOMAS JEFFERSON, 1813

success in battle won him incredible support. Warriors from across the Great Lakes flocked to his cause.

Miami chief Little Turtle was shrewd, tireless, diplomatic, and strategic. He built a powerful alliance with Shawnee chief Blue Jacket and other tribes in the Ohio River Valley during the Old Northwest War, between 1785 and 1795. When he led 1,000 warriors into battle against General Arthur St. Clair along the banks of the Wabash River, he was able to control his eager braves and maintain concealment of 1,000 people as they snuck within 100 yards of the enemy camp and attacked with surprise. He routed 1,200 enemy soldiers, militia, and support personnel. As they tried to break his line with bayonet charges, time after time he retreated his center and pressed the flanks in a double envelopment, a military tactic first employed by Hannibal at the Battle of Cannae in 216 B.C. Little Turtle never went to a military college, but he was a deft strategist. He destroyed all but 24 of St. Clair's force in a resounding tribal victory. His coalition grew in response.

Like Pontiac and Little Turtle, Tecumseh built a tribal alliance through powerful oratory, deft diplomacy, and peerless leadership on the battlefield. At the Battle of Brownstown, his warriors ambushed more than 200 U.S. troops and won decisively. At the siege of Detroit, he tricked the U.S. garrison into believing he had thousands of warriors. They surrendered the fort even though there were 2,500 soldiers and militia in the fort and only 400 warriors with Tecumseh.

Other tribal leaders such as Cherokee chief Dragging Canoe and Ojibwe chief Hole in the Day made their mark with clever leadership in peace and war. These are the stories of the leaders and alliances that shook the continent in the clash of empires. ■

POWERS COLLIDE The clash of empires involved new tactics for diplomacy and war. Although early wars of resistance focused on isolating tribes to enable conquest, these wars engulfed North America's largest and most powerful Indian confederacies, motivating them to fight either with or against various European armies.

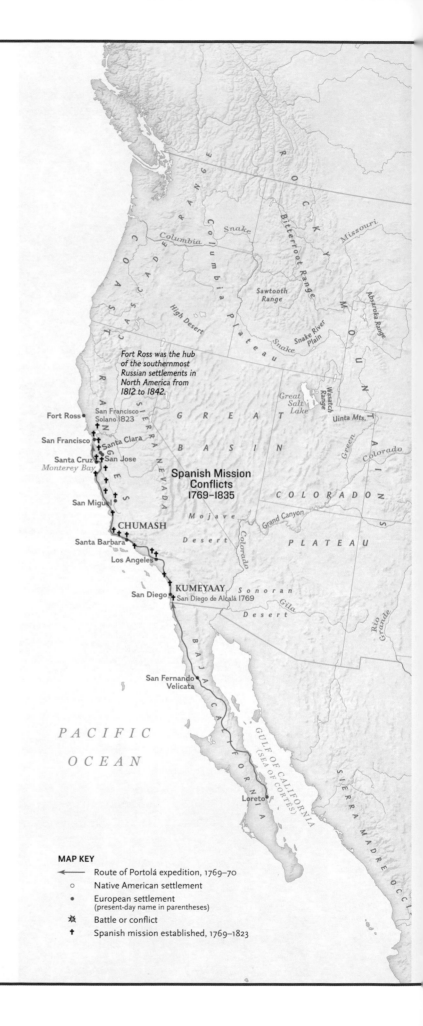

MAP KEY

← Route of Portolá expedition, 1769–70
○ Native American settlement
● European settlement
(present-day name in parentheses)
✹ Battle or conflict
✝ Spanish mission established, 1769–1823

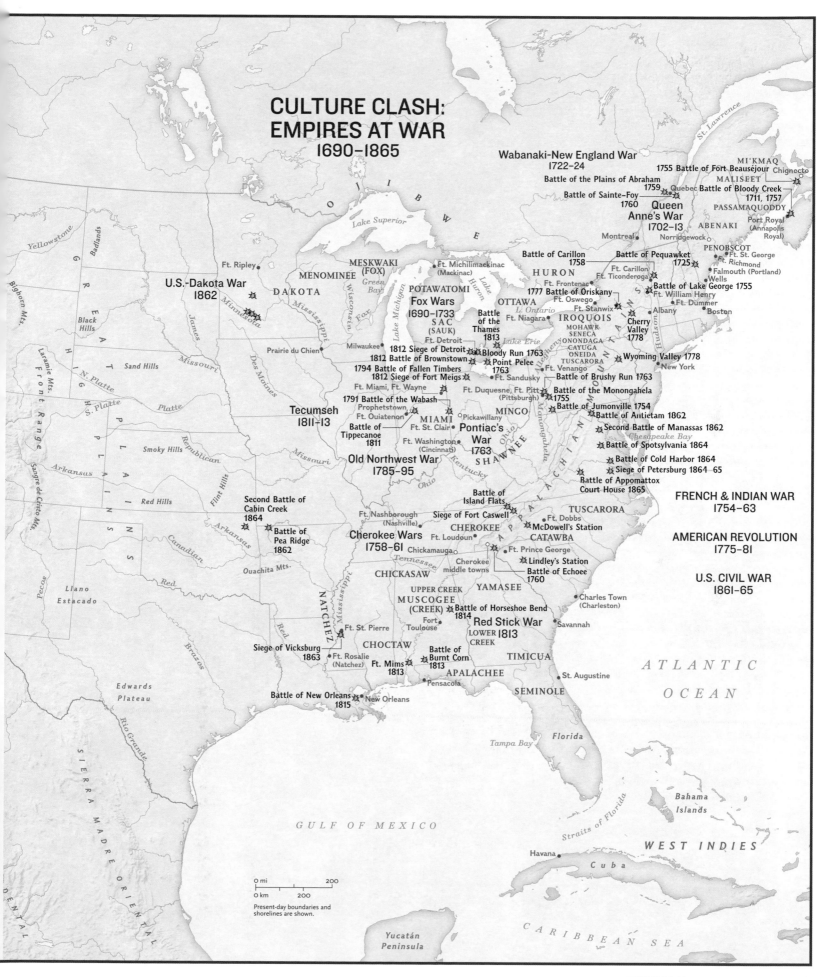

CULTURE CLASH: EMPIRES AT WAR
1690–1865

Wabanaki–New England War
1722–24

1755 Battle of Fort Beauséjour
MI'KMAQ   Chignecto

Battle of the Plains of Abraham   MALISEET
1759
Battle of Sainte-Foy   Quebec   Battle of Bloody Creek
1760   Queen   1711, 1757
Anne's War   PASSAMAQUODDY
1702–13   Port Royal
Montreal   (Annapolis Royal)
ABENAKI
Norridgewock   PENOBSCOT
Ft. St. George
Ft. Ripley   Battle of Carillon   Battle of Pequawket   Ft. Richmond
Ft. Michilimackinac   1758   1725   Falmouth (Portland)
MENOMINEE   (Mackinac)   HURON   Ft. Carillon   Wells
MESKWAKI   Ft. Frontenac   Ft. Ticonderoga   Battle of Lake George 1755
(FOX)   1777 Battle of Oriskany   Ft. William Henry
U.S.–Dakota War   POTAWATOMI   OTTAWA   Ft. Oswego   Ft. Dummer
1862   Fox Wars   Ft. Niagara   Albany   Boston
DAKOTA   1690–1733   IROQUOIS
SAC   Battle   MOHAWK   Cherry
(SAUK)   of the   SENECA   Valley
Thames   ONONDAGA   1778
1813   CAYUGA   Hudson
Ft. Detroit   L. Erie   ONEIDA   New York
Milwaukee   1812 Siege of Detroit   Bloody Run 1763   TUSCARORA   Wyoming Valley 1778
1812 Battle of Brownstown   Point Pelee   Ft. Venango
Prairie du Chien   1794 Battle of Fallen Timbers   1763   Battle of Brushy Run 1763
1812 Siege of Fort Meigs   Ft. Sandusky
Ft. Miami, Ft. Wayne   Ft. Duquesne, Ft. Pitt   Battle of the Monongahela
1791 Battle of the Wabash   (Pittsburgh)   1755
Tecumseh   Prophetstown   MINGO   Battle of Jumonville 1754
1811–13   Ft. Ouiatenon   MIAMI   Pickawillany   Battle of Antietam 1862
Battle of   Ft. St. Clair   Pontiac's   Second Battle of Manassas 1862
Tippecanoe   Ft. Washington   War   Battle of Spotsylvania 1864
1811   (Cincinnati)   1763
Old Northwest War   SHAWNEE   Battle of Cold Harbor 1864
1785–95   Ohio   Siege of Petersburg 1864–65
Kentucky   Battle of Appomattox
Court House 1865
Battle of
Island Flats   FRENCH & INDIAN WAR
Second Battle of   Battle of   1754–63
Cabin Creek   Ft. Nashborough   Siege of Fort Caswell   TUSCARORA
1864   (Nashville)   Ft. Dobbs
CHEROKEE   McDowell's Station   AMERICAN REVOLUTION
Battle of   Ft. Loudoun   CATAWBA   1775–81
Pea Ridge   Cherokee Wars   Chickamauga   Ft. Prince George
1862   1758–61   Cherokee   Lindley's Station   U.S. CIVIL WAR
middle towns   Battle of Echoe   1861–65
CHICKASAW   1760
Tennessee   Charles Town
UPPER CREEK   YAMASEE   (Charleston)
CHOCTAW   MUSCOGEE
(CREEK)   Battle of Horseshoe Bend   Savannah
Ft. St. Pierre   1814
NATCHEZ   Fort   Red Stick War
Toulouse   LOWER   1813
Siege of Vicksburg   CHOCTAW   CREEK
1863   Ft. Rosalie   Battle of   TIMICUA
(Natchez)   Ft. Mims   Burnt Corn
1813   1813   APALACHEE   St. Augustine
Pensacola
Battle of New Orleans   SEMINOLE
1815   New Orleans

Tampa Bay   Florida

ATLANTIC
OCEAN

GULF OF MEXICO

Bahama
Islands

WEST INDIES

Havana   Cuba

Straits of Florida

CARIBBEAN SEA

0 mi   200
0 km   200
Present-day boundaries and
shorelines are shown.

Yucatán
Peninsula

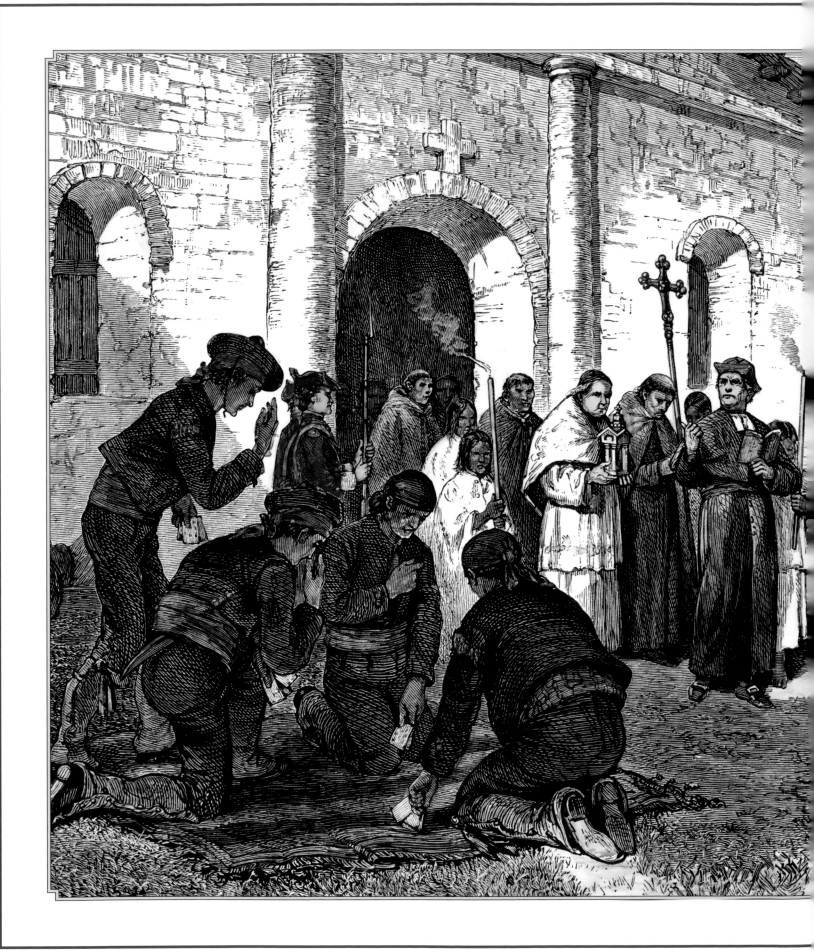

Spanish Mission Conflicts
EMPIRES OF FURS AND SLAVES

For centuries, it didn't matter at all to the many Indians in California that Spain, England, and Russia all laid claim to the land. Juan Rodriguez Cabrillo had done so for Spain in 1542, Francis Drake for England in 1579. No European power was capable of actually exercising a claim until the 1700s, when Russia and Spain both expanded into the region. In 1769, Spanish conquistadors had been pushing the empire north from central Mexico to the American Southwest for 200 years. The Russian Empire had been colonizing Alaska and British Columbia, working their way south to California since 1732. As they vied for resources and colonial rights, it was evident that the winner would be the European power that had the deepest ties with native communities. The Russians and Spanish were astounded by the numbers and diversity of the native people they saw in California and the potential for new colonial experiments. Few of California's tribes had significant military experience or allies. The peacetime advantages of the California tribes turned out to be disadvantages when the Spanish and Russians descended.

SPANISH MISSIONS

The Spanish intended to colonize the tribes, convert them to Christianity, claim their lands, and subjugate the entire population as forced labor in the *encomienda* system. In California, the Catholic Church administered not just religious conversion, but also military and political operations. King Charles III recalled the Jesuit

ESTRACTO DE NOTICIAS del Puerto de Monterrey, de la Misſion, y Preſidio que ſe han eſtablecido en él con la denominacion de San Carlos, y del ſuceſſo de las dos Expediciones de Mar, y Tierra que à eſte fin ſe deſpacharon en el año proximo anterior de 1769.

DESPUES DE LAS REPETIDAS, y coſtoſas Expediciones que ſe hicieron por la Corona de Eſpaña en los dos ſiglos antecedentes para el reconocimiento de la Coſta Occidental de Californias, por la mar del Sur, y la ocupacion del importante Puerto de Monterrey, ſe ha logrado ahora felizmente eſta empreſſa con las dos Expediciones de mar, y tierra que à conſequencia de

PORTOLÁ EXPEDITION In 1769, the Spanish sent their first expedition to present-day California. Soon, the small tribes had to fend off conquistadors, Russian traders, and then American gold rushers.

missionaries in 1767 and sent in the Franciscans two years later. It was a new chapter in an old game for the Spanish, who had perfected coerced labor and subjugation strategies. They established 21 missions on the California coast. Because the movements and numbers of both the Russians and the inland tribes were unknown, the Spanish focused on the coastal missions, which could easily be fortified, supplied, and linked by a system of nearby inland roads and naval communications. Father Junipero Serra was tapped to lead the effort. He founded the early Spanish missions in California. Gaspar de Portolá, the governor of California, worked side by side with Serra to realize the goals of the empire.

The Mission San Diego de Alcalá in San Diego anchored the southern tier of California Spanish missions; the northernmost mission was Mission San Francisco Solano in Sonoma, north of modern-day San Francisco. Many California cities and towns were established on Indian village sites where the missions exerted their heaviest influence, including San Jose, Santa Clara, Santa Cruz, San Miguel, and Santa Barbara.

Spanish clergy, soldiers, and settlers unwittingly brought diseases to which the tribes of California had no natural immunity. Throughout the missions, the tribal population was ravaged by one epidemic after another. Mortality rates were as high as 95 percent. Through the mission system, the Spanish also systematically demolished tribal governance structures, cultures, and economies.

JUNIPERO SERRA **Serra built and oversaw the mission system in California, in charge of religious, political, and military administration.**

From 1812 to 1841, the Russians maintained Fort Ross in northern California, in what is now Sonoma County, and their subjugation of the northern Pomo was especially harsh. The Russians wanted to build a fur empire and did not pursue colonization farther south than San Francisco because they did not find abundant sea otters or other furbearing animals there.

The Chumash were one of the larger tribes in California, indigenous to what are now San Luis Obispo, Santa Barbara, Ventura, and Los Angeles Counties from Morro Bay to Malibu, and also living on three of the large Channel Islands. The Chumash and their neighbors, the Kumeyaay, were immediately targeted for Spanish colonization. With so much at stake, even the peaceful California tribes answered the call for war when empires clashed in California.

RISING UP

The Europeans brutally suppressed military resistance by the Kumeyaay and other tribes. In 1775, more than 800 Ipai and Tipai at Mission San Diego de Alcalá rose up, killing the local priest, Luís Jayme, and taking control of the mission. The other mission Indians, unaccustomed to any kind of coordinated military or political endeavor, stayed out of the conflict. That enabled the Spanish to send reinforcements from other missions. There ended up being a dozen other such resistance efforts, but always independent and never coordinated. They were crushed one at a time.

CONQUISTADOR OF THE CLOTH

Father Junipero Serra arrived in Mexico from Spain in 1749 and landed in the middle of several intersecting conflicts—wars between the Spanish Empire and Indians, between the Jesuit and Franciscan Orders of the Catholic Church, and between religious and secular positions on the administration of empire. In 1752, he was named inquisitor for the Catholic Church and oversaw several inquests at the Sierra Gorda missions.

He wrote reports of witchcraft, sorcery, and devil worship. When Serra's pen moved, increasingly, so did the empire. While still in Mexico, Serra put down an Indian uprising, leading the Spanish authorities to put him in charge of the new slavery-based missions in California in 1769. More than half his party died or deserted on the trip from Baja to San Diego.

It took years to build the missions, and the effort was fraught with conflict. When Serra landed in California, 20 Indians attacked. In 1773, Serra argued with Pedro Fages, a military official, who Serra ultimately removed. He also resisted Felipe de Neve's effort to bring enlightenment principles to the missions, mainly because that would have countermanded slavery as an institution, a principal function of the missions. Despite Serra's role in genocidal treatment of the Indians, his personal confirmation of 5,308 converts won him sainthood in 2015.

In 1785, Toypurina, a Chumash medicine woman at present-day Los Angeles, led the first of two truly formidable resistance efforts. She united the Chumash, and they overwhelmed the garrisons at several missions. It took months for the Spanish to isolate the resisters and retake the missions. In 1824, the Chumash rebelled again and captured two missions. Although unarmed, they overwhelmed the Spanish garrison and then used Spanish guns to hold off reinforcements. Eventually, the Chumash leaders agreed to a cease-fire. As soon as everyone laid down their arms, the Spanish put people back in shackles. Leaders were executed, and all the Chumash were immediately returned to slavery at the missions. As awful as the suppression of tribal resistance was, the Spanish were reluctant to sell and relocate entire populations or annihilate them as they had in other parts of their empire.

> "THAT SPIRITUAL FATHERS SHOULD PUNISH THEIR SONS, THE INDIANS, WITH BLOWS APPEARS TO BE AS OLD AS THE CONQUEST OF THE AMERICAS."
>
> FATHER JUNIPERO SERRA, 1780

In part, they needed the Indians as laborers, and mortality rates were very high for Indian slaves, so they always needed more. But they also could not afford to enable the tribes to ally themselves with the Russians or with inland tribes. The web of relationships among empires ironically stayed Spanish hands at times.

When Mexico gained independence from Spain in 1821, the new nation included all of California. The Mexican government continued the mission system until 1834, when it abolished slavery and secularized the missions. But secularization did not end brutality. Most mission Indians were forced to live and work in a state of serfdom—disempowered and landless in their own land. Most ended up working for Mexican landowners for poverty wages until the American period, which brought a new wave of violence to the region. ∎

CHUMASH The Chumash were one of the largest tribes in southern California, and thrived on the abundant ocean fish, often harvested from plank canoes like this.

WISCONSIN HEIGHTS The Wisconsin River connected French outposts in the Great Lakes with
Louisiana. The Fox struggled on its heights against the French and later against the Americans.

FOX WARS

LINCHPIN OF EMPIRES

The incredible Fox, or Meskwaki (also spelled Mesquakie), Indian story spans centuries of conflict, military betrayal, and perseverance through battle. From their villages in Michigan's Upper Peninsula, the Fox fought numerous Indian enemies from 1600 on. Their closest neighbors, the Ojibwe, were among their most feared enemies, and the two tribes waged a brutal conflict that started before European contact and continued through its initial phases. The Fox and Ojibwe are linguistically and culturally related, but political and military allegiance was an entirely different matter. Over the next few decades, the Fox slowly moved their villages south to the Green Bay region of present-day Wisconsin.

France and England fought for decades over colonial rights and trade networks in the Great Lakes. The French eventually backed the Three Fires Confederacy (Ottawa, Potawatomi, and Ojibwe) while the British backed the Iroquois Confederacy (Mohawk, Seneca, Onondaga, Cayuga, Oneida, and Tuscarora). The conflict between those tribal confederacies and their European allies disrupted many tribes in the Great Lakes, depopulating the Huron region, and driving war refugees from conflict zones to Fox territory. The Fox temporarily allied themselves with the Wisconsin Dakota to expel the war refugees when they became so numerous that they drained critical resources.

NEW FRANCE BLUNDERS

Fox politics changed abruptly in 1679. The Ojibwe and Dakota forged a peace and both tribes were trading with the French. Hoping to expand their trade and trapping territory, the two tribes attacked the Fox. Fox chiefs sent emissaries to the French, threatening war if the French did not trade with the Fox and use their influence to back off their tribal aggressors. The Ojibwe and Dakota each outnumbered the Fox by more than three to one, and the tribe had no access to guns or ammunition. The French dismissed Fox threats.

In 1690, the Fox attacked several French canoe trade convoys. The French, squeezed by the British in Hudson Bay and their American colonies, connected their Great Lakes colonies and those in Louisiana through Green Bay on Lake Michigan, to the Fox River, then to the Wisconsin and Mississippi Rivers. The Fox dominated the Fox River connection, and they quickly forced the French to abandon the trade route. That put the French in an unsustainable economic, military, and political position, so they directed incredible resources to crushing the Fox. That year, the Ojibwe and Dakota responded to French requests for aid, bringing huge war parties of 1,200 warriors into Fox territory to press the attack. In 1692, the French reopened the trade route and built several new forts to protect it in Wisconsin.

The Fox regrouped, strengthening defensive palisades, earthworks, and protections for their villages. Then they struck back directly at the French. In 1698, the government of New France was again forced to close the Fox River portage, cutting off vital supply chains and communication between

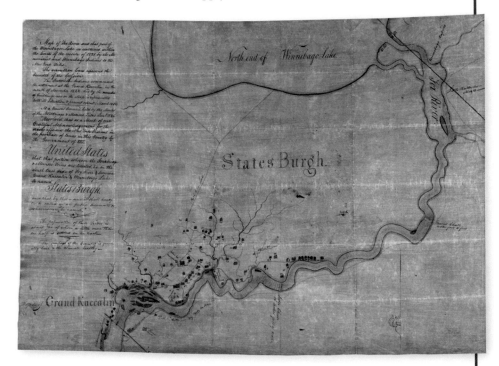

FOX RIVER The Fox River, the heart of Fox territory in the 1720s, connects the Lake Superior and Mississippi watersheds.

Louisiana and Montreal. Even though they had no guns or ammunition and were outnumbered six to one by their enemies, geography gave the Fox the upper hand, allowing them to sporadically close the portage, and consistently disrupt French trade and travel. They forced the French to abandon several of their new forts and trading posts.

FOX SURVIVAL

In 1720, the French resolved to expel the Fox from northern Wisconsin even if the cost in human lives and financial resources was truly significant. They brought overwhelming pressure to bear. Again, the Ojibwe and Dakota did most of the fighting for the French, but New France sent troops into the field as well. Reeling, the Fox moved their primary villages farther south again, about 100 miles to southern Wisconsin, near present-day Milwaukee.

Even with the Fox on the defensive by 1729, the French took no chances that they might regroup and further threaten their empire, especially as the displaced Fox relocated closer to British forts and settlements. That year, the French and

their allies killed more than 300 Fox warriors. In 1730, they launched an all-out assault on Fox villages in southern Wisconsin, killing 200 more warriors, and at least as many women, children, and elders, as well as capturing 500 more. The captives were all sold into slavery and shipped out of the Great Lakes to other parts of the French Empire.

In 1732, the government of New France made the policy of genocide official. The Fox were displaced from most of their villages and desperately sought asylum. In 1733, they even approached their longtime enemies the Dakota for mercy and

FRENCH GENOCIDAL EDICT, 1732

In 1732, the government of New France issued a genocidal edict against the Fox Indians that called for them to be eradicated from the Earth. France had a special hatred of the Fox after the small tribe had successfully fended off decades of assaults. In 1709, New France abolished slavery in its territory, but colonists routinely kept Fox slaves for many more decades.

In 1733, in compliance with the edict, French officials refused to accept the surrender of Fox war refugees. A large band tried to flee to New York to seek refuge with the Seneca, but was annihilated by the French and their Potawatomi, Ojibwe, and Menominee allies. Survivors from other bands sought refuge with the Sac. The French then marched on the Sac, demanding the surrender of all Fox Indians. When the Sac refused, the French attacked, but were driven back. The French sent one more major expedition against the Fox in 1736, but it too had little success.

The Ojibwe and Dakota peace shattered during this time, throwing New France's western trade networks into turmoil. In 1736, France annihilated the Natchez in Mississippi, but blundered into a major military campaign against the large and powerful Chickasaw tribe, which closed their trade corridor on the southern end of the Mississippi. The colonizers just could not fight everyone at once. The Marquis de Beauharnois, governor-general of New France, retracted the genocidal edict in 1738, and issued a general pardon of the Fox. At that time, only 500 Fox survived of the more than 20,000 at the start of the Fox Wars.

surrender. Their plight was so severe that the Dakota were ready to grant the request. The French leaned heavily on the Dakota, and the Fox had to keep running. Later that year, they came to the French and offered to surrender, but the French refused the offer and attacked the Fox war refugees.

Scattering, the Fox approached another Algonquian tribe, the Sac (Sauk), for help. In 1733, they found refuge there. Over the next two years, most of the scattered bands and refugee families made their way out of the Great Lakes to the great Sac villages on the Mississippi River at Prairie du Chien, Wisconsin, and in Illinois and Iowa. Greatly reduced in numbers, the Fox and Sac, two distinct and independent tribes, slowly merged their bloodlines and politics. They traded with Spanish and eventually English traders. By 1763, some Sac and Fox bands allied themselves with the British to help defeat the French in the French and Indian War. ∎

WAR DANCE The Sac and Fox displayed their military tradition in war dances. Because they had no major European trading partner for guns, they used precontact weapons against the French for decades, to deadly effect.

QUEEN ANNE'S WAR

TRIBES, FRANCE, AND ENGLAND CLASH IN THE WAR OF SPANISH SUCCESSION

When the Spanish monarch King Charles II died in 1700, Europe was thrown into turmoil, and France, England, and Spain came to blows over control of their empires. The conflict began in 1702, lasted for 10 years, and in North America engulfed several tribes, who often fought for their European allies as proxies. The North American theater of conflict was known as Queen Anne's War, waged on three tribal fronts—Acadia, Carolina, and Florida.

ACADIAN FRONT

Acadia (modern-day New Brunswick, Nova Scotia, Maine, and Massachusetts) was home to the powerful Wabanaki Confederacy (Mi'kmaq, Maliseet, and Abenaki). The Penobscot and other Acadian tribes were soon pulled into the conflict, usually on the side of the French. For most of the

QUEEN ANNE **The English queen directed massive expenditure and troop deployment to push back the French and their Indian allies.**

10-year war, the tribes held the British at bay, successfully raiding as far south as Boston, and avoiding comparable damage to their own communities. In 1703, Michel Leneuf de la Vallière de Beaubassin led a force of 500 Wabanaki warriors and a handful of French Canadians against British settlements, killing or capturing 300 English at Falmouth (present-day Portland, Maine) and Wells. In 1704, the Wabanaki raided the English settlement at Deerfield, taking more than 100 captives. In 1705, Anglo-Wabanaki conflict ravaged English settlements and tribal villages alike.

The English escalated troop deployments, bringing 1,600 English soldiers to lay siege to the French hub at Port Royal in 1707. The French were on the defense, but their powerful Indian allies repulsed English attacks on Port Royal repeatedly that year. In 1709, farmers around Boston abandoned planting crops and retreated to English forts because of occasional French and repeated Indian raids. The tide turned in 1710, when 3,600 English troops conquered Port Royal, forcing the French to abandon military defense of Nova Scotia. The Wabanaki Confederacy fought on for another two years, with moderate success. At the Battle of Bloody Creek in 1711, the Abenaki killed 16 English soldiers and captured many more. The English increased troop deployments, and by the time France and English signed an armistice in 1712, all were ready for a reprieve from fighting.

CAROLINA AND FLORIDA FRONTS

While the Wabanaki held their own in Acadia, even in the face of French defeat, some tribes in the English colonies of North and South Carolina ascended while others paid a heavy price for resistance. The Chickasaw, Creek, and Yamasee were strongly allied with the English throughout Queen Anne's War. The English had coastal colonies in Carolina, but the French had been expanding trading posts throughout the Southeast from Louisiana. As the English pressed their claims militarily, the French relied primarily on their Choctaw allies to hold the English at bay. The English isolated potential rivals such as the Tuscarora and vented their full force on them, crippling the expansion of French alliances.

In 1702, James Moore, the English governor, moved to

FIGHTING THE WABANAKI Hannah Dustin and Mary Neff, painted here, fought alongside their men when the Wabanaki attacked English settlements in Acadia at the height of Queen Anne's War.

impede French trade expansion throughout the Southeast. He sent 500 English troops and 300 tribal allies against the Spanish garrisoned at St. Augustine, Florida. They burned the main Spanish settlement but could not breach the walls of the stone fort. Eventually, the Spanish navy arrived with reinforcements from Havana, Cuba, and broke the siege.

The Spanish were in a vulnerable position in Florida. They refused to arm the Indians because the Spanish colonial economy required heavy use of Indian slaves, and they did not want to enable an Indian slave revolt. That left them with few allies and few troops to fend off attacks from the English and their Indian allies. The English brutally ravaged the remnant Timucua and Apalachee villages in 1704. The Spanish relied on 8,000 Indian slaves in Florida, but the English killed so many that the tribal population under Spanish control was reduced to 200. The Spanish, without the enslaved labor force needed to sustain their empire, were poised to abandon their colonies in Florida in the next major conflict.

In 1706, Spanish and French forces launched an amphibious assault on Charleston from Havana. The English held on, and their successes elsewhere soon changed the French plans. The French and English signed an armistice in 1712, and then the Treaty of Utrecht in 1713. The French ceded Acadia and Hudson Bay to the English. The tribes fought on. ∎

WABANAKI-NEW ENGLAND WAR
ENGLISH MUSKETS, FRENCH MANIPULATIONS, AND INDIAN LIVES

The French and British were at each other's throats for most of the 1700s, and their conflict embroiled the Wabanaki homeland. The Wabanaki were a loose confederacy of Mi'kmaq, Maliseet, Penobscot, Passamaquoddy, and Abenaki Indians. In spite of all the fighting between France and England, and the competing claims and colonies of the Europeans, the tribes had not ceded title to their lands in New England, Nova Scotia, or New Brunswick to any European nation. Even after Queen Anne's War, which brought the conflict to their lodges and involved many of their warriors, the Wabanaki had no representation at the Treaty of Utrecht, which was signed at the conclusion of Queen Anne's War. Some Wabanaki tribes signed the Treaty of Portsmouth after Queen Anne's War to affirm peace and friendship, but they never consented to British rule or new English colonies. Wabanaki lands, which encompassed the region often called Acadia by the Europeans, were coveted and increasingly encroached on by English settlers after Queen Anne's War. The failure of the English to obtain Indian consultation and permission proved deadly for all sides.

CHIEF PAUGUS Instrumental in leading Wabanaki forces against the English, Paugus was killed during a punitive scalp raid by English militia in 1725.

Wabanaki Offensive

The English built new forts in Wabanaki territory in 1720—Fort George and Fort Canso. The move inflamed the tribes. The French encouraged the Wabanaki to attack the English, essentially taking greater risks to promote the French agenda, which included dislodging the English from Acadia. In 1722, the arrival of Father Sébastien Rale at the Abenaki town of Norridgewock inflamed the English. They correctly suspected that he was an agent of New France planning to supply the Indians with weapons and ammunition if they rose up against the British. The British government built new forts in Maine, Massachusetts, and Vermont in anticipation of renewed conflict with the French and Wabanaki. Rale refused to leave Norridgewock. Instead, the tribes delivered a written statement to the British, defining Wabanaki territory. The English sent 300 troops to arrest Rale. He escaped, but they found letters in his strongbox confirming their suspicion that he was an agent of New France.

At Jeddore Harbour, Nova Scotia, the Mi'kmaq repeatedly attacked English settlements and fishing villages, taking numerous prisoners. They even obtained larger ships from the French and occupied a strategic position near the harbor, cutting off access for the English settlement. The English mustered a naval force, led by John Elliot and John Robinson, that stormed the Mi'kmaq ships and recovered many of the captives. The Mi'kmaq warriors swam for safety, and more than 30 were shot in the water. The Battle of Winnepang, as it was sometimes called, strengthened the English position, but the conflict was far from over. The Mi'kmaq resumed raiding rather than blockading English settlements.

While the Mi'kmaq attacked the English in Nova Scotia, Gray Lock led Abenaki warriors in a series of raids on English settlements in northern Massachusetts and New Hampshire. His initial success at the Battle of Northfield put the English on the defense. By 1724, they had built Fort Dummer at the site of present-day Brattleboro, Vermont, as a new base of military operations against the Wabanaki. Gray Lock pressed attacks at Northfield, Deerfield, Brookfield, and Sunderland. The English retreated from outlying settlements to Fort Dummer, and Gray Lock then focused small raids on the fort itself. The strategy worked through the duration of conflict. Gray Lock's primary village, Woronoke, was untouched in English counterattacks.

English Retaliation

As the war progressed, the Abenaki raided Fort George and took 60 prisoners. Then Maliseet and Mi'kmaq warriors attacked Port Royal (Annapolis Royal). Five hundred Wabanaki attacked Fort Richmond. There were 14 Wabanaki raids in 1723, and another 10 in 1724 in Maine, Vermont, and Nova Scotia. The warriors attacked British merchant vessels and fishing ships. The English abandoned their blockhouses and consolidated people at the forts.

Then England declared war on the Wabanaki. Instead of battling local militia, the tribes soon faced royal troop deployments from England. Unlike local militia, who had to farm and tend to families, British regulars were solely focused on destruction of the Wabanaki. They marched on Norridgewock, the Abenaki center, on August 22, 1724. More than 200 British rangers routed tribal defenders and killed Father Rale.

John Lovewell and other bounty hunters were paid by the scalp for Indians they killed, including Chief Paugus. The Wabanaki and English eventually agreed to a cease-fire. The British learned hard lessons from the conflict even though they emerged victorious. Afterward, they actively sought tribal permission for new settlements. ∎

> "THE WARRIORS THAT FOUGHT FOR THEIR COUNTRY, AND BLED, HAVE SUNK TO THEIR REST; THE DAMP EARTH IS THEIR BED."
>
> HENRY WADSWORTH LONGFELLOW, "THE BATTLE OF LOVELL'S POND," BASED ON THE BATTLE OF PEQUAWKET IN THE WABANAKI-NEW ENGLAND WAR

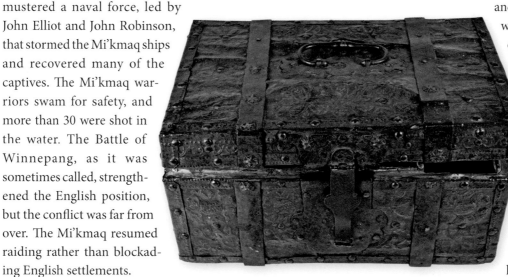

FATHER RALE'S STRONGBOX
When the English captured Father Rale's strongbox, its contents confirmed the priest was a French military agent.

FRENCH AND INDIAN WAR
TRIBAL WARRIORS JOIN THE EPIC STRUGGLE

The French and Indian War, from 1754 to 1763, was fought in North America contemporaneously with the global Seven Years' War, 1755–1764. France and England were the primary protagonists, but each had numerous tribal allies whose lives and homelands were transformed by the dispute. France had just 75,000 colonists in North America, but numerous Abenaki, Mi'kmaq, Lenape, Ojibwe, Ottawa, Shawnee, and Wyandot allies. The English had two million colonists plus powerful Catawba and Cherokee allies. It was a complicated and brutal conflict for all involved, fought along the Allegheny and Monongahela Rivers, throughout the Ohio River Valley, the Great Lakes, and Acadia.

FIRST SALVO: ACADIAN THEATER

After Father Rale's War and sustained Anglo-Wabanaki conflict in Acadia, the region was never fully at peace. The English were intent on displacing their French rivals and any Indians allied with them. They encroached on Mi'kmaq lands in Acadia, intentionally violating the Treaty of Portsmouth, which they had signed in 1726.

In a nasty prelude to the main conflict in the French and Indian War, in 1749, Edward Cornwallis resettled more than 3,000 English colonists in Mi'kmaq lands without permission and built four British forts to protect them, angering the Mi'kmaq. The English were begging for a fight. Hundreds of French Acadians refused to switch religious affiliation from Catholic to Anglican as new settlers engulfed them. Many fled to Quebec.

The English pressed their luck. Charles Lawrence and John Gorham led colonial militia and British regulars deep into Mi'kmaq territory in defense of their encroaching colonists. French Acadian militia under the command of Jean-Louis Le

LOUISBOURG **The British took the Canadian port from the French during the War of the Austrian Succession in 1745, bartered it back into French control, then retook it in the French and Indian War in 1758.**

For John Bowles at N° 13 in Cornhil

Loutre fought alongside the Mi'kmaq warriors. The Mi'kmaq and French Acadians fought 24 engagements with the English in Acadia, 13 of them Mi'kmaq raids around Halifax. In 1749, the English assaulted Canso. The Mi'kmaq counterattacked against Chignecto and Dartmouth later that year. Some French Acadians and Mi'kmaq tried to barter a peace, but British regulars razed a Mi'kmaq village and the conflict escalated. In 1750, British troops assaulted Chignecto successfully with significant casualties. By 1752, in spite of British aggression and resupply, the Mi'kmaq and French appeared to be winning more battles than they were losing. The British signed a peace treaty in 1752, only to rip it up several months later.

By 1755, French and British troops around the globe were preparing to collide. At the Battle of Fort Beauséjour, a French Acadian named Thomas Pichon spied for the British, who sent more than 2,000 troops against the stronghold. It fell after heavy fighting in naval engagements and on land. The British expelled the Acadians, and solidified control over most of Acadia outside of Nova Scotia, cutting off French supply routes. The Mi'kmaq were on their own. Many retreated to Canada to avoid punitive raids by colonial militia.

FRENCH VICTORIES IN OHIO, NEW YORK

While Acadia burned, the tribes in the Ohio River Valley watched English and French troop deployments with a sense of great foreboding. In 1752, the French attacked the British-allied Miami at Pickawillany, killing 14 warriors. Conflict did not widen afterward as the tribes sought to solidify alliances and play the Europeans off one another for weapons and trade terms. Both the French and British initiated troop buildups and constructed more forts in the Ohio. The tribes were bristling.

In 1754, British General Edward Braddock met with four English colonial governors, and decided to send royal troops and colonial militia against the French in a large surprise four-pronged attack. George Washington, an officer in the British Army, ambushed a French patrol in present-day Pennsylvania at the Battle of Jumonville Glen. Washington was accompanied by

MOOSE ANTLER COMB Indian warriors used these moose antler combs to braid their hair before fighting alongside French soldiers in wigs and brass-buttoned coats.

THE TREATY OF UTRECHT, 1713

The English and French warred constantly in the 18th century. In Acadia (present-day Massachusetts, Maine, New Hampshire, Nova Scotia, and New Brunswick), both settled and resettled areas over decades, evicting the other nation's colonists whenever control changed. Neither power had formal authorization to settle there from the indigenous owners of the land—Abenaki, Mi'kmaq, Passamaquoddy, Maliseet, and Penobscot. After the English pushed the French and their Indian allies back during Queen Anne's War, the Europeans tried to divide their empires and avoid further bloodshed. With the Treaty of Utrecht, signed in 1713, they agreed that England would have exclusive colonial rights to Rupert's Land (present-day Hudson Bay and thousands of adjacent acres), as well as its Atlantic coast colonies. The French would have rights to the Great Lakes, Mississippi, and Louisiana.

The Treaty of Utrecht bought peace for only a few years. All sides in Acadia still seethed with anger, including the encroached-upon tribes. Ultimately, areas addressed in the Treaty of Utrecht became battle lines in the subsequent wars between France and England. The English outnumbered the French in North America 20 to 1, but neither would surrender empire without a fight. For the Indians, the fight was not for colonies or empire, but survival, lifeways, homeland, and families.

Tanacharison, a Mingo chief, who was courting British favor even though most of his fellow tribesmen were likely to support the French. When the battle started, the Mingo chief charged the field and split the head of the French commander, Joseph Coulon de Jumonville, with a tomahawk.

Washington withdrew under heavy counterattack by French, Shawnee, Delaware, and Mingo warriors. All parties planned more major military campaigns. The British pressed attacks from Albany, Fort William Henry, and Oswego on French positions at Niagara, Ticonderoga, Frontenac, and Duquesne. The French were vastly outnumbered, but had the more formidable Indian allies. That made all the difference between 1754 and 1755. Aside from British success at Beauséjour in 1755 in Acadia, British efforts in New York and Ohio stalled as France's Indian allies launched successful counterattacks and raids. French troops stayed close to major fortifications.

BATTLE OF THE MONONGAHELA

Pennsylvania was bathed in blood on July 9, 1755. Braddock led a large force of 2,200 British regulars and colonial militia into the Ohio River Valley, planning to engage the French at Fort Duquesne, at what is now

BATTLE OF THE PLAINS OF ABRAHAM British troops appeared suddenly on the field near Quebec, overwhelming the French and their allies. Pictured here is the death of French officer Louis-Joseph de Montcalm.

Pittsburgh. Braddock's expedition had a miserable time cutting overland through the thick Pennsylvania woods and arrived on the banks of the Monongahela River exhausted, with a thin and poorly defended supply line. Braddock, overconfident and without military intelligence, ordered his troops to form ranks and march on the fort.

The French were outnumbered two to one, but reinforced by Ottawa and Potawatomi warriors. They introduced British troops to a radically different style of fighting. Indian warriors set up snipers on both sides of the access road to the fort and fired on the neatly lined British ranks. The British were used to fighting organized troops in rows, marching at and firing on one another. Unprepared for attack by concealed enemies, they suffered significant casualties without inflicting much harm on the tribal force. The British advance stalled. Sensing opportunity, French troops marched out of the fort and engaged the British head on.

Braddock was now directly engaged with French regulars, and flanked on two sides by Ottawa and Potawatomi warriors. The Monongahela River was behind them, making retreat especially difficult. The battle reached a frenzy as all sides realized that the British were about to be enveloped and likely

TRIBAL COUNCIL After the war, the British tried to win over tribes once allied
to the French. Pictured here is a peace conference set up by Colonel Henry Bouquet.

wiped out. The war whoops and eagle whistles of the warriors added to the terror of the British troops, who fell into disarray. Braddock had three horses shot out from under him as he tried to rally his forces. The warriors pressed their flanking attack, and Braddock was mortally wounded. When he fell, the British forces ran for the river, sustaining heavy losses. Washington arrived, trying to cover the retreating troops from the other side of the river, with minimal success. The casualty rate was 85 percent for the British force. Humiliated by their defeat, the British permanently changed the structure of their military, developing a new position of skirmisher and deploying skirmishers in every conflict to counter the impact of concealed fighters and snipers.

FRENCH DEFENSE AND INDIAN CAMPAIGNS

For three years the British struggled to make inroads against the French. They outnumbered the French 20 to 1, but Indian allies strategically reinforced the French and disrupted British actions, keeping their troops bottled up in forts. A British attack at Louisbourg failed, and the attempted siege of Fort William Henry was broken. Then, in 1756, the French took Fort Bull, and destroyed 45,000 pounds of English gunpowder.

With Indians raiding English settlements across Ohio and New York, French troops engineered a strategic feint, doubling back to successfully attack Oswego.

Here the French won a major military victory but started to lose the peace by failing to honor native traditions in war. France's Indian allies were used to pillaging overrun English settlements, but the French stopped them, causing great offense. The tribes rallied again for another French victory at the Battle of Fort William Henry, but once more the French denied the Indians the right to loot. Frustrated, the tribes attacked the retreating British column, taking hundreds of prisoners.

CHARLES LAWRENCE Governor of Nova Scotia and brigadier general, he played a critical role in the British actions in Acadia.

TURNING THE TIDE: BRITISH CONQUEST

Trouble turned to disaster for the French and their allies in 1758, when a devastating wave of smallpox hit the tribes especially hard. Without a vigorous tribal campaign against smaller English settlements, the British were able to reinforce positions and go on the offensive. It was like uncorking a bottle.

That year, the British crushed French troops at Fort Duquesne, taking control of the Ohio River Valley. Then they took Louisbourg in a major naval and land battle, thus taking control of Nova Scotia and solidifying Acadia in British control. Then they captured Frontenac in the Great Lakes. Now the British were looking for a decisive blow.

They assembled a force of 18,000 British regulars and colonial militia to march on major French forts in the Great Lakes. Overconfident, brash, and miscalculating, James Abercrombie led British troops in a direct frontal assault on an entrenched French force with no artillery support or flanking maneuvers, hoping to overwhelm the defenders. On July 8, 1758, at the Battle of Carillon (Ticonderoga), around 3,600 French troops and Indian allies defeated Abercrombie's 18,000-man force. The French suffered 400 casualties and the British more than 2,000. The decisive blow the English hoped to land turned into a humiliating retreat.

Despite that stunning victory, French positions were isolated and now defensive. In 1759, the British regrouped and dislodged them, wresting Carillon from French control permanently. In 1759, they conquered Quebec in bloody fighting where the generals for both forces died. The French counterpunched at the Battle of Sainte-Foy in 1760. The British Army suffered more than 1,000 casualties, the French more than 800, but the British held Quebec. In 1760, the British enveloped Montreal and the French surrendered. ∎

PONTIAC'S WAR
TRIBAL JUGGERNAUT

The French surrender after the French and Indian War shocked the Great Lakes tribes. France lost Quebec and Montreal. But the major battles that had involved the tribes had mainly been victories for the Indians. By 1763, General Jeffrey Amherst, who led the British at Montreal in 1760, treated the tribes as conquered vassals. He discontinued the ancient tribal custom, long accommodated by the French, of paying tribute to tribal leaders. He limited the amount of ammunition and guns traded to Indians. And although the French brought traders to tribal villages, often to live with and marry native women, the English brought settlers who wanted to displace tribal people and take their land. The British were warned when they first occupied Detroit, "This country was given by God to the Indians." By 1763, Pontiac was ready to prove it.

Pontiac persuaded many tribes to join a formidable alliance against English rule in April 1763. Pontiac was Ottawa, and his name, Baandiyaag (later corrupted into Pontiac), meant "he who binds them together." He lived up to that name. Hundreds of Ottawa warriors were joined by their close cousins, the Potawatomi and Mascoutens (prairie Potawatomi). Huron, Miami, Wea, Kickapoo, Piankeshaw, Delaware, and Wyandot rounded out the alliance. The Iroquois Confederacy, which had fought the Ottawa, Potawatomi, and Ojibwe during the Beaver Wars, honored their allegiance to the British, established in the Covenant Chain alliance that stood throughout the French and Indian War.

BATTLE OF BUSHY RUN Pontiac (above) united tribes against the British. They burned 9 of 11 forts in the Great Lakes and besieged the rest until Bushy Run (left), when British soldiers broke the siege at Fort Pitt.

But the Seneca, who were part of the powerful Iroquois Confederacy, broke their alliance. The Mingo (Senecas of the Ohio River who were not part of the Iroquois Confederacy) joined Pontiac, as did some of the main Seneca.

INTRIGUE CONQUERS BRITISH FORTS

Pontiac was a calculating diplomat and military tactician. His first several attacks were successful exercises in intrigue and manipulation. In April 1763, he tried to sneak into Fort Detroit with 300 warriors, but the British were suspicious, so he pulled back, starting a siege two days later to cut off communication between Detroit and other British forts. Then his warriors attacked British supply columns from Fort Niagara, defeating a major British deployment at Point Pelee. Word spread of trouble in Detroit, and the British sent reinforcements to attack Pontiac's camp. But he was warned and ambushed their force a mile out, wounding 34 and killing 20, including commander James Dalyell. The British survived in an organized retreat, but the creek at the battlefield ran red with English blood. The English called the attack the Battle of Bloody Run. Amherst issued a 200-pound bounty for Pontiac's scalp.

In May 1763, Pontiac peacefully entered Fort Sandusky, held the commander prisoner, and executed 15 British guards. Then he repeated the process at Fort St. Joseph. At Fort Miami, the British commander was lured out of the fort to rendezvous

DEVIL'S HOLE AMBUSH

At the time Pontiac rose up against the British, the Seneca in the eastern Great Lakes were tired of English encroachment on their lands. At the Niagara Gorge, more than 300 Seneca warriors under the leadership of Chief Farmer's Brother ambushed a supply train heading to British posts nearby. They closed ranks quickly, making musket fire ineffective. In brutal hand-to-hand combat they overwhelmed the teamsters and their security detail, killing all but three of the men.

The British dispatched two companies of light infantry to deal with the Seneca, but the well-prepared warriors at Devil's Hole ambushed them. Fighting from heavy brush on a nearby knoll, the Seneca repelled the British troops, who moved into an unorganized retreat. The Seneca circled and cut off the troops from the fort, forcing a close confrontation where their superior numbers overwhelmed the British. They killed 81 British regulars and wounded eight, suffering only one warrior wounded.

The British then reinforced their strongholds in Niagara, thwarting the long-term goal of Farmer's Brother, which was to drive them out. The Seneca fought on with Pontiac, but never regained the initiative in the Niagara region.

with his native mistress and was shot dead by Pontiac's warriors. The British garrison at Fort Ouiatenon was so outmatched that the British surrendered without contest.

On June 2, 1763, Pontiac's warriors staged a game of lacrosse in front of Fort Mackinac. Hundreds of players were on the field. British soldiers lined the walls of the fort to watch. As they did, Ottawa women smuggled concealed guns into the fort. Then one of the warriors tossed the ball over the wall of the fort. The warriors charged through the open gate, grabbed the concealed weapons, and killed most of the British garrison. From there, Pontiac swept down through the Ohio River Valley. The Seneca conquered Fort Venango. They captured the commander and made him write down their grievances. Then they burned him at the stake.

Fort Le Boeuf fell shortly after, then Fort Presque Isle. The British there surrendered with a promise of safe passage to Fort Pitt, but some of Pontiac's warriors were unwilling to honor the agreement and ambushed the unarmed troops as they left, killing most.

On June 22, Pontiac besieged Fort Pitt. Pitt and Detroit were the only remaining British

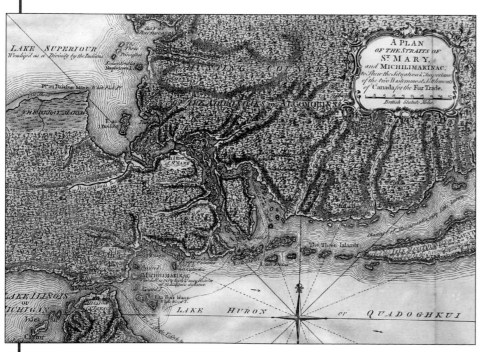

STRAITS OF MACKINAC **Pontiac staged a brilliant conquest of the fort at Mackinac, and the British strongholds toppled like dominoes.**

LACROSSE PLAYERS Sometimes called the little game of war, lacrosse was an intense contest, and players often dressed in full war regalia for games, making possible Pontiac's ruse at Mackinac.

military posts in the Great Lakes; nine other forts were under Pontiac's control, most of them burned. Pontiac flew a French flag in his village. He sent runners to seek French assistance, but it never came. Amherst ordered smallpox-infected blankets to be sent to the tribes. Henry Bouquet and William Trent carried out the orders. At the Battle of Bushy Run, Bouquet broke through Pontiac's line at Fort Pitt with 500 troops and relieved the beleaguered garrison. Almost immediately after that, the Seneca defeated a large British force at Devil's Hole, killing 81 British regulars.

PEACE THROUGH MUTUAL ACCOMMODATION

Pontiac was close to victory, but the sieges dragged on, and many of his warriors needed to go home to provide for their families. As his force dwindled, Pontiac lifted the sieges and pulled back to the Maumee to initiate a punishing guerrilla war, raiding throughout Appalachia. Amherst was recalled to London, and Major General Thomas Gage sent to relieve him. The British never defeated Pontiac in the field, but the tribes could not drive the British out either. In 1764, the Seneca rejoined the Covenant Chain in a treaty at Niagara, ceding Niagara Portage for peace with no other consequences. Colonel John Bradstreet negotiated two major treaties in Ohio, and Bouquet arranged a transfer of prisoners. Pontiac released more than 200. In 1766, Pontiac traveled to New York and signed a peace and friendship treaty with the British. Some of his old allies fought on, including Shawnee chief Charlot Kaské, who eventually retreated west of the Mississippi. Most other tribes accepted British trade while the British promised to honor the Royal Proclamation of 1763, which pledged no new settlements west of the Appalachians. ■

CHEROKEE WARS
BETRAYAL IN THE SOUTHEAST

The Cherokee were the largest tribe in the Southeast, occupying 50 major towns in present-day North Carolina, South Carolina, and Tennessee. They were clever, adaptive, politically sophisticated, and militarily powerful. They fought their Indian neighbors to preserve territory, but had no interest in colonizing them. They accommodated the English in the early settlement period because they valued English trade goods, profited from the deerskin trade, and saw little risk in alliance. Disease and encroachment by the English colonists eventually caused tension, but the Cherokee kept the peace and the British courted their friendship, especially in conflict with other tribes.

The French eventually approached the Cherokee as well. They built forts along the lower Mississippi River and courted Cherokee trade and alliance. The Cherokee never broke their military alliance with the English, although the western Cherokee towns often traded with the French and some of the Cherokee chiefs felt greater affinity with them. Tensions in Cherokee alliances were tested in the 1700s, and the dynamic came to a head when the French and Indian War broke out.

TESTING THE ANGLO-CHEROKEE ALLIANCE

English colonists, with full backing from the British Army, systematically encroached upon and displaced various tribes in the Carolinas. The Cherokee were never bothered and often helped English militias do the dirty work because the first tribes to be displaced were Cherokee enemies. From 1711 to 1715, the Cherokee helped Carolina militias defeat the

Tuscarora. From 1715 to 1716, the Yamasee War engulfed the region. Some Cherokee factions supported the Yamasee; most sided with the British. By the end of that conflict, even the Cherokee who had been inclined to help the Yamasee tried to avoid direct conflict with the British or the pro-British Cherokee.

The French and Indian War broke out in 1754. At first, the western Cherokee who were friendly with the French, led by Mankiller and several other prominent chiefs, stayed neutral. The eastern Cherokee joined the British war effort. They rallied more than 700 warriors to help the British Army assault Fort Duquesne, in Pennsylvania. They also fanned out and assisted in other attacks in the Ohio River Valley, even occupying another fort for British defense at the mouth of the Ohio River.

CREEK CHIEF The Creek often fought the Cherokee, but Dragging Canoe persuaded some to ally against Americans.

In 1758, pro-British Cherokee aided in the eventual takeover of Fort Duquesne. The British force was stretched thin and low on supplies after the attack. The soldiers even butchered some of their horses for food. The Cherokee were not allowed to loot or receive British assistance in being resupplied. After providing so much critical support to the British, the Cherokee felt unappreciated and left Duquesne. While returning home, they helped themselves to supplies at several English farms. This was an established British custom—to commandeer supplies for a critical war effort. But the colonists did not see the Cherokee as part of the British Army. When some Cherokee commandeered horses from English farms, the colonists called out the local militia and attacked.

The Cherokee were surprised, thinking that commandeering supplies from the colonists they were protecting was in keeping with colonial customs. It is not known how many Cherokee were killed, but the colonists scalped 30 to 40 Cherokee, collecting bounties on their scalps as pro-French Shawnee. The colonial militia then attacked several Cherokee towns and the British-loyalist Cherokee garrison at Fort Loudoun, in a brutal massacre.

The French fortified Fort Toulouse in Alabama, and Fort St. Pierre and Fort Rosalie in Mississippi. Then they reached out to the Cherokee for alliance. In 1758, some Cherokee started retaliatory raids on British settlements. In 1759, Big Mortar, a Creek (Muscogee) chief tried to unify Cherokee, Creek, Shawnee, Chickasaw, and Catawba villages against the British. His efforts failed, but sowed seeds that Dragging Canoe harvested in a later pan-Indian resistance. In 1759, violence escalated and the Cherokee declared war on the British, not as French allies, but independently.

THE ANGLO-CHEROKEE WAR

William Lyttelton, the governor of South Carolina, knew that the English could not fight everyone simultaneously and realized that the English had unnecessarily escalated conflict with the Cherokee. He agreed to a peace parley with the Cherokee, but his delegates there took 23 Indian peace

FORT LOUDOUN COUNCIL Fort Loudoun was the westernmost British fort in Cherokee territory. Colonel Henry Bouquet met the Cherokee there in 1758 in a vain effort to save the alliance after settlers murdered several chiefs.

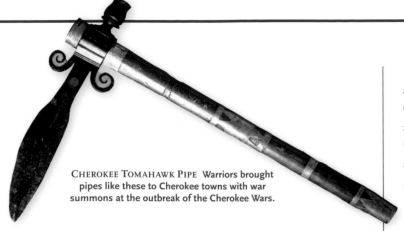

CHEROKEE TOMAHAWK PIPE Warriors brought pipes like these to Cherokee towns with war summons at the outbreak of the Cherokee Wars.

delegates hostage. Infuriated, the Cherokee attacked Fort Prince George in a desperate attempt to rescue their captive chiefs. In the course of their attack, they killed the British fort commander. His replacement ordered the execution of the 23 Cherokee hostages.

The Cherokee saw no way forward but war. Fort Dobbs and Fort Prince George withstood major attacks, but English backcountry farms and trading posts fell to the Cherokee. Then the Cherokee besieged Fort Loudoun and took control of the buildings and garrison. With the Cherokee winning the backcountry battles and keeping the British bottled up in major forts, the colonists sent a request to Jeffrey Amherst, commander of British forces in North America, for assistance. Amherst sent Archibald Montgomerie and 1,200 British regulars, joined by 300 colonial rangers. They razed several of the lower towns, taking 100 Cherokee captives.

At the first Battle of Echoee, the Cherokee ambushed Montgomerie and the main troop deployment in a deep valley. The Cherokee had acquired rifled muskets from the French, more accurate than standard British military issue, and set up a withering fire on British ranks. Several British officers were killed. Fifty colonial rangers feared being enveloped, so they deserted.

Montgomerie tried to lead his company of Highlanders on a flanking move while the Royal Scots pushed the center of the Cherokee line. The Cherokee fell back, displaced to a high hill, and could not be dislodged. Other Cherokee warned nearby towns of danger, and a third group outflanked the Highlanders and attacked Montgomerie's supply train. They destroyed so many supplies and pack animals that Montgomerie was forced to retreat to Fort Prince George. He left numerous wounded soldiers at the fort, and then retreated to Charleston. The battle halted the British advance into Cherokee territory.

By 1760, the Cherokee controlled Fort Loudoun. They executed 23 British soldiers in retaliation for their 23 murdered chiefs. They kept 100 British soldiers as prisoners, hoping to barter an exchange for the 100 Cherokee captives the British held. Then they released the rest of the British garrison with an agreement that they would retreat unarmed. Those soldiers rearmed, so the Cherokee attacked them.

Montgomerie was recalled to England, and Amherst sent James Grant to muster British regulars and militia, along with Catawba, Chickasaw, and Mohawk allies—a total of 2,800 fighters—to crush the Cherokee middle towns. At the Second Battle of Echoee, the Cherokee killed most of the British pack animals, but could not force the English to retreat. Grant pushed on the middle towns until 300 of his men were too sick to walk. His hard drive produced the desired result.

The Cherokee had to remove their families from the conflict zone, and the British force entered the middle towns with little resistance. Most of the 15 middle towns were razed and their food supplies destroyed. More than 4,000 Cherokee were now homeless and without food. In 1761, with a fresh outbreak of smallpox and many of their people starving, the Cherokee sued for peace.

NICKAJACK EXPEDITION

Dragging Canoe built and defended the Chickamauga Cherokee towns from 1776 to 1792. His passing was a great loss, but the Chickamauga fought on. They raided American settlements and defended their territory from encroachment. Nickajack Town and Running Water Town were especially resistant.

William Blount, who was governor of the Southwest Territory before helping to create the state of Tennessee, tried and failed to broker a peace. Local settlers wanted more than the Cherokee would ever give, and the Cherokee had little trust that Blount would protect their interests. Blount sensed weakness in the Cherokee after the passing of Dragging Canoe. He abandoned diplomacy and called up the local militia.

As the militiamen marched on Nickajack Town, the Cherokee residents fled to Running Water Town. The evacuation was nearly complete when the militia arrived, but Cherokee warriors doubled back to buy more time for their families to reach sanctuary. Along the banks of the Tennessee River they fought a fierce but one-sided battle. Three Americans were wounded and 70 Cherokee were killed. The militia razed Nickajack Town, then marched on to Running Water and demolished it. The Cherokee fled in disarray.

FORT NASHBOROUGH The future site of Nashville, Tennessee, this fort was a focus of Dragging Canoe's resistance at the start of the American Revolution. It had 20 log buildings within a wooden picket, and could shelter hundreds of people.

The Cherokee signed two treaties with the English after that. In 1765, Henry Timberlake brought three Cherokee chiefs to London, still trying to cement the Anglo-Cherokee peace. The colonists did not share his goodwill, and it was one of the many issues of contention between them and the British government in the brewing American Revolution.

DRAGGING CANOE

By 1775, the Cherokee alliance with the English was for the most part repaired. Dragging Canoe, a prominent Cherokee war chief, was an especially strong British loyalist. But tensions between the Cherokee and many American colonists rarely eased, especially after the 1775 Henderson Purchase, which sold Cherokee lands south of the Kentucky River to a private party that opened them for settlement. Dragging Canoe refused to consent to the sale of Cherokee land. George Washington, who had fought with and against Cherokee warriors in several campaigns, warned colonists against driving a wedge between themselves and the Cherokee.

When the American Revolution broke out, Dragging Canoe committed Cherokee warriors to the British cause. He was instrumental in the British war effort on the frontier, leading successful Cherokee attacks at McDowell's Station, Lindley's Station, the Battle of Island Flats, and the Siege of Fort Caswell. At Island Flats, Dragging Canoe was wounded, and his brother Little Owl was shot 11 times but miraculously survived. The Cherokee were on the defensive in several other battles in which American militia prosecuted scorched-earth campaigns against Cherokee towns, with devastating results.

Dragging Canoe led his people to build new towns at Chickamauga, and from there he led a successful off-and-on military campaign against the United States until his death in 1792. He did not win all battles, but his military successes forced settlers to keep a healthy distance from the Chickamauga homeland, preserving its integrity for three generations. When he died, Dragging Canoe was formally memorialized by the Cherokee Council. ∎

OLD NORTHWEST WAR
BLOODLETTING ON THE AMERICAN FRONTIER

The Ohio River Valley was in a state of perpetual conflict from the early English settlement of New York, through the French and Indian War, and into the American Revolution. The tribes were inundated by foreigners who both had designs on their land and needed them as military allies. After the Revolutionary War, American plans for their homeland came to a head in the region's bloodiest conflict.

When the United States and Great Britain signed the Treaty of Paris in 1783, ending the American Revolution, England ceded what was then called the Northwest Territory (the Ohio River Valley) to America. No Indians had ever ceded land there, so America's understanding of

DEATH OF MONTGOMERY U.S. General Richard Montgomery was killed in action in 1775. British forces successfully beat back the American invasion of Canada with help from Indian allies.

title to the Ohio was guaranteed to bring the new nation into conflict with the occupants and owners of the land. After the Treaty of Fort Stanwix in 1784, the United States got the Iroquois Confederacy in New York to release any claims to the Ohio, but they were not living there and for years had been trying to dislodge the resident tribes. The Treaty of Fort McIntosh in 1785 stated peace and friendship between America and some tribes, but did nothing meaningful to avoid conflict, especially when America paid its war veterans in land grants in Ohio and New York without getting land cessions from the tribes.

Miami chief Little Turtle and Shawnee chief Blue Jacket helped forge a coalition between their tribes and Dragging Canoe's Chickamauga

Cherokee as well as the Wyandot (Huron), Ojibwe, Ottawa, Potawatomi, Lenape, Kickapoo, Kaskaskia, Wea, and Piankeshaw at a major tribal conference in 1785. Some tribes, like the Chickamauga Cherokee, had never stopped fighting American colonists, but now there was a truly formidable tribal alliance.

Little Turtle and Blue Jacket were not rash. Their warriors were seasoned fighters from decades of sustained conflict with the Iroquois and in wars between France and England. The two leaders made careful calculations, diplomatically built their confederation, and waited for the right opportunity to strike. White settlers started to flood into the Ohio River Valley, especially after the Northwest Ordinance of 1787, which gave squatters ownership rights even if they were squatting on unceded Indian land. Little Turtle and Blue Jacket went into action. One by one, isolated settlers were picked off—killed or taken hostage. Unprepared for another major military conflict so soon after the Revolution, America tried to placate the tribes at the Treaty of Fort Harmar, but continued encroaching on the tribes, building Fort Washington in 1789. The tribes raided white towns and settlements with devastating effect, killing or capturing 1,500 settlers. George Washington sent General Benjamin Logan to raise a militia, attacking several Shawnee towns on the Mad River. The Old Northwest War was on.

Harmar Campaign, 1790

Little Turtle and Blue Jacket could call upon 2,000 warriors, and in smaller engagements they overwhelmed minor settler outposts. Washington now sent General Josiah Harmar at the head of a large militia force of 1,500 against the Shawnee and Miami. But Harmar, who received little military intelligence, proceeded slowly and methodically. Little Turtle and Blue Jacket waited for the right time to attack.

Harmar sent Colonel John Hardin and 400 of his militia out of Fort Wayne, Indiana. At Heller's Corner, 1,200 warriors ambushed Hardin. He lost 60 men, as his force was nearly enveloped in a brutal fighting retreat. Little Turtle did not press the attack against the main force, preferring to engage when he had tactical advantage. At Hartshorn's Defeat, the tribal coalition ambushed a small detachment led by Phillip Hartshorn, killing 20 soldiers. Harmar refused to reinforce Hartshorn's position because

> "**If ever we are constrained to lift the hatchet against any tribe, we will never lay it down till that tribe is exterminated, or driven beyond the Mississippi.**"
>
> Thomas Jefferson

of risk to his larger force, leading some of his officers to accuse him of cowardice.

At the Battle of the Pumpkin Fields, Hardin fought a defensive gambit as he waited for reinforcements. Harmar again proved tepid and unwilling to reinforce the smaller regiment, which was dislodged and retreated with 129 killed and 94 wounded. The battlefield was strewn with the bodies of dead militiamen, their scalped heads steaming in the cool air like pumpkins on an autumn morning, giving the battle its name.

Battle of the Wabash, 1791

George Washington recalled Harmar and ordered Major General Arthur St. Clair to deal with Little Turtle and Blue Jacket. St. Clair brought 1,000 militia and 200 support personnel into the field. They bivouacked along the Wabash River. Little Turtle deployed the bulk of his force, sneaking more than 1,000 warriors undetected within 100 yards of the American military camp. They attacked at dawn, catching the militia by surprise and chasing them across the river.

TREATY OF FORT STANWIX

After the Revolutionary War, the new government of the United States was bankrupt. It had little authority to tax. It was delinquent in payment of soldiers, but desperately needed the loyalty of the army and its citizens, who still included many British sympathizers. Britain remained intent upon reclaiming America, a matter not fully resolved until the War of 1812. The United States decided to pay Revolutionary War veterans in land grants in Indian territory, even though the new nation had yet to acquire the land it was promising to give away.

The United States engaged the Iroquois Confederacy in a major diplomatic effort, which resulted in the Treaty of Fort Stanwix in 1784. The Iroquois Confederacy (Seneca, Cayuga, Onondaga, Oneida, Mohawk, and Tuscarora) ceded their claims to the Ohio River Valley. They had been moving into the Ohio for many decades at the expense of other tribes, but it was fiercely contested terrain. The Iroquois lost a territorial claim more than they did a homeland. But for the Shawnee, Mingo, Cherokee, Ottawa, Potawatomi, Wyandot, and many other tribes, the region was home. And none of those tribes agreed to the treaty. The U.S. government paid its veterans in land grants and opened the Ohio River Valley to white settlement, igniting a ferocious war between America and the owners of the land.

Little Turtle quickly deployed marksmen who sniped out the soldiers who were manning artillery support from a nearby hill. Surrounded and demoralized, one of St. Clair's officers, William Darke, led a bayonet charge, hoping to break Little Turtle's line and escape. Little Turtle retreated his central line in a feint and then enveloped the charging force, annihilating the charge. Facing destruction of the entire force, the militia tried the same tactic several times with the same result.

St. Clair had three horses shot out from under him as he desperately tried to rally the survivors. He concentrated his force and issued another bayonet charge, which Little Turtle allowed through so he could envelop them, but the Americans sprinted from the camp toward Fort Jefferson. Little Turtle's warriors pursued them for three miles and then broke off the chase. They executed the wounded survivors and looted the camp. Little Turtle's

"MAD" ANTHONY **General Anthony Wayne crushed a major tribal force at the Battle of Fallen Timbers in 1794.**

force killed 632 of the 920 soldiers and wounded another 264. All 200 support personnel were also killed. Only 24 militia were unharmed. It was the highest loss for any battle with Indians in U.S. history—three times the number at the Battle of the Little Bighorn.

Washington demanded St. Clair's resignation. In 1792, Cornplanter and Red Jacket, who were Iroquois and not directly involved in the conflict, wanted to sue for a regional peace while the Indians had military advantage. Little Turtle paid no heed, still leading successful raids, ambushes, and attacks, including a large one on Fort St. Clair. In 1793, a peace parley at Sandusky failed as the Iroquois refused to back Shawnee territory claims. They were determined to fight it out rather than surrender their territory while undefeated in battle.

BATTLE OF FALLEN TIMBERS, 1794

Washington now turned to "Mad" Anthony Wayne, a daring Revolutionary War general. Wayne took time to build and train a new military host. He started in 1792, then marched to Fort Washington in 1793, just as the peace conference in Sandusky failed. Wayne built Fort Greeneville and Fort Recovery (at the site of the Battle of the Wabash), recovering several cannon St. Clair lost. He spent the winter preparing for conflict. In spring of 1794, 1,200 Indian warriors destroyed a U.S. military supply team and escort and attacked Fort Recovery, but failed to take the fort, which was guarded by U.S. troops and their Chickasaw allies.

Wayne advanced his main force to the Maumee River (near present-day Toledo). There was a bramble of blown-down trees there, and Little Turtle and Blue Jacket had the bulk of their 1,500 warriors concealed among the fallen timbers. With 2,000 American troops, Wayne had both numerical and tactical advantage. Instead of slowly advancing, using snipers, or surrounding and starving out the Indians, Wayne ordered an all-out bayonet charge. That put his numerical advantage to best use. Closing ranks made Indian musket fire less effective, and mitigated the concealment advantage the fallen timbers gave the warriors. While most of his force pressed the center, Wayne sent his cavalry on a flanking maneuver and routed the tribal force.

JOSEPH BRANT: MOHAWK WAR CHIEF

◇◇◇◇◇◇◇◇◇◇◇◇◇◇◇◇◇◇◇◇◇◇◇◇◇◇◇◇◇

Joseph Brant was a prominent Mohawk war chief and British loyalist. As a teenager, he fought with other Mohawk warriors as a British ally in the French and Indian War. He personally took part in at least five major engagements, earning distinction on the battlefield.

When the Revolutionary War broke out, Brant was commissioned as a British officer. He led a segregated unit of Mohawk warriors in independent actions and cooperative campaigns with British regulars. He helped lead Mohawk and Seneca warriors at Wyoming Valley and Cherry Valley, waging a withering series of attacks on the colonists.

After the war, Brant moved with many of his people to Quebec, fearing backlash from American settlers and unfair treatment from the U.S. government. He traveled to Philadelphia and met with George Washington as part of an American effort to woo the Mohawk. Brant also traveled to England and met with King George III, effectively maintaining resources and protection for his community. He was offered pensions from both the U.S. and British governments and maintained a large plantation in Canada. During the Old Northwest War, Brant refused formal war invitations from American Indians, but stayed engaged in diplomatic ties with all parties and eventually persuaded British officials to send weapons and supplies to the Indians.

Shawnee chief Blue Jacket and Miami chief Little Turtle tried to regroup at the British-controlled Fort Miami, but were locked out. They had been allies of the British throughout the Revolutionary War and afterward, and the betrayal by their allies came as a terrible shock. The United States and Great Britain were negotiating a new peace accord, the Jay Treaty. France was in turmoil, Great Britain was overextended, and America was recovering from the Revolution. They all needed a break from fighting one another.

Caught in the open at Fort Miami and lacking any cavalry to fend off Wayne's advance, the tribal force dispersed. They had little ability to effectively stop Wayne from a slow, methodical scorched-earth campaign against the Miami and Shawnee villages. In defensive mode, the warriors worked to get their families out of the path of Wayne's marauding army. Most of their homes and food supplies were torched. In 1795, the United States and Great Britain approved the Jay Treaty, which defined the Canadian border and bought nearly 20 years of peace between the United States and Great Britain. Then the United States signed the Treaty of Greeneville with the remnants of Little Turtle's alliance. It involved a major land cession. The Northwest Territory flooded with white settlers, and soon the states of Ohio and Indiana were created. The tribes were pushed out, retreating west and regrouping until out of the ashes, Tecumseh, in later years, tried to bring them back together again. ∎

BATTLE OF FALLEN TIMBERS The defeat of a multitribe coalition forced
the signing of the Treaty of Greeneville in 1795, ending the Old Northwest War.

AMERICAN REVOLUTION

ALLIED AND BETRAYED

W hile the Cherokee were engulfed in conflict with colonists before the Revolutionary War and continued to defend their territory during and after the war, the American Revolution posed a different challenge for tribes in New York and Florida. The conflict tore apart their ancient alliances and eventually their homes as America sparred with Great Britain while Spain and France intervened opportunistically, all with devastating effects on the natives.

Prior to European contact, five major Iroquoian tribes based in New York—Seneca, Cayuga, Onondaga, Oneida, and Mohawk—formed a ceremonial union of their independent tribes. The tribes had been at war, and their new union was symbolized in burying their war hatchets at the base of a great tree of peace, a metaphor and symbol that transferred into English usage. The Tuscarora formally joined the league in 1722. The spiritual foundation for the Iroquois League still stands today, but the overlapping political and military confederacy among the member tribes was torn asunder during the Revolutionary War.

In 1677, the Iroquois formed a political and military alliance with the English known as the Covenant Chain. For decades it served both the Iroquois and English well. The Iroquois fought with and for the English throughout their many conflicts with the French and other tribes, including Queen Anne's War and the French and Indian War. King George III's Royal Proclamation of 1763 stated that there would be no settlement west of the Appalachian Mountains.

CROSSING THE DELAWARE George Washington's trip was a dramatic moment in the war. His Oneida allies brought him reinforcements and supplies. Washington smoked many Iroquois pipes (above) making alliances with the tribes.

> "WHEN YOUR ARMY ENTERED . . . WE CALLED YOU TOWN
> DESTROYER; AND TO THIS DAY WHEN THAT NAME IS HEARD OUR
> WOMEN LOOK BEHIND THEM AND TURN PALE, AND OUR CHILDREN
> CLING CLOSE TO THE NECKS OF THEIR MOTHERS."
>
> CORNPLANTER TO WASHINGTON

The first hint of trouble for the military cohesion of the Iroquois Confederacy had come in the French and Indian War, when a small group of Catholic Mohawks supported the French at the Battle of Lake George. That pitted Mohawks against one another, but did not further fracture the confederacy. The American Revolution, however, challenged the Iroquois as never before. To them, the colonists and the English government were one and the same. That they would fight one another was confusing enough, but even more so when both sides recruited the tribes individually as military allies. They tried to remain neutral, but that proved impossible.

CHOOSING SIDES IN THE REVOLUTION

Ultimately, the Tuscarora and Oneida, heavily influenced by Presbyterian missionary Samuel Kirkland, sided with colonists. The Oneida resupplied and reinforced Washington during his 1776 crossing of the Delaware River and fought in a series of important battles. The Cayuga, Seneca, and Mohawk sided with the British and were instrumental in many clashes in New York. The Onondaga stayed neutral as long as they could, but eventually were attacked by American troops and joined the British.

In 1776, Joseph Brant, a distinguished Mohawk leader, returned from a formal state visit to London. He fought at the Battle of Long Island and then came home to gather Mohawk warriors for a major campaign against the colonists. Brant led Mohawk warriors against colonial settlements, including the attack at Cherry Valley. Seeing the value of the disruption the tribal campaign was causing the colonists, the British commissioned another Mohawk leader, Joseph Louis Cook, as a lieutenant colonel, the highest rank bestowed on a Native American in the conflict.

The Iroquois had a terrible test in 1777 at the Battle of Oriskany. Tuscarora and Oneida warriors accompanied a colonial relief expedition led by General Nicholas Herkimer, trying to break the siege at Fort Stanwix. The column was ambushed by British loyalist Mohawk scouts led by Joseph Brant and numerous Seneca allies, including Cornplanter. It was the first major battle that pitted Iroquois Indians against one another. Afterward, Brant led Mohawk warriors in a raid on the Oneida village of Oriska. The Oneida responded with attacks on three Mohawk villages. Many Mohawk fled to Canada for the duration of the war, and most stayed there afterward.

George Washington said, "Indians and wolves are both beasts of prey, tho' they differ in shape." Determined to crush the Mohawk and Seneca and reduce their power to engage in attacks on colonists, he sent concurrent campaigns led by

CORNPLANTER: SENECA WAR CHIEF

Cornplanter was a Seneca war chief and diplomat. His father, Johannes Abeel, was Dutch, and his mother Seneca. Cornplanter, sometimes known as John Abeel, played prominent roles in Seneca society for most of his extraordinarily long life—he was born around 1732 and died in 1836.

During the French and Indian War, most Iroquois honored the Covenant Chain, the 1677 economic and military alliance with the British. Cornplanter was an opportunist, however, and although he did not want to undermine the cohesion of the Iroquois Confederacy, he was among the Indian allies to the French during the defeat of General Edward Braddock at the Battle of the Monongahela.

During the American Revolution, Cornplanter played an even more pivotal role. He organized Seneca warriors and helped lead major attacks at Wyoming Valley and Cherry Valley in 1778. Those attacks put the colonists in defensive positions, but also inspired George Washington to send troops against the Mohawk and Seneca.

Cornplanter remained a prominent diplomat after the Revolution, signing the Treaty of Fort Stanwix in 1784 and keeping the Seneca neutral during the Old Northwest War. In 1796, as reward for his efforts to keep the Seneca from joining other tribes against the Americans, Cornplanter was given title to a 1,500-acre tract of land in New York known as the Cornplanter Tract. He and his heirs lived there for decades. The land was flooded by development of the Kinzua Dam in 1965, and most residents were relocated to the Allegany Reservation.

Colonel Daniel Brodhead and General John Sullivan to upstate New York on a scorched-earth campaign. Throughout the Finger Lakes area they attacked tribal villages. Even the Onondaga, who had remained neutral through most of the conflict, were attacked. Methodically, the colonial force, which numbered more than 5,000, burned food supplies and houses. Homeless and without supplies, more than 5,000 Iroquois sought refuge in Canada. More than 40 tribal towns were destroyed. Even though the campaign did not result in decisive military victory, Washington got his desired result—the Iroquois were far less effective as a fighting force for the British. Cornplanter called George Washington "Town Destroyer" afterward, and even today many Iroquois still refer to him that way.

TRIBAL CAMPAIGN IN FLORIDA

While the Iroquois Confederacy imploded, American colonists were pushing the Cherokee farther west in the Carolinas. Thomas Jefferson said, "I hope that the Cherokees will now be driven beyond the Mississippi and that this in future will be declared to the Indians the invariable consequence of their beginning a war. Our contest with Britain is too serious and too great to permit any possibility of avocation from the Indians." The Choctaw and Creek were bracing for conflict and their neutrality would not stand. The tribes had to pick sides as the conflict enveloped their homelands.

The Revolutionary War spilled farther south and soon brought the Spanish into the fray. At the conclusion of the French and Indian War, France had ceded Louisiana to the Spanish to keep it out of British hands. Spain retroceded it later, giving the French permission to be the principal European occupiers and trade beneficiaries. Years later, France sold the land to the United States in the Louisiana Purchase. Regardless of the European shenanigans around title, it was still tribal land, and no tribe had sold the property to any European power.

The British and Spanish had a tense tug-of-war over Indian trade prior to the Revolutionary War. Now those relationships were tested militarily. The British occupied New Orleans at the outbreak of the war. In 1778, the British fleet took control of Savannah. The Creek reinforced and supported the British as they pushed to St. Augustine. In 1780, the Spanish allied with the American colonists and took New Orleans from the British, threatening the British stronghold at Pensacola. The Creek sent 2,000 warriors to reinforce the British and held off the Spanish attack. The tide turned when the Creek retreated in 1781, and the Spanish conquered Pensacola and Savannah. The English retreated from St. Augustine in 1783. Although the Creek were instrumental in advancing British interests, that assistance only served to set the American colonists and their government against the Creek in subsequent conflicts. The battle for control of the Southeast had just begun. ∎

RED JACKET Red Jacket, a Seneca chief and British loyalist during the Revolution, was instrumental in campaigns that broke the Iroquois Confederacy.

TECUMSEH'S WAR
TRIBAL DIPLOMAT IN THE CAULDRON OF CONFLICT

Shawnee chief Tecumseh, who lived from 1768 to 1813, was one of the most celebrated Indian leaders of all time, even outside native communities. Ironically, even William Tecumseh Sherman, architect of America's deadly strategy in the Plains Indian wars, was named after him. Tecumseh united a coalition of tribes in the southern Great Lakes to rebuild their communities and lifeways. His efforts were not military at first, but American expansion soon engulfed his people in war, especially after the outbreak of the War of 1812. In that effort, too, Tecumseh proved exceptional.

Tecumseh traveled tirelessly, using deft diplomacy, inspiring oratory, military action, and knowledge of several tribal languages to unite

TIPPECANOE William Henry Harrison was catapulted to fame when he attacked Prophetstown in Tecumseh's absence in the Battle of Tippecanoe, a severe setback for Tecumseh's coalition.

Native American people in common purpose. Many Shawnee were displaced from Ohio during the height of the conflict with the Iroquois during the Beaver Wars. But his relationships internally among the Shawnee and externally with other tribes were earned over and over through diplomatic effort.

Tecumseh had many reasons to hate white settlers. His father was killed in 1774, during Lord Dunmore's War, at the Battle of Point Pleasant. In 1779, his childhood village was destroyed by Kentucky militia. In 1780, his family moved to another village, but that too was torched by marauding militia. In 1782, his village was destroyed again, and Tecumseh moved to yet another new home at Bellefontaine, Ohio. He saw many of his relatives, including small children, killed by settlers and militia. Tecumseh resolved to change the course of history so his people would never have to live in fear again.

With both of his parents dead, Tecumseh was raised by his older brother, Chiksika. Tecumseh fought along with him as a teenager and young man in the Old Northwest War. In the middle of the conflict, Tecumseh moved with a dozen Shawnee to live with the Chickamauga Cherokee because his brother married a Cherokee woman. There, Tecumseh met Dragging Canoe, famous leader of the Cherokee resistance and a brilliant military tactician. Chiksika was killed while leading a raid, and Tecumseh assumed leadership of their small band of Shawnee. He returned to Ohio and fought in several battles of the Old Northwest War, including the Battle of Fallen Timbers. In spite of the tribal loss in that battle, Tecumseh refused to sign the Treaty of Greeneville.

BUILDING PROPHETSTOWN

Tecumseh also refused to sell any more land. That put him at odds with Black Hoof, a rival Shawnee chief, who tried to reconcile with the United States while Tecumseh pursued his dream of independent and thriving native communities. In 1807, Tecumseh parleyed with American officials, and Tecumseh told U.S. officials and Blue Jacket, the dominant Shawnee chief during the Old Northwest War, that he wanted peace, and to move west, farther away from white settlement.

In 1808, he did just that and established Prophetstown in the heart of Miami territory, in what is now Indiana. Miami chief Little Turtle was disgruntled, but still friendly with the Shawnee.

In 1809, the Kickapoo and Wea ceded three million acres of land in the Treaty of Fort Wayne. The Shawnee did not cede anything, and Tecumseh started to speak against the growing American presence in their land and on their borders. He was ready to take affairs into his own hands when he approached Indiana Governor William Henry Harrison at his home at Grouseland with 400 warriors. Tecumseh demanded the land that

> "SELL A COUNTRY!
> WHY NOT SELL THE
> AIR, THE GREAT SEA,
> AS WELL AS THE
> EARTH? DID NOT
> THE GREAT SPIRIT
> MAKE THEM ALL FOR
> THE USE OF HIS
> CHILDREN?"
>
> TECUMSEH

TECUMSEH Tecumseh was the ultimate diplomat, uniting tribes in a formidable resistance effort.

was sold be given back. Harrison ignored him, but a Potawatomi chief intervened and persuaded Tecumseh to leave in peace. Tecumseh threatened to ally with the British if the treaty was not redressed. Then he started to court more Indian allies—Cherokee, Creek, Choctaw, Osage, and Kickapoo.

In 1811, Tecumseh was traveling without stop, and left his brother Tenskwatawa in charge of affairs at Prophetstown, with strict instructions to retreat if Harrison called up militia to attack the village. Harrison saw an opportunity and did just that, bringing more than 1,000 militiamen to Prophetstown to destroy Tecumseh's center. Tenskwatawa rashly rallied the warriors, but Harrison's force was overwhelming and the Indians retreated. Casualties were minimal, but Tecumseh was livid and Tenskwatawa's reputation among the people suffered for his choice. Harrison razed Prophetstown and destroyed its food supply. The Battle of Tippecanoe, as Americans later called it, catapulted Harrison to national fame—eventually the presidency—and was a major setback for Tecumseh.

THE WAR OF 1812

Tecumseh reached out to the British during the War of 1812 and demonstrated his military genius in several major actions.

One of his first battles in the war was the Battle of Brownstown. Tecumseh fearlessly set an ambush with only 24 warriors. He waited until the much larger U.S. force was fording a wide stream and sprung the ambush at incredibly close quarters. His 24 warriors killed 18 soldiers, wounded 12, and routed the entire force of 200 soldiers. The American troops were so terrified by the sudden hand-to-hand combat, war whoops, and casualties that more than 70 deserted in a chaotic stampede.

At the Siege of Detroit in 1812, Tecumseh again showed clever strategy against a larger force. The fort was well supplied, garrisoned, and in charge of 33 cannon, making a full frontal assault difficult and costly. Tecumseh asked British Major General Isaac Brock to pull his force back and out of range from the

DEATH OF TECUMSEH The killing of the coalition's leader at the Battle of the Thames doomed the resistance. The tribes soon sued for peace.

brigadier general in the British Army, but Tecumseh declined the appointment, gave away the sash, and said all he needed was the validation of his warriors.

At the Siege of Fort Meigs in 1812, Tecumseh again distinguished himself, crushing a relief effort by feinting into the woods and drawing the Kentucky militia into an ambush. He also defeated a major sortie from the fort. Despite Tecumseh's success, the British did not conquer the fort. Afterward, some of his warriors started to execute their American prisoners. Tecumseh stopped them, publicly rebuking Major General Henry Procter for not stopping the executions himself. "I conquer to save; you to kill," he said.

Tecumseh wanted to press the attack on the Americans while his side had the tactical advantage and momentum, but Procter wanted to retreat to Canada for the winter. Although Tecumseh had Brock's full support, his relationship with Procter was frosty, especially after their exchange during the Siege of Fort Meigs. Tecumseh finally persuaded Procter to reinforce him in a major offensive, redeploying his warriors to a staging ground at Moraviantown.

American forces converged on his position at the Battle of the Thames. Procter was close by, deploying cannon in a

fort's long guns, but to offer neither retreat nor surrender. Then Tecumseh led approximately 400 warriors to a copse of dense woods bordering the open area in front of the fort. Methodically, he marched his warriors in long rows from the woods to the field in view of the fort, along the British flank to reinforce Brock. As soon as his warriors were positioned on the high ground near Brock, he secretly redeployed the warriors to the original point of concealment in a repeated, circling march. The clever ruse gave the impression that Tecumseh had a massively overwhelming force, and it worked. American Brigadier General William Hull, who had command of the fort, thought Tecumseh had thousands of warriors and surrendered the fort without contest. There were more American captives than warriors and British soldiers combined. Tecumseh took 2,500 captives (582 regulars and more than 1,600 militia, plus civilians, 33 cannon, and more than 2,500 muskets). His force amounted to at most 600 warriors accompanied by 400 Canadian militia and 330 British regulars. Brock was so impressed that he persuaded the British government to offer Tecumseh appointment as

TENSKWATAWA

Tecumseh partnered with his brother, Tenskwatawa, a prophet who advocated for the people to abstain from alcohol use and to abjure the economic, cultural, and political influences of Europeans. Many Indians believed that both brothers had special powers. In 1806, William Henry Harrison, Indiana's territorial governor, disputed Tenskwatawa's claim that the Great Spirit guided him. Harrison challenged the prophet to demonstrate his spiritual power by making daytime turn to night. That challenge was soon followed by a dramatic solar eclipse.

Tecumseh's name meant Shooting Star. Although he deferred to his brother in spiritual matters, a brilliant comet streaked through the night sky in 1811 when Tecumseh was trying to persuade the Creek to join his confederacy. Later that same year, the New Madrid earthquakes shook the Midwest and South, lending further credence to the claims that the Great Spirit blessed the efforts of Tecumseh and Tenskwatawa.

Tecumseh and Tenskwatawa were not primarily interested in fighting the Americans. They wanted to build a new cultural and political foundation for all the tribes in the southern Great Lakes. They founded villages in Greeneville, Ohio, in 1805, and in Prophetstown, Indiana, in 1808, both of which were inhabited by several tribes. When the inhabitants were encroached upon, they rallied warriors for the defense of their communities.

defensive array. Tecumseh rode to the British lines and shook hands with each officer before deploying his warriors in a flanking move along a black ash swamp. Tecumseh's old nemesis, William Henry Harrison, led the 3,500-strong U.S. force, which included a cavalry detachment. There were about 800 British troops in a defensive position, and Tecumseh had about 500 warriors on the field. Harrison ordered a full frontal assault on the British position. Tecumseh flanked the Americans, but failed to stop the charge. Procter got the British regulars to fire one volley and then fled the field with 250 of his troops. The rest of the British surrendered. That left the Indian force vulnerable. Tecumseh rallied his warriors, but was at a strategic disadvantage with a smaller force and an exposed position. He had no cavalry. He fought valiantly,

using musket fire to successfully suppress a frontal cavalry charge. Casualties were not overwhelming, with about 33 warriors killed, but Tecumseh was mortally wounded. When he fell, tribal resistance dissolved. The American force controlled the field.

With Tecumseh gone, his confederacy crumbled. Most of the tribes sued for peace. Although the Americans did not send punitive expeditions against Tecumseh's confederacy immediately, over the next few decades, each tribe in the region was systematically displaced, some retreating to Canada and others relocating to Kansas and Oklahoma. Tecumseh's death was a blow for the British too, although Procter was loath to admit it. Their front in the Great Lakes collapsed, ultimately leading to defeat in the War of 1812. ∎

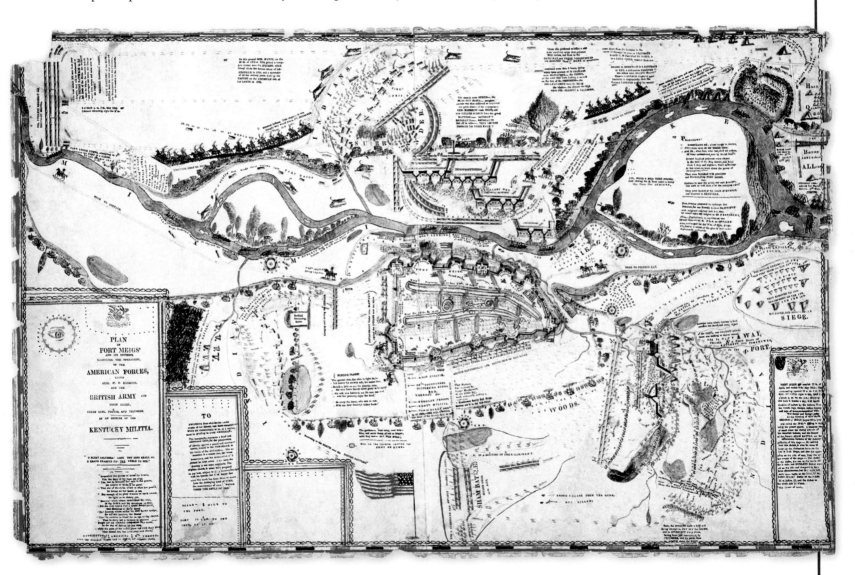

SIEGE OF FORT MEIGS Tecumseh coordinated attacks and subterfuge with British General Henry Procter in 1813, inflicting heavy casualties on U.S. defenders.

RED STICK WAR
THE CREEK CIVIL WAR

The Creek deftly played the French, Spanish, and English off one another and traded with all of them in the 1700s. The Creek sold 50,000 deerskins every year out of Savannah alone. The trade was so profitable that it transformed the Creek from farmers to specialists in various aspects of trade, harvest, and diplomacy.

The Creek accommodated English colonists and then American settlers. They willingly accepted Benjamin Hawkins, who was appointed by George Washington to "civilize" the Creek. The Lower Creek towns in particular had very close economic ties with white colonists, while the Upper Creek were more isolated and independent. The Lower Creek granted the American nation a series of smaller land cessions in Georgia. They also gave permission for a road through their land that connected Georgia with New Orleans. The Lower Creek towns were close to the new highway and in increasingly close contact with Americans.

Shawnee chief Tecumseh rearranged Creek allegiances in the early 1800s. He courted their alliance in 1811, and when he did so, a comet blazed across the night sky. Because Tecumseh's name meant Shooting Star, many took it as a sign.

> "NO ONE NEED THINK THAT THE WORLD CAN BE RULED WITHOUT BLOOD. THE CIVIL SWORD SHALL AND MUST BE RED AND BLOODY."
>
> ANDREW JACKSON

The New Madrid earthquakes followed soon after, shaking many of the Creek villages. A large group of traditionalist Upper Creek who had misgivings about the pace of cultural change in their land pledged support to Tecumseh. Most of the Tecumseh-allied Creek came from the Upper Creek towns, and they were opposed by the Creeks from the Lower Creek towns. The rift among the Creek coincided with the American-British conflict in the War of 1812. A brutal civil war erupted, often called the Red Stick War.

A WAR BOTH SIDES LOST

In Creek culture, red "sticks," or war clubs, represented war, and white ones represented peace. The Upper Creek who were swayed by Tecumseh were also suffering from the implosion of the deerskin trade and were extremely upset with increasingly forceful efforts to assimilate them. They called themselves the Red Sticks because they were ready to fight for the land and ancient lifeways.

Some Red Sticks traveled north to fight with Tecumseh. There were several isolated attacks on white farms and settlements as some of the Red Sticks traveled between Prophetstown, Detroit, and the Upper Creek towns. The Americans

---

ANDREW JACKSON

Andrew Jackson, the seventh president of the United States, built his career as an Indian fighter. He continued that effort even as president.

Jackson was a Tennessee planter, slave owner, and merchant. He had a 1,000-acre plantation and successful civilian life. In 1801, he was named commander of the Tennessee militia. He spent his first years dealing with the Cherokee, but when the Red Stick Creek attacked Fort Mims, he really made a name for himself. Commanding a massive force, he decisively beat the Red Sticks at Horseshoe Bend and forced punitive terms on the Creek in the Treaty of Fort Jackson afterward.

Jackson earned the nickname Old Hickory fighting the British at the Battle of New Orleans, where his 5,000 soldiers and militia defeated a British force of 7,500. Afterward, he continued to press the Red Sticks, most of whom took refuge with the Seminole in Florida. During the First Seminole War in 1817 he invaded Spanish territory and executed two British agents, even though America was not at war with either European nation. He avoided a call for censure and went on to a brilliant political career.

Many U.S. presidents, including Washington, Jefferson, and Adams, advocated for removing Indians out of the east. Jackson picked areas of land west of the Mississippi River for relocating the tribes. During his tenure as president, 1829 to 1837, America imposed more than 70 treaties on different Indian tribes and began the removal era. Most of the tribes Jackson fought in the Southeast were relocated to Oklahoma.

FORT MIMS In 1813, "Red Stick" Upper Creek warriors descended on Fort Mims for a one-sided victory over the U.S. force and their Lower Creek allies. This drawing depicts warriors executing captives afterward.

did not intervene with the Creek beyond their efforts to fight Tecumseh and his allied force. Most Red Stick Creek stayed in their ancestral villages, but increasingly started to harass the White Sticks, killing livestock and occasionally torching buildings.

The civil war began in earnest when White Sticks under William McIntosh, Little Prince, and Big Warrior attacked a party of 150 warriors traveling to join the Red Sticks, then attacked several Red Stick towns. The entire Creek nation was in an uproar, and everyone had to choose sides.

In July 1813, some of the Red Sticks traveled to Pensacola, Florida, to trade with the Spanish. The Spanish, who had supported the Americans during the Revolutionary War, were now trying to curb American encroachment and were happy to arm anyone willing to fight the Americans. American troops, deployed to fight the British in the War of 1812, surprised the Red Sticks and pillaged their camp, so the warriors regrouped and attacked in the Battle of Burnt Corn. Casualties were low on both sides, but the U.S. government made plans to attack the Creek.

The Red Sticks struck preemptively at Fort Mims in Alabama. In August 1813, Red Stick chiefs William Weatherford (Red Eagle) and Peter McQueen led a force of nearly 1,000 warriors to Fort Mims. Two black slaves reported sighting painted warriors near the fort, but Major Daniel Beasley discounted what they said and had one slave flogged for giving a false report. He posted no pickets or sentries. The fort was garrisoned with 265 militia and had at least as many civilians and White Stick Creek. In a complete surprise, the Red Sticks attacked at noon, swiftly stormed the outer defenses, and bottled up the remaining resistance in a blockhouse inside the fort. The Red Sticks sustained heavy losses of more than 100 warriors, but pressed the attack, torched the buildings, and slaughtered all the militia, civilians, and White Sticks—more than 500 people. They spared only the slaves, although 36 of the residents and militia escaped. Most were scalped.

Panic gripped white settlements and the Lower Creek towns. Many people fled to Mobile for protection. The main army was in the northern theater, fighting Tecumseh and the

British. Tennessee, Georgia, and Mississippi rallied local militia to fight the Red Sticks. The conflict transitioned from a Creek civil war to an American campaign against the Red Sticks. General Andrew Jackson was given command of the militia.

Jackson marched through the Lower Creek towns with 2,600 militia, 500 Cherokee warriors, and 100 White Stick Creeks. He found a major fortified Red Stick camp at Horseshoe Bend, Alabama. About 1,000 Red Sticks guarded the camp, which was protected by a large bend in the river, an elevated position, and significant breastworks. Jackson deployed artillery and started a two-hour barrage. Then he ordered a bayonet charge, storming the breastworks and engaging in hand-to-hand combat. The Creek refused to surrender. Casualties were overwhelming. A total of 800 Creek warriors were killed, devastating their fighting force. Chief Menawa and 200 Creek escaped and fled to Florida, where they sought refuge with the Seminole. There was retributive warfare afterward, and more Red Sticks fled to Florida and joined the Seminole, tripling that tribe's population and fighting on for their freedom, land, and way of life.

CREEK DIASPORA

The remaining Creek had no choice but to sign the Treaty of Fort Jackson or face annihilation. The Creek sold 21 million acres of land—more than half the Creek territory, including most of present-day Alabama and much of Georgia. None of the Creek were spared in the treaty, including the loyal White Stick Creeks who helped defeat the Red Sticks. The terms of the treaty were so unfair that President John Quincy Adams nullified the treaty and negotiated a new one in 1826 with provisions that the Creek did not have to relocate. But there was pressure on the government not to honor the renegotiated treaty. The Indian Removal Act of 1830 forced relocation of many tribes. Another treaty in 1832 established the process for Creek removal to Indian Territory in Oklahoma. It was the 20th major land cession treaty signed by the Creek. ■

RED STICKS ON THE RUN Andrew Jackson defeated a Red Stick Creek force at Horseshoe Bend (map above), killing 900 and capturing 500. The Creek fled to Florida, where they joined their Seminole cousins (right) in guerrilla fighting.

"ARE YOU THE SMARTEST MAN THAT OUR GREAT FATHER COULD SEND
IN A TRYING TIME LIKE THIS? BECAUSE IF YOU ARE THE SMARTEST MAN
THE GREAT FATHER HAS GOT, I PITY OUR GREAT FATHER."

HOLE IN THE DAY TO COMMISSIONER WILLIAM P. DOLE

MINNESOTA, 1862 While white civilians fled the U.S.-Dakota War in southern
Minnesota, Hole in the Day led a challenge to U.S. authority in central Minnesota.

SHOWDOWN AT FORT RIPLEY

OJIBWE INTERVENTION IN MINNESOTA

Minnesota was rife with conflict in 1862. The Dakota killed between 400 and 800 white civilians in the U.S.-Dakota War that year. More than 2,000 Dakota died, and thousands more were either held prisoner or ran for their lives, many to Canada. Abraham Lincoln signed off on the largest mass execution in the history of the United States—38 Dakota hung simultaneously the day after Christmas. Two full regiments were recalled from the Civil War to deal with Indians in Minnesota.

At Fort Ripley, in central Minnesota, Ojibwe chief Hole in the Day rallied his warriors to best take advantage of the chaos. The Ojibwe were furious about Indian agents refusing to release payments for land they had already sold and also for selling their annuities for personal profit. Fort Ripley was poorly garrisoned with about 20 soldiers. Hole in the Day had traveled to Washington and knew that although a quick victory was possible at the fort, winning a war against the United States was unrealistic. He deployed his warriors, sent runners to other Ojibwe communities, and instructed his warriors to take missionaries captive and destroy the Indian agencies. At Gull Lake, Leech Lake, and Ottertail City, Ojibwe warriors took prisoners and marched on Crow Wing. The Ojibwe killed nobody, hoping to force the government to listen to demands, but the region braced for confrontation.

HOLE IN THE DAY Brilliant, cunning, and brash, Hole in the Day taunted and manipulated American officials at Fort Ripley.

DIPLOMACY AT GUNPOINT

William P. Dole, commissioner of Indian Affairs, arrived in Minnesota just in time to be summoned to an emergency parley with Hole in the Day at Crow Wing. Dole dispatched a runner to tell Hole in the Day that he would confer with the chief privately and that he should come unarmed and alone, and that the commissioner would do so as well. Secretly, Dole planned to arrest Hole in the Day. He traveled to the conference with 100 soldiers who had just arrived to reinforce Fort Ripley, as well as about 25 vigilantes. Hole in the Day was ready to match wits. He showed up at the conference with 100 loyal Ojibwe warriors and lined them up facing the U.S. troops. Dole demanded that Hole in the Day surrender. The army captain chirped that the chief better do so, or he would be "blown to hell in five minutes." Hole in the Day motioned with his hands and another 100 Ojibwe warriors appeared behind the U.S. troop deployment, surrounding the soldiers and outnumbering them two to one. Hole in the Day said he did not want a fight but could not stop his warriors from defending themselves.

Humiliated, Dole listened to Hole in the Day's demands. The chief insulted the commissioner's intelligence and the government's ineptitude. When the conference was over, Dole fled back to Washington only to learn that the U.S. secretary of state had received a letter from British authorities stating that Hole in the Day had relatives in Canada and that he was preparing to send Ojibwe families there to keep them out of conflict zones while he started a war with the Americans. Fighting the Ojibwe—and possibly sending U.S. troops to pursue them into Canada—might trigger a conflict with the British in Canada. The U.S. government could not fight the Civil War, the Dakota, the Ojibwe, and the British simultaneously.

Chagrined again, Dole assigned commissioners to negotiate terms with Hole in the Day, who got exactly what he wanted. Tribal leaders dictated the terms of a new treaty. The Indian agents were recalled and formally investigated. The annuities were released, and the Ojibwe were paid funds past due. Hole in the Day was even compensated for the burning of his house by U.S. troops in the midst of the turmoil. It was hard for Indians to win a war against the U.S. government, and even harder to win a peace, but Hole in the Day did. Afterward, trader Augustus Aspinwall declared, "He was the smartest Indian chief the Chippewa Indians ever had." ∎

INDIANS IN THE U.S. CIVIL WAR

TRIBAL WARRIORS SHAPING AMERICA

During the Civil War, both the Union and the Confederacy continued to support white settlers who encroached on Indian land. There were major military actions by the Union against the Dakota in Minnesota and across the Plains and Great Basin. But for most tribes, there was a lull in military force directed at them. Most tribes were happy to remain neutral and let white folk kill one another.

For more than 20 tribes, though, the Civil War was their war, too. A total of 28,693 Native Americans served in the Civil War in either the Union or Confederate armies. At Pea Ridge, the Second Battle of Manassas, Antietam, Spotsylvania, Cold Harbor, and Petersburg, they fought with the blue and the gray. Most tribes that engaged in the conflict fought for the Union, such as the Delaware, who made tribal declaration of war against the Confederacy. Company K of

GRANT'S STAFF Lieutenant Colonel Ely Parker (second from the right), a Seneca Indian who was Ulysses S. Grant's military secretary, drafted Robert E. Lee's surrender.

the 1st Michigan Sharpshooters, made up of Ojibwe, Ottawa, Potawatomi, Delaware, Huron, and Oneida soldiers, fought for the Union in several major engagements. At the Siege of Petersburg the unit stormed Shand House east of the trenches in a bold attack, surprising the Confederate regiment there and capturing 600 Confederate troops.

Others, like the Choctaw, fought for the South. And a few, including the Cherokee and Creek, were deeply divided and ended up with men on both sides. Some Ojibwe and Iroquois warriors donned uniforms and fought as integrated members of regular units. Most fought in segregated units as part of larger troop deployments.

STAND WATIE: THE LAST CONFEDERATE

Divisions in the Cherokee nation were deep. Since the arrival of Europeans, the Cherokee had adopted economic and political attributes of foreigners. They incorporated plantation economies and the ownership of slaves into their culture. Some Cherokee were very wealthy, but most were not. Some, like Stand Watie's family, signed the Treaty of New Echota that set up their relocation to Oklahoma. Others, like John Ross, considered it a capital offense to sell Cherokee land. When the Civil War broke out, the divisions between north and south followed these ancient fault lines.

Stand Watie, the descendant of treaty signers and slave owners, built a Cherokee unit for the Confederacy. They called the unit the 1st Cherokee Mounted Rifles. Watie was given command and a commission as colonel. He distinguished himself and his unit, winning promotion to brigadier general. He was one of only two Native Americans to gain that rank. The other was Ely S. Parker, a Seneca Indian from New York, who fought for the Union. With Watie's promotions came command of a larger unit, the Confederate Indian Cavalry of the Army of the Trans-Mississippi, which included Seminole, Creek, and Osage men plus three full battalions of Cherokee.

Watie sparred politically with John Ross inside the Cherokee nation. Ross supported neutrality, but he did not have sufficient support to stop Watie from embroiling Cherokee men in the Confederate war effort. The Cherokee nation signed a treaty with the Confederacy and agreed to furnish 10 companies of cavalry. John Ross was subsequently captured by Union troops, proclaimed for them, and spent the rest of the war in Philadelphia. Watie was named head of the Cherokee nation, and there was nothing else blocking Cherokee involvement in the fighting.

ELY PARKER AND LEE'S SURRENDER

Ely S. Parker was a Seneca sachem, accomplished engineer, lawyer, and U.S. public servant who left an indelible mark on U.S. history. He was a descendant of Red Jacket, and in spite of his deep community connection and service tradition to his community, Parker aspired to be a lawyer in the white world as well. He completed law school only to be denied the right to take the bar exam because he was Seneca, and the Seneca were not U.S. citizens. Parker went back to school and earned an engineering degree. When the Civil War began, Parker offered to organize a segregated unit of Seneca volunteers to fight for the Union, but was denied. He applied for a position as an engineer in the Union Army and was again denied because of his race. He doggedly pursued that goal until Ulysses Grant, depleted of engineers at the Siege of Vicksburg, gave Parker a commission.

Grant, impressed with Parker's field record, brought him into his direct command as adjutant. Parker wrote most of Grant's personal and professional correspondence during the war and drafted the Confederate terms of surrender for the Union. When Robert E. Lee surrendered at Appomattox, Parker recalled that Lee stared at Parker for a moment and then extended his hand, saying: "I am glad to see one real American here." Parker shook his hand and replied, "We are all Americans."

Watie brought his unit to the Battle of Pea Ridge in 1862. They captured a major Union artillery battery and then covered the main body of Confederate troops while they retreated from the field. In 1864, Watie deployed 400 tribal soldiers along the Arkansas River in a clever ambush of the steamboat *J. R. Williams.* He disabled the vessel with artillery fire and killed or captured most of the Union guard and crew.

At the Second Battle of Cabin Creek, Watie led Cherokee troops in an attack on Union haymaking operations at Flat Rock, inflicting more than 100 casualties. The Cherokee engaged a segregated unit of black Union soldiers, and there were reports that the Cherokee and Texan units executed their black prisoners. Three days later, a successful artillery barrage dislodged Union troops from a major supply train and Watie's forces routed the ground support. They confiscated a massive supply depot valued at more than one million dollars.

At the end of the war, Watie refused to surrender. He kept his troops in the field long after Robert E. Lee surrendered at Appomattox, finally agreeing to a cease-fire on June 23, 1865. Afterward, John Ross returned to Oklahoma, and Watie was deposed as leader of the Cherokee. ∎

ARROWS AND BULLETS

As soon as two different groups of people occupied the same part of the planet, competition and conflict became inevitable. Even before Europeans arrived in North America, some tribes had been enemies longer than any living person could remember. Others were allies. The Europeans changed these ancient balances. They brought guns, horses, and deadly illnesses. Many tribes, debilitated by disease, were toppled or transformed. In some cases, conflict intensified as groups sparred for trade alliances with the newcomers, who treated the Indians as pawns in their own long-standing conflicts.

The nature of Indian relationships and the ways they waged war with one another would never be the same. In the wars between the tribes, the chiefs who led the tribes in council and on the battlefield carried a heavy burden as they rallied warriors, inspired the masses, and changed the course of history.

THE CHANGING NATURE OF TRIBAL RELATIONSHIPS

Tribes fought and befriended one another across North America prior to European contact. After the Europeans arrived, the stakes rose. Some tribes were so diminished by disease that they were politically destabilized. Conflict at a vulnerable time sometimes doomed them. Tribes such as the Pequot and Natchez were devastated by their Indian enemies during the early contact era, which would have been impossible just a couple generations before, when populations were larger.

Some of the tribes fought the tide. The Mohawk, Oneida,

> "THE MASTER OF LIFE HAS GIVEN TO ALL THE INDIANS THE LAND TO LIVE ON IN PEACE, BUT UNHAPPILY, WE ARE ALL FOOLISH."
>
> BEAR HEART (OJIBWE)

Onondaga, Seneca, and Cayuga formed the Iroquois Confederacy in New York. That monumental diplomatic accomplishment enabled the member tribes to direct their military power at external enemies rather than at each other. It propelled the Iroquois to dominance in the eastern Great Lakes. The confederacy systematically displaced its western tribal neighbors throughout the Beaver Wars until the Ojibwe, Ottawa, and Potawatomi forged an alliance of their own and forced the Iroquois out of their homelands. The power of alliance was more important than ever as the scale and duration of conflict increased.

In the upper Midwest, the Ojibwe and Dakota fought a century of terrible territorial wars. But the tribes still grew, not by what they took from one another, but by what they did not. In periods of peace, the tribes intermarried and even shared hunting and fishing resources. The relationship was complicated, but critical for the prosperity of both tribes.

1450
Mohawk, Oneida, Onondaga, Seneca, and Cayuga tribes form Iroquois Confederacy, which dominates eastern Great Lakes for centuries.

1641–1701
Beaver Wars dominate Great Lakes tribal life; Iroquois crush the Huron and expand until other tribes push them back to New York.

1680
The Pueblo Revolt disperses Spanish horses into the wild; the animals proliferate across the Plains and transform tribal life.

1721–1729
The Chickasaw emerge victorious in a series of conflicts with the French and Choctaw known as the Chickasaw Wars.

RAIDS AND RETALIATION
Lakota and Blackfeet Indians
clashed often on the Great
Plains. Horses dramatically
changed the range of war
parties and the consequences
of conflict.

In Hawaii, nearly a million Native Hawaiians occupied seven major islands and historically warred with one another. In the early 19th century, Kamehameha rose to power, defeating rivals on the Big Island of Hawaii and building a military force trained in both ancient war tactics and modern musketry. Through conquest and deft diplomacy he united the islands and created the Kingdom of Hawaii, ushering in a period of unparalleled peace and prosperity.

While the Hawaiians came together, the Cherokee fell apart. After they were exiled from the east to Oklahoma via the Trail of Tears, two factions of the tribe nearly started a civil war as they enforced Cherokee blood law to punish sales of tribal land. The repeated cycles of murder and reprisal lasted for decades.

Many tribes agreed to serve in the U.S. Army as scouts when the Americans came to conquer the West. This enabled them to leverage their warrior skills for financial benefits, while also,

more importantly, crippling the ability of their enemies to do them further harm.

In the wars between the tribes, the nature of relationships—new alliances, ancient enemies, and the cohesion of long-standing groups—made all the difference. Survival depended on relationships. In peace and war, everyone needed a strategy or paid the price.

THE CHANGING NATURE OF TRIBAL CONFLICT

Although intertribal relationships shifted during the early contact period, so did the nature of tribal conflict. The stakes became higher and the consequences more dire. Tribes that had known only sporadic or largely ceremonial war found themselves fighting for survival. Conflict increasingly affected children and extended families.

The Beaver Wars exemplified the changing nature of war. The Iroquois, who used to raid the Huron sporadically, vented their full military might on them. The conflict was

1737–1862	1810	1833	1839–1865
Ojibwe-Dakota conflict consumes both tribes as they fight for territory and revenge across hundreds of miles of rugged terrain.	King Kamehameha unifies the islands of Hawaii by conquest and diplomacy, establishing the Kingdom of Hawaii.	The Osage nearly annihilate an entire Kiowa village in the surprise Cutthroat Gap Massacre.	The Cherokee nation erupts into decades of murders and reprisal killings over enforcement of the Cherokee blood law.

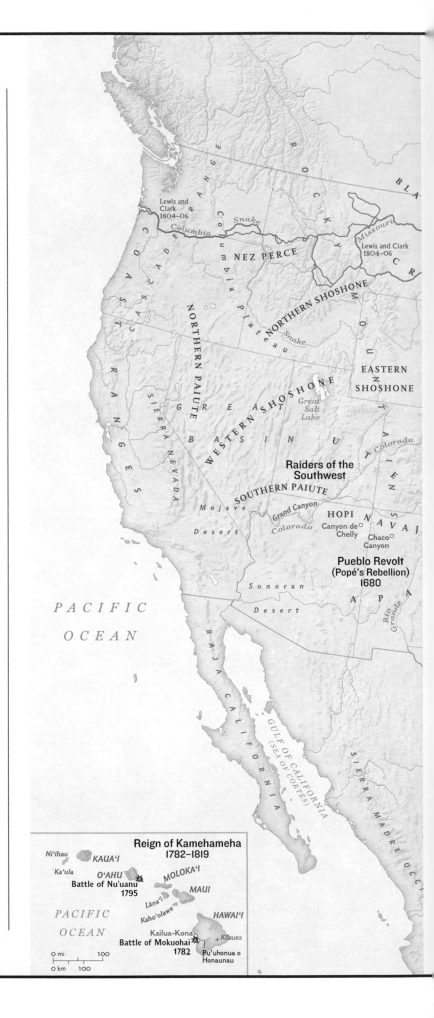

> ## "IF THEY HAD NOT RESISTED THE ENCROACHMENTS OF THEIR ENEMIES, THEY WOULD SOON HAVE BEEN DEPRIVED OF THE MEANS OF SUBSISTENCE AND MUST HAVE PERISHED. IF THEY WOULD HAVE GAME TO KILL, THEY MUST KILL MEN TOO."
>
> SAMUEL POND

compounded by devastating disease pandemics that hit the dense Huron villages especially hard. The Huron never recovered their territory or population. The Iroquois took thousands of captives over the course of the 60-year Beaver Wars. Responding to European demands for slaves, they adopted many captives into their tribes and sold many more. Taking captives went from ritual to a population-rebuilding strategy and economic enterprise. Depopulated villages never recovered.

In the Southeast, the goal of slave raiding also changed, from absorbing captives to selling them to feed the labor demands of the French, English, and Spanish Empires. Thousands of Indians were transported to the West Indies to work on plantations. They and their tribes were never the same again.

When the Pueblos rose up against Spanish colonization of the Southwest in 1680, they flung the corrals open and dispersed herds of horses into the wild. Within decades there were three million wild horses galloping across the Plains. The Apache and Navajo tamed them and thus went from disadvantaged hunter-gatherers trying to trade with the Pueblos for corn into prolific raiders of the Pueblos and other tribes. The Lakota acquired horses and expanded their territory twentyfold at the expense of other tribes as they emerged dominant in the northern Plains. The Comanche similarly rose to power on the southern Plains, fighting every tribe and European power they encountered. They surrendered nothing as they perfected horseback warfare, raiding, and buffalo hunting.

Many tribes suffered as war changed, but others grew. The Chickasaw, undefeated in their campaigns against Europeans and enemy tribes, fared well. So did the Lakota, Comanche, Apache, and Navajo. Adaptability to the shifting nature of conflict was essential. ■

RANGE OF CONFLICT Tribes across North America warred over territory, but did not colonize one another. In the Great Plains, Southeast, and Great Lakes regions few natural obstacles divided the tribes. Territory was enforced by the war club, not geography.

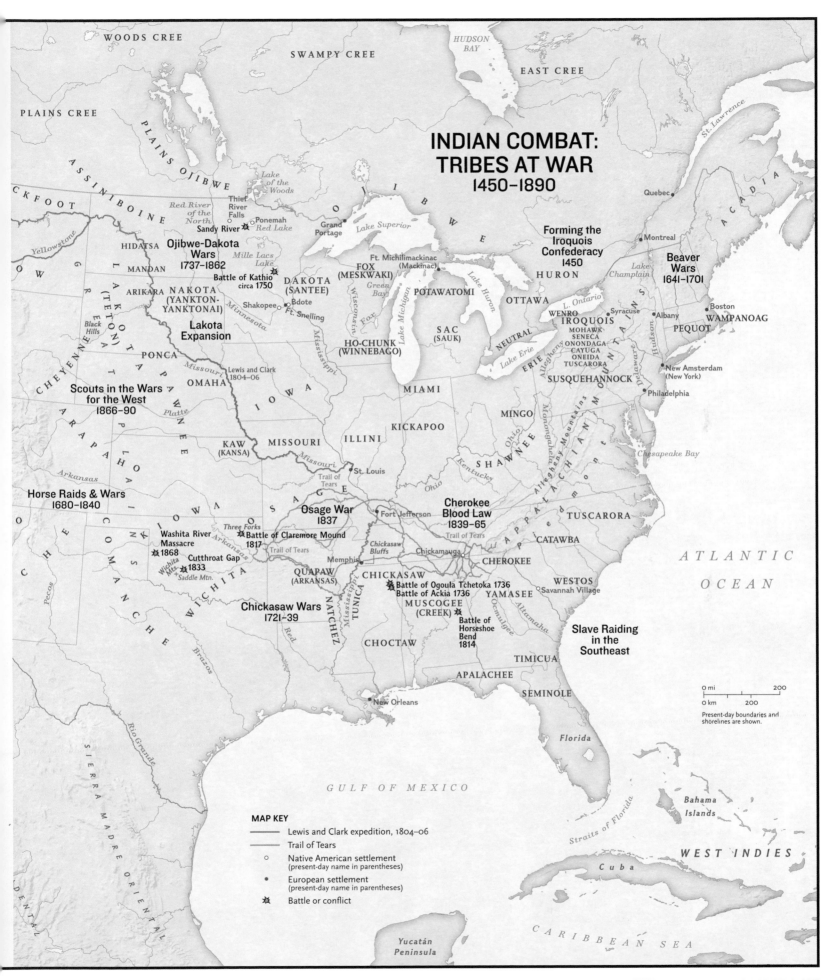

INDIAN COMBAT: TRIBES AT WAR
1450-1890

WOODS CREE

SWAMPY CREE

HUDSON BAY

EAST CREE

PLAINS CREE

ASSINIBOINE

PLAINS OJIBWE

BLACKFOOT

Yellowstone

HIDATSA

MANDAN

ARIKARA

NAKOTA (YANKTON-YANKTONAI)

LAKOTA (TETON) GREAT SIOUX

Black Hills

Missouri

Lake of the Woods

Thief River Falls

Red River of the North

Ponemah Red Lake

Sandy River

Lake Superior

Grand Portage

O J I B W E

Mille Lacs Lake

Battle of Kathio circa 1750

Ojibwe-Dakota Wars 1737-1862

DAKOTA (SANTEE)

Shakopee · Bdote
Ft. Snelling

Minnesota

Lakota Expansion

Wisconsin

Ft. Michilimackinac (Mackinac)

FOX (MESKWAKI)

Green Bay

POTAWATOMI

Fox

Lake Michigan

SAC (SAUK)

HO-CHUNK (WINNEBAGO)

Forming the Iroquois Confederacy 1450

HURON

OTTAWA

Lake Champlain

Quebec

Montreal

ACADIA

St. Lawrence

Lake Ontario

WENRO

IROQUOIS

NEUTRAL

Lake Erie

ERIE

MOHAWK
SENECA
ONONDAGA
CAYUGA
ONEIDA
TUSCARORA

Syracuse

Albany

Boston

WAMPANOAG

PEQUET

Beaver Wars 1641-1701

New Amsterdam (New York)

Philadelphia

SUSQUEHANNOCK

Chesapeake Bay

PONCA

CHEYENNE

ARAPAHO

Scouts in the Wars for the West 1866-90

Missouri

Lewis and Clark 1804-06

OMAHA

IOWA

PAWNEE

KAW (KANSA)

MISSOURI

Platte

Arkansas

Horse Raids & Wars 1680-1840

OSAGE

Trail of Tears

St. Louis

ILLINI

KICKAPOO

MIAMI

MINGO

SHAWNEE

Kentucky

Ohio

Monongahela

Allegheny

Ohio

APPALACHIAN MOUNTAINS

TUSCARORA

Osage War 1837

Fort Jefferson

Cherokee Blood Law 1839-65

Trail of Tears

Piedmont

CATAWBA

COMANCHE

KIOWA

Washita River Massacre 1868

Three Forks

Battle of Claremore Mound 1817

Cutthroat Gap 1833

Wichita Mts.

Saddle Mtn.

WICHITA

Arkansas

Trail of Tears

Memphis

QUAPAW (ARKANSAS)

Chickasaw Bluffs

Chickamauga

CHEROKEE

WESTOS

Savannah Village

NATCHEZ

TUNICA

CHICKASAW

Battle of Ogoula Tchetoka 1736
Battle of Ackia 1736

MUSCOGEE (CREEK)

YAMASEE

Ocmulgee

Altamaha

Chickasaw Wars 1721-39

Red

Mississippi

CHOCTAW

Battle of Horseshoe Bend 1814

TIMICUA

APALACHEE

SEMINOLE

Slave Raiding in the Southeast

ATLANTIC OCEAN

Pecos

Rio Grande

Brazos

New Orleans

GULF OF MEXICO

Florida

Straits of Florida

SIERRA MADRE ORIENTAL

0 mi 200
0 km 200
Present-day boundaries and shorelines are shown.

WEST INDIES

Bahama Islands

Cuba

CARIBBEAN SEA

Yucatán Peninsula

MAP KEY

——— Lewis and Clark expedition, 1804-06

——— Trail of Tears

○ Native American settlement (present-day name in parentheses)

● European settlement (present-day name in parentheses)

✦ Battle or conflict

DEATH OF HIAWATHA Co-founder of the great Iroquois League, Hiawatha has been revered in Iroquois communities for centuries and romanticized by the rest of the world.

FORMING THE IROQUOIS CONFEDERACY

THE GREAT LAW OF PEACE

Prior to European contact, the Iroquoian tribes of the eastern Great Lakes were at war with one another. Although they all descended from common ancestors, over time they developed separate languages, territories, and political structures. The Cherokee, Erie, Susquehannock, Huron (Wyandot), Mingo, Mohawk, Oneida, Onondaga, Cayuga, Seneca, and Tuscarora fought vindictive territorial battles. The debilitating conflict threatened the vitality of all the tribes.

It was then that the prophet Dekanawida, the Great Peacemaker, had a powerful vision. He called upon Hiawatha to be his spokesman, and together they built a powerful political, social, military, and ceremonial alliance of the five largest Iroquoian tribes in the eastern Great Lakes—the Mohawk, Oneida, Onondaga, Cayuga, and Seneca. Each tribe kept its own land, language, and polity. Each tribe gathered its implements of war and buried them at the base of a giant white pine tree. The tree would serve as a symbol of their unity, and the action—to bury the hatchet—became an enduring metaphor for peace. Collectively, they called themselves the Haudenosaunee.

Tadodaho, an Onondaga chief, was the last of the Haudenosaunee to accept the teachings of peace. He was named the titular head of the Iroquois League. His village at Onondaga Lake, near present-day Syracuse, became the ceremonial center for the united tribes. There were 50 chiefs, or sachems, each representing a primary clan in the member tribes. They formed a common council and wrote Dekanawida's law, known as the Great Law of Peace, on wampum belts. In 1722, the Tuscarora, one of the Iroquoian tribes not part of the league, was displaced from the Carolinas by war with the English. The Haudenosaunee admitted them to the Iroquois League as the

JOSEPH BRANT Charismatic and fearless, the Mohawk leader was prominent during the Iroquois alliance with the British.

sixth member tribe. The Iroquois League—the ceremonial and social compact between the Haudenosaunee—endures today in the form of modern longhouse ceremonies and social events. The overlapping political and military Iroquois Confederacy was tested through their colonial experience with England and the United States and ultimately dissolved.

Many early American political thinkers—Thomas Jefferson, James Madison, and Benjamin Franklin—wrote about the Iroquois League. Although the Western concept of democracy emerged out of early Greek political thought and action and its representative form evolved in the ideals of the Roman senate, some historians argue that the Iroquois League influenced the American idea of independent states united in a common political structure.

WAXING POWER

The military alliance of the Haudenosaunee made them the preeminent tribal power in the eastern Great Lakes. At the expense of other tribes, they expanded into the Ohio River Valley and west through the central Great Lakes. Their alliance usually meant that they had enemies only to their west and south. For most confrontations, they were able to keep their families safe from conflict zones while warriors raided, conquered, and expanded tribal domain.

In 1677, the Iroquois Confederacy formed a powerful alliance with the British, the Covenant Chain. In conflicts between England and France and between England and the American colonies, Iroquois allegiance was critical to British success. Over time, the Iroquois became enmeshed in both American and British colonial efforts and paid the price. The American Revolution set off a civil war among the Haudenosaunee. They later repaired the league, but not the military confederacy. ■

BEAVER WARS

EPIC CONFLICT IN THE GREAT LAKES

Abundant and varied sources of food in New England and the Great Lakes enabled the tribes there to grow and flourish, but periodic droughts sometimes caused conflict over resources and territory. Once entrenched, the conflicts persisted for generations, and the arrival of Europeans embroiled them all in more than 200 years of cyclical and increasingly devastating war.

The Iroquois Confederacy in the eastern Great Lakes continually sparred with the related Huron and Susquehannock. Further west, the Ojibwe, Ottawa, and Potawatomi formed a loose alliance of their own, the Three Fires Confederacy. With the Huron occupying territory between the confederacies, there was a rough balance of power in the Great Lakes. But the arrival of the Dutch, French, and English rearranged relationships and power dynamics.

BIRCHBARK CANOE The greatest technological advantage of the Algonquian tribes of the Great Lakes was not access to guns, but the buoyant and durable birchbark canoe.

In the 1540s, the French explorer Jacques Cartier wrote of the abundant beaver populations of the eastern Great Lakes, which he saw as untapped wealth. In the early 1600s, the French were ready to exploit that knowledge in a new commercial enterprise—the transatlantic fur trade. Beaver hats became fashionable in Europe, and there was only one place in the world to get the skins to make them. In 1608, the French started their first colony in Quebec. Samuel de Champlain, who orchestrated the colonial efforts of New France, reached out to the Huron and the Algonquian tribes, including the Three Fires Confederacy. In 1609, Champlain, with Huron allies, attacked the Mohawk at Lake Champlain, and killed three chiefs. The Mohawk raided the Huron in 1610, but the Huron defeated them.

However, from 1610 to 1614, the Dutch built trading posts at Albany and along the Hudson and Delaware Rivers, and by 1615, the balance of power began shifting. The Iroquois acquired guns and were eager to use them against both their ancient enemies and the French aggressors.

RISE OF THE IROQUOIS MILITARY MACHINE

By 1628, the Mohawk were well aware of how important a strong trade relationship was with Europeans and how much difference firearms could make. They pressed a series of attacks and defeated their Mahican neighbors, an Algonquian tribe unrelated to the Mohawk, driving them out of their villages and away from the Hudson River. This was a significant territorial change for the Mohawk; Fort Orange in Albany became an Iroquois-Dutch trade hub. The Iroquois had a monopoly on guns. Soon, almost every Mohawk warrior had a Dutch arquebus, a precursor to the musket.

The Iroquois Confederacy had strong allies in one another and in the Dutch. The French underestimated the impact the Dutch-Iroquois relationship would have. In the 1630s, the French quit trading guns to Indians, but the Dutch continued doing so. That created a power differential between tribes. At the same time, the Iroquois trapped beavers to extinction in the Hudson River Valley in a frenzy of harvesting to pay for their weapons. They then looked with covetous eyes on the land of their native neighbors, the Wenro, Erie, Neutral, and Huron. In 1638, they began a methodical and strategic expansion west at the expense of these smaller tribes. They used a divide-and-conquer tactic, focusing first on the Wenro, then later the Erie and Neutral.

> "FEAR OF THE NATION'S CENSURE ACTED AS A MIGHTY BAND, BINDING ALL IN ONE SOCIAL, HONORABLE COMPACT."
>
> GEORGE COPWAY

These early victories, coupled with their ready access to guns, enabled the Iroquois to expand even farther west in the 1640s, beginning the six bloody decades known as the Beaver Wars. The Huron and Three Fires tribes were more numerous than the Iroquois, but the French would not sell them guns, and the Huron and Algonquian villages were dispersed across a wide front. The Iroquois used strategic raids and attacks to dislodge the powerful Huron.

In 1645, the French, surprised by the success of the Iroquois attacks, brokered a peace between Iroquois, Huron, and French. Then the French reneged on the deal and refused to trade with the Iroquois, reigniting the war. The Huron and Susquehannock allied against the Iroquois. To compensate for inferior numbers, the Iroquois relied on their superior weapons and strategy.

In the war culture of the Great Lakes, winter attacks were rare. Travel was difficult and dangerous. If warriors were far away, their families faced starvation. Prolonged attacks or sieges were not possible without a supply chain. The Iroquois broke with ancient tradition and in 1648 put together a massive offensive against the Huron, with devastating effect. They gathered more than 1,000 warriors and attacked in the winter. They overwhelmed Huron defenses in their fortified villages, one at a time. The invaders burned all structures and food supplies they could not carry away. They killed most warriors and captured everyone else. They sold the men to the French as slaves and dispersed the women and children throughout Iroquois territory. They assimilated the dependents and isolated those old enough to resist. Thousands of Huron were captured or killed. Most of the remaining Huron relocated west, seeking refuge with the Ojibwe, Potawatomi, and Ottawa. Villages on Lake Superior swelled with war refugees from New York. The Iroquois moved quickly to expand their trade, trapping and settling to absorb Huron land into their tribal empire.

Emboldened by their success against the Huron, the Iroquois stepped up

FLINTLOCK
The flintlock rifle aided in the fur trade and on the battlefield.

attacks on the Erie and the Neutral. In the 1650s, they began attacking French settlements, including Montreal. Even though the Iroquois were vastly outnumbered by their conquered enemies, they pressed attacks in the Ohio River Valley as well, turning on the Susquehannock. Iroquois offensives bogged down then because the Susquehannock were allied with the English and successfully resisted initial attacks. In 1664, the Dutch lost their colonies to the English, and the English made peace with the Iroquois. The Susquehannock folded without English intervention. The Iroquois were becoming overextended, and their dominance would soon be put to mighty test.

RISE OF THE THREE FIRES

The French, reeling from Iroquois attacks and the disruptions they caused to native trading partners, changed policy and started selling guns to the Ojibwe, Ottawa, and Potawatomi. They also deployed their own troops against the Iroquois. In 1666, they sent 1,300 soldiers against the Iroquois and burned three Mohawk villages. Casualties were low, but the Iroquois, who had relied on strong offense to deter attacks, now had to think about defense and food shortages.

By 1670, the Iroquois had attacked and displaced the Catawba, Huron, Neutral, Erie, Susquehannock, and Shawnee. They continued to push for more territory, focusing their attacks on the Miami and Shawnee in Ohio. Their alliance with the English in 1677, the Covenant Chain, strengthened

BEAVER CONTRACT
The French made many contracts like this one, where the Ojibwe agreed to transport furs to French markets from Michilimackinac.

them further and shaped their military actions in all English conflicts with the French and Americans.

In the face of this strength, the Ojibwe, Ottawa, and Potàwatomi ramped up their attacks on the Iroquois. The French deployed troops against them, too. In 1687, 3,000 French militia routed Mohawk and Seneca villages, destroying 1.3 million bushels of corn. From 1688 to 1697, King William's War engulfed the region. This war, which echoed the French and English conflicts in Europe, was really a series of campaigns in the larger Beaver Wars. Ojibwe, Ottawa, Potawatomi, and French forces attacked the Iroquois and English across New England. Reeling from a series of defeats, the Iroquois abandoned their Great Lakes offensives and retreated to New York to defend their home villages. Three Fires warriors mopped up Iroquois enclaves in Michigan and Ohio. The Iroquois sued for peace.

THE GREAT PEACE OF MONTREAL

In 1701, 39 chiefs from a dozen tribes convened a peace conference with the French. They agreed to a cease-fire. The Iroquois defined territory in New York as their homeland. The Huron were so depopulated that they would never reclaim their territory. The Ojibwe, Ottawa, and Potawatomi expanded both east and west. In each subsequent confrontation between European powers, the divisions from the decades-long Beaver Wars haunted the Great Lakes. ∎

ENGINE OF WAR: THE FUR TRADE

Europeans went crazy for beaver furs. They traded with Indians for the pelts, which were thick, water-resistant, and lustrous. They shipped the skins to England, France, and the Netherlands, where hatters used mercury to remove the long hairs, transforming the fur into supple, soft felt material for a variety of garments, including popular stove top, derby, and colonial hats. The process gave mercury poisoning to the European workers, causing birth defects and mental illness, hence the caricature of the "mad hatter."

In North America, the popularity of beaver fur and the wealth the beaver trade could bring led some tribes to kill nearly all the animals in their territory to meet demand. That in turn increased pressure on tribes that had become dependent on European trade to press territorial claims against both ancient and new enemies. The fur trade–based economy drove military action across North America.

The fur trade transformed the economies of many tribes, making them dependent on European goods and the specialized labor needed

to produce furs to acquire those goods. The eventual implosion of the fur trade devastated those tribes. They turned to the next most available resource, the one most demanded by foreigners—the land. Selling land became a vicious cycle that drove many tribes into abject poverty, because with less land, they had fewer and fewer resources to sustain them through disease pandemics and military campaigns. As they sold even more land for goods, poverty intensified. Ironically, the promise of easier access to prosperity led to decline.

JESUIT SURGE As the French cemented trade relations with Algonquian tribes,
they sent Jesuit missionaries in an effort to convert them to Christianity.

SLAVE RAIDING IN THE SOUTHEAST

CHANGING THE NATURE OF CONFLICT

Prior to the time of European contact many tribes took war captives. Children especially were usually adopted and raised as part of the captor tribe. For the matrilineal Creek tribe, adult male captives sometimes replaced a warrior who died in battle as a husband for the widow. Their children were regarded as full members of the tribe, with matrilineal clans and rights to ascend to prominent positions in society. What set native customs apart from European slavery most of all is that the tribes did not

OCMULGEE SLAVE RAID
Slave raiders pass through the Spanish trading post on the Ocmulgee River in Georgia.

practice chattel slavery—where people are legally regarded as property.

Contact with Europeans dramatically altered practices. Tribes were under pressure from the Dutch, English, French, and Spanish to sell captives to Europeans. Because most tribes quickly became engaged in a complicated economy revolving around deerskin and beaver fur, land transactions, and European goods such as guns, they accommodated requests for captives. The impact cascaded through tribal cultures on many levels.

"THEY WOULD MAKE FINE SERVANTS . . . WITH 50 MEN WE COULD SUBJUGATE THEM ALL AND MAKE THEM DO WHATEVER WE WANT."

CHRISTOPHER COLUMBUS

FROM WAR CAPTIVES TO SLAVES

European chattel slave sales of Indians began in 1636. By 1661, the practice was legal in all the British mainland colonies. The Virginia Slave Codes of 1705 further racialized the institution of slavery by declaring that all Indian, mulatto, and black slaves were real estate. Because Indians were so susceptible to disease, Europeans transported African slaves to America. For generations, the slave force was mixed Native American and African.

Chattel slavery in America first evolved as an export business. The colonies in the West Indies developed plantations and thus a market for chattel slavery before the mainland colonies. The West Indies was the primary destination for native slaves. From New England to Florida, the Dutch, English, French, and Spanish captured Indians and sold them in the West Indies. Even more commonly, they purchased war captives and sold them as slaves there. Increasingly, the Europeans used slavery as a military tactic. Throughout the Beaver Wars and immediately after the Pequot War and King Philip's War, thousands of Huron, Pequot, and Wampanoag warriors who fought against England and their families were shipped off the mainland to live the rest of their lives as slaves. The Tuscarora and Yamasee were similarly depopulated in English conflicts. Although Indians across the continent experienced European-run chattel slavery, the effect was most pronounced in the Southeast.

FROM SLAVES TO SLAVERS

Tribes such as the Chickasaw and Westos that previously adopted war captives, then shifted to selling their captives, eventually started raiding smaller tribes for the sole purpose of acquiring captives to sell. They depopulated many small enemy villages solely for economic reasons. The tribes were changing the custom of war.

Between 1670 and 1715, English slavers in Charleston sold and shipped 50,000 native slaves out of the Southeast, most to the West Indies. As the plantation economy took hold on the mainland, some slaves remained there—a 1708 census of South Carolina reported 4,100 black slaves, 1,400 native slaves, and 4,080 white colonists. By 1715, South Carolina's native slave population had grown to 1,850. The English who used the Westos as slave raiders turned on their former allies and wiped out most of the tribe. The Westos were no longer a viable cultural, linguistic, or political group.

Chattel slavery transformed tribes in the Southeast. The British-allied Chickasaw raided the French-allied Choctaw, Tunica, and Arkansas and sold their slaves to the British. Chickasaw slave raiding escalated to a major Choctaw-Chickasaw war in 1705. The warfare and the higher exposure to disease from slave trading with Europeans reduced the Chickasaw population more than 40 percent. The French and their Indian allies engaged in genocidal wars against the Natchez in Mississippi and the Fox in Wisconsin. Soon the entire Natchez population was enslaved by the French. The Creek were active slave raiders for the Spanish. They systematically destroyed the Timucua and Apalachee in Florida.

Slaving escalated conflict as large tribes picked on smaller ones, and then turned on one another. The Shawnee and Cherokee both raided and sold one another's captive members to the English and French. The impact was profound. The English estimated there were 200,000 Indians in the Southeast in 1685, falling to 90,000 by 1715. By 1750, the English gave up on enslaving Indians because there were so few left nearby that it no longer made economic sense, compared with buying African slaves from professional European slave raiders. In other parts of America, such as California, enslaved Indians remained the dominant form of labor until the mid-1800s. ∎

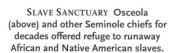

SLAVE SANCTUARY Osceola (above) and other Seminole chiefs for decades offered refuge to runaway African and Native American slaves.

OJIBWE-DAKOTA WARS
BLOOD IN THE WATER

The Ojibwe and Dakota fought off and on for more than a century. War defined their relationship, but other things did, too. They shared a common geographic space, economy, and military culture. They shared common struggles with European and American encroachment. Most Ojibwe and Dakota people have blood from both tribes running through their veins. Today the tribes are fast friends—politically, economically, and culturally cooperative. The differences are notable too, but never more so than when they fought an epic struggle across the prairies, timbered northland, and icy blue waters of the western Great Lakes and tallgrass prairie.

MASSACRE ISLAND

The long relationship between the Ojibwe and Dakota started peacefully. The Dakota had lived throughout the Wisconsin, Minnesota, and Ontario lake region for generations before the Ojibwe arrived. The Ojibwe came from the Atlantic coast, a densely populated area where occasional droughts triggered conflict. In addition to such practical reasons, the Ojibwe were following a series of prophecies that told them to move to the wild rice beds, home to the Dakota. The tribes traded and saw no cause to fight.

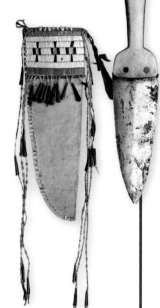

The arrival of French traders among the Ojibwe in the Great Lakes in the 1600s enabled the two tribes to extend and deepen their friendship. The Ojibwe served as middlemen in Dakota trade with the French. The Ojibwe benefited from their position as financial arbiters. The Dakota got French guns before anybody else in their area. In 1679, the Ojibwe and

BDOTE The Dakota call the confluence of the Minnesota and Mississippi Rivers Bdote, the birthplace of their people. The Americans built Fort Snelling here (left) starting in 1819. Above, a Sioux scalping knife.

Dakota formalized their peace, and it lasted for generations. The Ojibwe and Dakota together expelled refugees from the Beaver Wars. They even fought the Cree together north of Dakota land.

By 1729, the French were in a difficult position, which would soon cause trouble for the tribes. The 1713 Treaty of Utrecht restricted their colonization and trade to the Great Lakes, Mississippi River, and Gulf Coast regions while giving the English exclusive colonial rights to the Atlantic coastal colonies and Hudson Bay. The two powers were sparring for control of Acadia and the Ohio River Valley. The French wanted to find a passage to the Pacific Ocean and had no idea how long and arduous that route really was. They sent Pierre Gaultier de Varennes, sieur de La Vérendrye, to explore. The Cree he encountered at Grand Portage, Minnesota, drew him a map that still survives. The French poured resources into exploring Cree territory. La Vérendrye even allowed the Cree to adopt his son, Jean Baptiste.

> "THEY . . . TOOK EVERY MEANS IN THEIR POWER TO ESCAPE THE NOTICE OF THE OJIBWAYS— EVEN DISCARDING THE USE OF THE GUN ON ACCOUNT OF ITS LOUD REPORT, AND USING THE PRIMITIVE BOW AND ARROWS."
>
> WILLIAM WARREN, ON THE SECRET DAKOTA VILLAGE AT THIEF RIVER FALLS

The Cree took Jean Baptiste along on a war party against the Dakota. The Dakota and Cree fought constantly, but the French were trading with both. In a minor attack at Red Lake, Minnesota, the Dakota saw a white man among their attackers, and called out, "Who is attacking us?" The Cree responded, "It is the Frenchman." Even though this was not the full truth, the Dakota took them at their word and planned retribution. It took some time, but in 1736, the Dakota brought a war party of around 130 men to Lake of the Woods on the present-day Ontario-Minnesota border. They found Jean Baptiste and 20 other Frenchmen, killing them all. The victims were beheaded and left on a nearby island, known afterward as Massacre Island.

La Vérendrye was beside himself with grief. Forgetting entirely his mission to chart a path to the Pacific, he took all resources at his disposal and begged every Indian ally he had to wage a genocidal war against the Dakota. This presented a dilemma for the Ojibwe. They had to choose between their French allies and their Dakota allies. The French were not just military allies. They were married into and living among the Ojibwe in large numbers. The Ojibwe also stood to fight against other native allies, including the Ottawa and Potawatomi, if they betrayed the French. The Cree even offered the Ojibwe settlement rights to some of their territory if they joined the alliance against the Dakota. In the end, the Ojibwe had to betray someone, and they buried their tomahawks deep in Dakota backs.

Hundreds of Ojibwe warriors descended on the Dakota at Lake Pepin in southern Minnesota in 1737. The Cree and Assiniboine were to attack the Dakota as well, but a smallpox epidemic prevented them from mustering much strength. The Dakota had expected the Cree or French to attack, but instead only Ojibwe warriors came at them. The Dakota vented their entire military might on the Ojibwe, displacing many from northern Wisconsin.

In 1744, La Vérendrye was fired for starting the war and neglecting his mission. By 1763, the French had lost all hope of maintaining colonies or trade networks in North America after their defeat in the French and Indian War. But the Ojibwe and Dakota fought until 1862, radically transforming the composition of tribal populations across a 500-mile front. By the time the war ended, few even knew La Vérendrye's name or what started it all.

TO ENTER ONE ANOTHER'S LODGES

Even during times of heightened conflict, the Ojibwe and Dakota people who lived on the border of their territory with one another had sustained contact not just through war, but also through peaceful pursuits. The culture of war for the two tribes evolved into conflict as a fair-weather pursuit. During the winter, war was taboo. People from both tribes camped together to fish the abundant lakes in the north woods, snare rabbits, and hunt big game. The animosities from years of sustained conflict often bubbled beneath the surface, but they maintained the peace. This custom was called "to enter one another's lodges."

Throughout the winter it was common for the Ojibwe and Dakota to share their homes and food. Many Ojibwe and Dakota people married one another. Today, most Ojibwe and Dakota people along the ancient tribal border have ancestors from both tribes. For the Ojibwe, the clan system is still a vibrant part of tribal culture, and two of the largest Ojibwe clans—the wolf and the kingfisher—come from Dakota paternity in cross-tribal marriages. Despite the connections made through this ancient winter custom, when the snows melted and the lakes opened in the spring, both tribes sent canoes full of warriors against one another in renewed conflict.

BATTLE OF KATHIO: SHIFTING TERRITORY

The Dakota initially succeeded in displacing Ojibwe people from their villages in northern Wisconsin to large islands in Lake Superior or points east or north from there. But within a few years, the Ojibwe had the Dakota on their heels. The Ojibwe had tremendous advantages in war with the Dakota. They had greater ease of access to firearms and more numerous allies (Ottawa, Potawatomi, Cree, Assiniboine, French). The Dakota were fighting different tribes in all directions (Ojibwe, Cree, Assiniboine, Fox, Osage, Mandan). The Ojibwe also used birchbark canoes, which were larger and more buoyant than

OJIBWE WAR DANCE The Ojibwe, inspired by prophets who told them to move to "the land where food grows on water," a reference to wild rice beds, came to the home of the Dakota and won control of the land through bloody conflict.

Dakota canoes dug out from tree trunks. Between the canoes and the fact that Ojibwe villages were upstream from the Dakota across most of their combined front of contact, the Dakota had to paddle against the current for weeks to attack Ojibwe villages, then flee for their lives in slower craft. The Ojibwe could float downstream for a few days, attack with surprise, and escape in faster vessels.

Most battles were short—anywhere from a few minutes to an hour. But occasionally there were longer encounters with far-reaching consequences. The Battle of Kathio, at the outlet of the Rum River from Mille Lacs Lake, was just such a battle. This was a primary Dakota village, with hundreds of residents, perhaps as many as 2,000. When the Dakota took this land from the A'aninin (Gros Ventre) who were there before them, they moved into the large earthen lodges left by the A'aninin. Geothermal action kept these homes cool in summer and warm in the winter. They were also impenetrable to arrow or musket fire. The Ojibwe brought a huge force to bear on the village, vastly outnumbering the Dakota warriors, who also had to protect their young children nearby. Nonetheless, the Ojibwe could not penetrate Dakota defenses. There was no way to pick off Dakota warriors or besiege the village, which was well supplied.

The battle lasted three days. Ojibwe warriors rushed the village many times, but were sniped out by Dakota defenders or blocked at the doors of the earthen lodges. Eventually, the Ojibwe regrouped and came up with a devastating technological innovation. Combining all the gunpowder they had, they wrapped bundles of powder in cloth or birchbark. They then massed all their warriors and stormed the village in a coup de main, running not to the doors of the Dakota lodges, but over the tops. They dropped the gunpowder bundles through the smoke holes. Explosions echoed across the lake. The Dakota who did not die from the concussions had to leave the lodges to find breathable air. The Ojibwe fell on them with war clubs. The dazed Dakota had little chance to make an even fight of it. The Ojibwe killed most of the inhabitants, routed those able to run, and captured surviving children.

LUTHER STANDING BEAR **The Lakota chief wrote about the Dakota, Nakota, and Lakota experience in peace and war.**

The Ojibwe then brought hundreds of people to Kathio and moved right into the Dakota lodges. The Dakota tried to retake Kathio many times, but Ojibwe numbers and defenses were too strong.

BATTLE RIVER: THE MEANING OF WAR

After the Ojibwe took Kathio, they pressed attacks on other Dakota settlements. Their effort was audacious and risky. Warriors had to move their families with them because they were full-time providers as well as fighters. Nobody was beyond conflict zones. Ojibwe families moved into Ponemah on the north shore of Lower Red Lake. The Dakota still lived in villages on the south shore of the same lake, no more than 12 miles away. For the first winter they looked at the smoke from one another's fires with full knowledge that a conflict loomed in the spring. The Dakota sent scouts to Ponemah to ascertain the strength of the Ojibwe. Local elders still tell how medicine men in Ponemah used medicine and fire to create a mirage and Dakota scouts reported overwhelming Ojibwe numbers. Some Dakota families moved west rather than face the onslaught. That flight further weakened the Dakota.

Nonetheless, the Dakota brought the fight to the Ojibwe. They killed an Ojibwe trapper and wounded another at the mouth of a small creek south of Ponemah. Angry Ojibwe warriors started to converge on the Dakota. Some ran through the woods, armed with nothing more than war clubs. Others

SUN SHINING THROUGH: RED LAKE WAR CHIEF

Sun Shining Through (Mizhakiiyaasige) moved from Michigan to Red Lake in northwestern Minnesota in the early 1820s. He was lean and tough, quick to action, and an inspiring leader in battle. He and Moose Dung, a prominent Red Lake chief, rallied warriors from across the region when they learned that their enemies, the Dakota, had a secret village in Ojibwe territory. The Dakota village was protected by a massive earthen breastwork, 15 feet high. The occupants burned dry poplar wood for smokeless

fires and hunted with bows and arrows to avoid detection. They stayed hidden for more than 60 years. When the Ojibwe finally found the secret village, Sun Shining Through led hundreds of warriors in a charge over the earthen embankment. They annihilated the 100 Dakota residents. Sun Shining Through was wounded so severely he had to be dragged on a travois from the battle site to his home village, 60 miles away.

He recovered and led many other war parties. One time, he brought 200 Red Lake

warriors to attack Shakopee, a Dakota village with about 2,000 residents. His battle plan was a direct frontal assault. Hundreds of Dakota warriors sallied forth to defend their families. Sun Shining Through's two brothers fell, but he fought his way through the throng and survived. He led a retributive campaign afterward and came home with 30 Dakota scalps. He was so busy fighting that his fellow Red Lakers nicknamed him "Business." In spite of all the bloodshed, Sun Shining Through lived to be an elder statesman.

piled into birchbark canoes and came by water. When the Ojibwe arrived they came in waves. Even though they were outnumbered at first, they pressed a ferocious attack, driving the Dakota back, and gaining strength as more and more Ojibwe arrived. This attack lasted for hours. Eventually overrun, the Dakota survivors jumped into their wooden dugouts and paddled for their lives. The Ojibwe grabbed their birchbark craft and closed on them. At the outlet of the Sandy River they annihilated the Dakota survivors.

When the Ojibwe returned to the original site of the battle, so many dead Ojibwe and Dakota warriors were on the banks of the river that their blood ran into the lake in a great red plume. The lake had been called Red Lake for generations because of tannins in the creeks flowing into the lake. But now it took on a new meaning. The river is called Battle River in English and *Gaa-danapaniniding*—"the place of slaughter"— in Ojibwe. And Red Lake is Miskwaagamiiwi-zaaga'igan, the lake with the red body of water, the blood of two nations. ■

FORT SNELLING The U.S. fort at the confluence of the Minnesota and Mississippi Rivers became a focal point of Dakota resistance to American colonization.

Massacre at Cutthroat Gap
BLOODY AMBUSH ON THE SOUTHERN PLAINS

The Osage, like the Dakota, belong to the Siouan language family. They made their homes in present-day Missouri and Arkansas, then slowly expanded their territory west at the expense of other tribes. Conflict was ferocious on the southern Plains, where large tribes such as the Comanche dominated huge swaths of territory. The Osage hung on to their land by strength of arms and well-timed raids designed not just to steal horses, but also to disrupt enemy battle capabilities. At various times, they fought tribes all around them—the Choctaw to the east, and the Kiowa, Comanche, Cherokee, Cheyenne, and Arapaho in every other direction. They allied with the French for trade, and even accepted French Jesuit missionaries in the 18th century.

As the Osage pushed west into Oklahoma and Kansas, they clashed frequently with the Kiowa. In 1833, a large band of Osage warriors from Three Forks tracked Kiowa families en route to a major Kiowa council near the Wichita Mountains along the banks of Rainy Mountain Creek. There were more than 2,000 Kiowa at the council, and the thought of Osage warriors lurking nearby must have seemed absurd. When Kiowa hunters found an Osage arrow in the buffalo grass nearby, the council took precautions, posting sentries and even erecting hasty breastworks around the camp. After a few days, with no evidence of any danger, the bands broke off the council to spread out for hunting.

A band of Kiowa under Chief Islandman traveled to Saddle Mountain and then along the winding prairie creeks looking for buffalo. They camped at a shallow bend in the creek, setting up camp on both sides of the water. The Kiowa took few defensive precautions. Chief Islandman took most of the warriors with him to raid the Ute. Osage warriors, still carefully concealed nearby, took advantage of the opportunity to prepare a devastating attack.

> "THEY ARE MY PEOPLE, AND I AM NOT GOING TO LET YOU HAVE THEM. YOU AND I ARE GOING TO DIE RIGHT HERE."
>
> KICKING BIRD (KIOWA)

SURPRISE ATTACK

Two Kiowa girls reported seeing a pebble fall into the water, but their warning was dismissed as the work of boys playing tricks on them. The next morning, a young boy was bringing horses out to pasture and spotted an Osage warrior in full war regalia. He screamed an alarm. Then, seemingly out of nowhere, hundreds of Osage warriors charged the camp. The Kiowa were in disarray, as men and women scrambled for weapons to defend themselves or fled with their small children.

One Kiowa woman had no chance to escape as she held the hand of her child and strapped another baby in a cradleboard to her back. With a tomahawk she fought off repeated attackers until she was able to break free and run with her children. Another Kiowa man fought with a cradleboard grasped in his teeth. In spite of heroic efforts, the Kiowa suffered a terrible defeat. Some escaped on foot. Two were taken captive. More than 150 were killed.

The Osage decapitated most of the dead Kiowa. They grabbed the sacred Tai-me medicine bundle, critical to performance of the Kiowa sun dance. Then they torched the teepees. The Kiowa recorded the event on winter counts and oral histories as "the summer they cut their heads off." The location of the massacre, long favored by the Kiowa for summer camps, was renamed Cutthroat Gap. The Kiowa never camped there again. Afterward, Chief Islandman was chastised and removed from office, replaced by Chief Dohasan.

The Osage later made a peace overture. They returned their sole surviving captive, a child named White Weasel, and also returned the Tai-me medicine bundle.

Conflict between the two tribes persisted. The Osage were soon embroiled in treaty politics with the Americans. They eventually scouted for Custer in America's wars against the southern Cheyenne and were present at the Battle of Washita River in which Cheyenne chief Black Kettle was killed. ∎

OSAGE WARRIORS The Osage land offered little sanctuary from enemies—no islands,
major bodies of water, or mountains. They protected themselves with arms and diplomacy.

BATTLE ON THE CLIFFS OF NU'UANU

KAMEHAMEHA AND THE UNIFICATION OF HAWAII

Around 1736, a proud family of *ali'i*, or Hawaiian nobles, announced the birth of their son Kamehameha on the Big Island of Hawaii. The Big Island was a beautiful place, full of resources. At the high point of Hawaiian civilization there were as many as a million Native Hawaiians, and a large percentage of them lived on the Big Island. They did not always get along, and conflict engulfed the ali'i on a regular basis. When Kamehameha's parents died, his uncle Kalani'ōpu'u raised him. Kamehameha grew up at court and was formally schooled in diplomacy and in war.

An ancient Hawaiian legend foretold that the person who could move the giant Naha Stone was destined to move the people in war and peace. Although there are different versions of how it happened, Hawaiians agree that as a young man, Kamehameha lifted and overturned the stone. Only one other Hawaiian previously had been known to so much as budge the enormous rock. It was an auspicious beginning for the man destined to unite all the Hawaiian people on all the islands into one kingdom.

CONQUEST OF THE BIG ISLAND

When Kamehameha's uncle died, his position passed to Kamehameha's cousin, Kīwala'ō, but Kamehameha was given a prominent position as *konohiki,* or "guardian," at Waipio, the lushest and most prosperous part of the Big Island. He was also honorifically named religious guardian of the island. Goodwill between Kīwala'ō and Kamehameha was not destined to last.

In 1782, Kīwala'ō came to visit Kamehameha in Kona. Kīwala'ō was worried about his charismatic cousin's potential to challenge his authority and tried to force the issue before the other man could gain strength. Kamehameha offered his king a drink, but Kīwala'ō gave it to a subordinate, a great insult in ancient Hawaiian etiquette. Such an attack to his dignity forced Kamehameha to defend his honor, even though he was not looking for a fight and was vastly outnumbered by the king's entourage. Kamehameha was fighting for his life, but also, ultimately, for the right to lead. The two cousins took their warriors into the bay for a ritual battle on the water. They paddled war canoes toward one another, first engaging with basalt sling stones, which could be thrown with the force of a musket ball. As they closed in, warriors hurled kauila spears at one another. Then the canoes collided and combat was hand to hand with shark tooth knives and clubs. The clash between Kīwala'ō and Kamehameha was later known as the Battle of Mokuohai.

Despite overwhelming odds, Kamehameha's warriors got close enough to fell Kīwala'ō with a sling stone. While he lay stunned on the deck of his war canoe, Ke'eaumoku Pāpa'iahiahi, the head

KAMEHAMEHA I The Hawaiian noble united the Hawaiian Islands by conquest. Here, he is depicted receiving Russian explorer Otto von Kotzebue.

konohiki from Kona, himself severely wounded, swam to the fallen king and slit his throat with a shark tooth knife. Kīwalaʻō's warriors abandoned the battle. Kamehameha captured his cousin's red feather cloak and declared himself konohiki of most districts on the Big Island. In 1790, he gathered warriors for the conquest of the Puna district on the island's east side. While he was away, a rival subordinate chief named Keōua led an uprising in his home district. Kamehameha returned and chased him past Mount Kilauea, which dramatically erupted and devastated Keōua's forces. Most died of asphyxiation from gas fumes and ash. The legitimacy of Kamehameha's rule on the Big Island was never questioned again.

PALI LOOKOUT At the Battle of Nuʻuanu, King Kamehameha I sent two divisions of his army to scale the sheer cliffs of Pali Lookout and seize the defenders' cannon. Some 400 enemy warriors died, including by being forced off the cliff.

CONQUEST OF THE ISLANDS

Secure at home, Kamehameha planned to conquer and govern all the Hawaiian Islands. He spent years planning, praying, and training. He purchased muskets, cannon, and ammunition from the British. He schooled his warriors in their use as well as ancient Hawaiian tools of war—shark tooth knives and kauila spears. He built a massive *heiau*, or temple, in the Kona district overlooking Maui and prayed regularly for success in uniting the islands. Each heiau was built to honor a specific god. When Kamehameha dedicated his temple to the war god Ku, there was no doubt of his intentions.

In 1795, he was ready to make his move. Kamehameha launched an armada of 960 war canoes filled with 10,000

KAMEHAMEHA THE GREAT The people of Hawaii called Kamehameha "the Great"
not only for his military accomplishments but also for his peacetime leadership.

well-trained Hawaiian warriors. The islands of Maui and Molokai fell with little resistance. His forces then converged on the smaller but densely populated island of Oahu.

When Kamehameha landed, he was betrayed. A high-ranking ali'i named Ka'iana defected to the principal chief at Oahu, Kalanikūpule. Undaunted, Kamehameha fought at the front of his army across Oahu, winning battle after battle. But his enemies were ready. They placed cannon at the top of a high cliff, Nu'uanu Pali. The cannon and strategically deployed defenders inflicted heavy casualties on Kamehameha's warriors.

In a daring move, Kamehameha ordered two divisions of his army to scale the cliffs. It was so dangerous as to seem preposterous, and Kalanikūpule could easily have destroyed Kamehameha's men if he only knew what they were doing, but he did not. The attackers reached the top of the cliff, killed the warriors manning the artillery, and assaulted Kalanikūpule's main force. Kamehameha enveloped the rest of the enemy warriors in a pincer move and fought a ferocious battle atop Nu'uanu. His forces destroyed 400 enemy warriors by cannon, musket, spear, shark tooth knife—and by pushing them off the 1,000-foot cliff. Ka'iana, who had betrayed Kamehameha, died in battle. Kalanikūpule was captured and ritually sacrificed. Oahu was folded into Kamehameha's kingdom.

KINGDOM OF HAWAII

Early in Kamehameha's rise to power, during his attack on Puna, his warriors descended on the fishing village there and routed the locals. Kamehameha was chasing them down, and while sprinting across the lava beds, he caught his foot in the rocks. A villager armed only with a canoe paddle turned around and smashed Kamehameha across the head, stunning him. Although killing the king would have been easy, the fisherman showed mercy and let him go. Years later, Kamehameha returned to Puna and summoned the man to his court. Although most in attendance expected the villager to be killed, the king honored him, thanked him, and issued a new decree. Elders, women, and children could not be harmed in war. Only able-bodied warriors engaged in fighting could be honorable targets. The decree was known as Kānāwai Māmalahoe, or the Law of the Splintered Paddle. It was often invoked by Daniel Inouye, decorated veteran and longtime U.S. senator from Hawaii, during his 58 years of public service; it remains part of human rights and military code nomenclature.

Kamehameha was equally successful as a peacetime leader. He sent warriors to help rebuild the villages of his enemies.

PU'UHONUA O HONAUNAU: THE PLACE OF REFUGE

The Hawaiian people lived by a code of cultural laws, or *kapu*. Kapu were considered inviolable. For anyone who dared to break them, the penalty was death. If someone entered an area reserved for the ali'i, or Hawaiian royalty, without permission or ate a taboo food, all Hawaiian people were obligated to enforce the sentence without delay. For a kapu breaker or a defeated warrior who might otherwise be put to death, the only hope was to elude capture and reach one of the sacred sites—*pu'uhonua*, or places of refuge. It was forbidden to kill anyone at a pu'uhonua.

The places of refuge were burial sites for the most revered chiefs, and their bones contained *mana*, or spiritual power, that protected everyone in times of peace and war. Their power was considered so great that the refuge was not just temporary sanctuary but also a place to receive permanent absolution.

Pu'uhonua o Honaunau is one of the oldest and most intact places of refuge on the Big Island of Hawaii. A large *heiau*, or temple, was built there. Kamehameha the Great's son was the last of the Hawaiian royalty to be buried at Pu'uhonua o Honaunau. The beautiful sacred site is now a national historical park that remains a place of sanctuary and reverence for Hawaiian people.

He offered medical care to wounded enemy warriors. He planted sweet potatoes and taro across the islands. His effort worked. Ancient rivalries and tensions eased. He enforced a system of independent territories with trade and cultural obligations and protections. He developed laws and a system of taxation. The rise of the Kingdom of Hawaii was among the swiftest, most peaceful, and most well organized in history.

In 1810, Kaumuali'i, the top ali'i nui of Kauai, diplomatically avoided conflict with Kamehameha by agreeing to place Kauai into the Kingdom of Hawaii as a vassal state that paid taxes. Without a shot being fired, the last of the major islands was brought into the kingdom.

Kamehameha deftly devised a plan to build and strengthen the kingdom and avoid further bloodshed, especially with foreigners. England, France, Spain, Portugal, Russia, and the United States were all busy trying to colonize parts of Polynesia. Kamehameha made it illegal for foreigners to own land in Hawaii, thwarting the efforts of early traders, missionaries, and diplomats. At the same time, he engaged all those nations in trade, making their financial success dependent on Hawaiian sovereignty. That accomplishment proved difficult for Kamehameha's descendants to match after the death of the king in 1819. ■

CHICKASAW WARS
UNDEFEATED TRIBAL POWER

Chickasaw warriors were among the most accomplished in the Southeast. They successfully defended their large territory in Mississippi through generations of pressure from their native neighbors. They occasionally fought with the Creek, Cherokee, and Choctaw, a larger tribe to whom they are closely related. The arrival of the French in Louisiana provided an entirely new challenge.

French Louisiana extended from New Orleans up the Mississippi River to Illinois and transected a huge swath of Chickasaw land. The French seized upon the tensions between the Chickasaw and Choctaw. They allied with the Choctaw in southern Mississippi and the Illinois tribes in the southern Great Lakes, especially the Peoria and Illini. The Chickasaw

CHICKASAW ALLIANCE The Chickasaw allied with the English under James Edward Oglethorpe at the outbreak of the Chickasaw Wars.

were as clever at diplomacy as they were adept at war. They reached out to the British for trade and military alliance. They played the English perfectly and soon fortified their towns with cannon and equipped their warriors with muskets.

CHICKASAW-CHOCTAW COLLISION

In 1721, Jean-Baptiste Le Moyne sieur de Bienville, the French governor of Louisiana, wanted the Chickasaw reduced. They were allied with the English, making the French vulnerable to tribal and English attack in the middle reaches of the Mississippi River. Bienville urged the Choctaw to attack the Chickasaw to disrupt British trade, but he underestimated the Chickasaw.

For defense, the Chickasaw coalesced a line of new villages around Savannah Village, South Carolina, on a British trade route. They then acted to preempt French attacks. They knew the Choctaw were largely French proxies. The Choctaw moved against the Chickasaw, with war in the Indian custom—small raids, attacks on isolated hunting and trading parties. The Chickasaw responded with overwhelming force not against the Choctaw, but rather against the French. They occupied Chickasaw Bluff, near present-day Memphis, Tennessee. From there, they blocked all French trade and military traffic on the Mississippi. The French were in a losing war with the British for trade influence and empire. Bienville was recalled to France in 1724.

After a 10-year hiatus, Bienville returned to Louisiana in 1734, determined to teach the Chickasaw a lesson. The Choctaw refused to fight Chickasaw alone when Bienville asked them to attack. Bienville took two years to build a force, but in 1736 he launched a major French campaign against the Chickasaw with allied Choctaw and Illini warriors.

Bienville's second in command led 130 French soldiers and nearly 400 Illini, Miami, and Arkansas warriors against the Chickasaw at the Battle of Ogoula Tchetoka near present-day Tupelo, Mississippi. But the Chickasaw were ready. They had cleverly fortified positions, with palisaded towns at high elevations, chosen for best natural defense. They cut down the French ranks in a withering cross fire while Chickasaw reinforcements arrived from a nearby town and flanked the

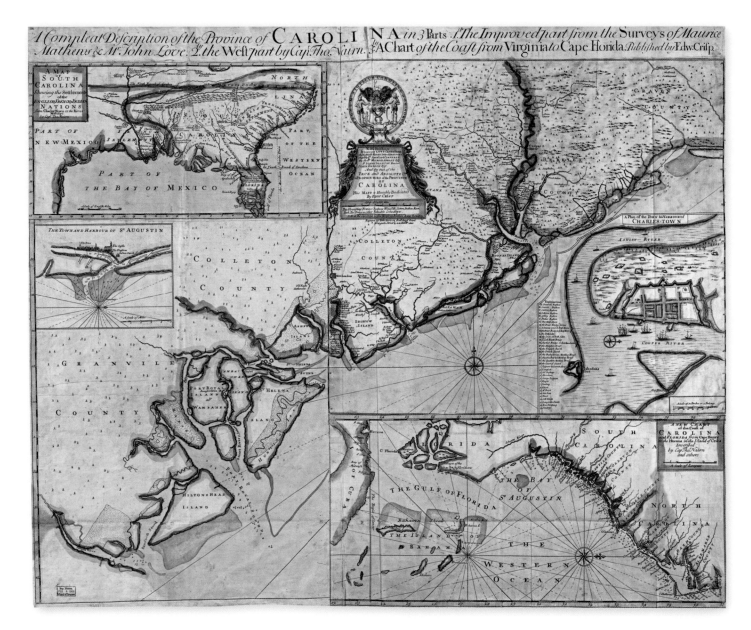

A Compleat Description of the Province of CAROLINA in 3 Parts. 1. The Improved part from the Surveys of Maurice Mathews & Mr. John Love. 2. the West part by Capt. Tho. Nairn. 3. A Chart of the Coast from Virginia to Cape Florida. Published by Edw: Crisp

French attackers. The French who could do so fled. The Chickasaw burned 17 French captives alive. Almost every French soldier was killed.

Bienville's main force of 600 French troops and 600 Choctaw warriors soon descended on the Chickasaw towns. At the Battle of Ackia, Chickasaw defenders inflicted 200 French casualties. Warriors snuck out to the flatlands and burned off the grass, leaving the French no cover and little option but to retreat in defeat.

Bienville tried to punish the Chickasaw one more time, in 1739, bringing a force of 2,400 Choctaw warriors and 1,200 French soldiers, siege equipment, and heavy artillery. More than 500 French died of disease. The siege equipment bogged

CHICKASAW POWER When Europeans arrived, Chickasaw control over a huge swath of territory in the Southeast was beyond dispute. They were never defeated in a major battle with their Indian enemies or the French.

down in the swamps, and Bienville abandoned the march. The Chickasaw were never defeated in a major battle by the French, Choctaw, Illini, or other enemies, through the American Revolution and up to the Civil War.

In 1780, Chickasaw warriors aided the British assault on Fort Jefferson in western Kentucky. They signed three treaties with the Spanish after the American Revolution and six with the United States, playing the nations off one another. In 1795, under the Treaty of San Lorenzo, Spain ceded all colonies north of the 31st parallel, keeping Florida and a small part of Louisiana. Undefeated in battle, the Chickasaw watched Mississippi become a state in 1798 and then had to contend with the removal era in U.S. Indian policy. ■

OSAGE WAR

SURROUNDED BUT NEVER OVERWHELMED

The Osage fought a long and sometimes desperate struggle to keep their land in the face of conflict with many tribes and later with the United States. Because the tribe's nexus of villages shifted west over a relatively short period, they are one of the few tribes that became deeply experienced in woodland waterborne conflict, assaults on large fortified tribal villages in the Southeast, and horseback hunting, raiding, and war on the Great Plains. They emerged from the cauldron of war with diminished lands but dauntless courage.

The Osage are part of the Siouan language family and especially closely related to the Ponca, Omaha, Kaw, and Quapaw. Once, those tribes were all likely one people, but they diversified in language and culture as they moved from the eastern Great Lakes to the Mississippi River Valley. They fought their way out of the Ohio River Valley, but historians disagree about when. Some say it was long before European contact, but others say that they were driven out of the Ohio during the Beaver Wars, when Iroquois warriors moved into the region to occupy the land for trapping and trade.

When the Osage were displaced from the Ohio River Valley, they regrouped in Missouri. Other tribes already occupied this land, including the mighty Choctaw. Osage-Choctaw conflict was sporadic and usually not debilitating to either

OSAGE VILLAGE The Osage built their homes in the European
style and incorporated metal tools and weapons into their culture.

"THEY LOOKED LIKE SO MANY NOBLE BRONZE FIGURES.
THE OSAGES ARE THE FINEST LOOKING INDIANS
I HAVE EVER SEEN IN THE WEST."

WASHINGTON IRVING

population, but it lasted a long time. By the time French traders came to Missouri in 1673, the Osage and Choctaw had been fighting as long as anyone from either tribe could remember. The Osage had fared well and controlled territory in Missouri, Arkansas, Kansas, Oklahoma, and Texas.

MOVING WEST ON HORSEBACK

The Osage maintained an agricultural economy—planting corn, beans, and squash. But like their woodland forebears, they were adept gatherers and deer hunters. In 1690, they acquired horses from other Plains tribes. As their horse herds grew, the Osage boldly pushed the western edges of their territory at the expense of the Kiowa and other Plains tribes. They hunted buffalo even more than deer, becoming skilled in horsemanship in both hunting and war.

With land in what would eventually become five U.S. states, the Osage were truly formidable. They took on the mighty Comanche in epic conflict on the southern Plains. They raided and fought densely occupied and well-fortified Choctaw towns to their east and nomadic Plains tribes to their west. They were also strategic diplomats. They formed an alliance with the French and used that friendship to work the Choctaw, traditional Osage enemies but also French allies. They accepted French Jesuit missionaries and helped the French in occasional conflicts with the Spanish. The French responded with obvious respect. In 1725, they brought a delegation of Osage chiefs to Paris, where they spent a great deal of time with King Louis XV, attending the opera with him and hunting the French woods with the king and most of his court.

The Osage proved their adaptability after the French lost the French and Indian War. In 1763, the French cleverly ceded their colonies in Louisiana to the Spanish before surrendering

OSAGE WARRIOR George Catlin, who painted this warrior in 1834, said Osage were the tallest Indians he ever saw, with most men over six feet.

to the English. That put Osage territory, which was still unceded tribal land, in the middle of Spanish domain. The Spanish courted Osage favor and built a new tribal trading post there. The tribe continued diplomacy where it worked and warred when it did not, which was still the case in regard to the Kiowa and Comanche.

U.S. EXPANSION TO OSAGE LAND

A smallpox epidemic ravaged Osage villages between 1801 and 1802, killing 2,000 and weakening the tribe in advance of America's Louisiana Purchase of 1803. France had ceded that land to Spain in 1763 and Spain had retroceded it back, so the transaction was between the French and the Americans, even though it was all Indian land.

The Louisiana Purchase uncorked American expansion into the West, after decades of steady American encroachment on tribes in the Southeast. The Lewis and Clark expedition set out from St. Louis in 1804 to cross to the Pacific coast. Then America came after the tribes. In 1808, 20,000 Osage, Iowa, Missouri, Sac and Fox, Kickapoo, Shawnee, and Delaware Indians ceded land in Missouri— more than 52 million acres—the entire eastern portion of the state. That was the first American expansion into Osage land. Thomas Jefferson paid annuities and gave ammunition to Osage enemies, encouraging them to attack and displace the tribe.

In 1817, at the Battle of Claremore Mound, Cherokee and Choctaw warriors assisted white settlers in an attack on an Osage village, killing 38 and capturing 104. The Cherokee sold the captives as slaves. The Osage were pressured to concede further land cessions in 1818 and again in 1825. A reservation was established for them in 1830 in Kansas. The Missouri militia started rounding up Osage from their Missouri villages in 1837 to deport them to Kansas. ■

LAKOTA EXPANSION
CULTURE IN MOTION

Long before European contact, intense conflict in the Ohio River Valley dispersed many tribes. Among them were the early Siouan forebears of the Lakota, even though their identity as Lakota had not yet been formed. As they spread out, they diversified and eventually became the Osage, Ponca, Quapaw, Kaw, Ho-Chunk (Winnebago), and Sioux.

As the Sioux moved into Minnesota and spread farther north, they slowly displaced the Hidatsa, Arikara, Cheyenne, and A'aninin (Gros Ventre). That process started around 1600, and was complete around 1700. The lodges of the A'aninin were used by the Sioux who displaced them, and were still visible in Minnesota to white traders and trappers in the 1850s.

BDOTE: RISING UP
In Minnesota, the Sioux underwent a major transformation, becoming culturally a people, distinct from all the other Siouan groups. They flourished there, farming corn, harvesting wild rice, hunting, and fishing. They maintained the Wakan Dance as their central religious society. They identify the birthplace of their people as Bdote, the confluence of the Minnesota and Mississippi Rivers near present-day Minneapolis-St. Paul. When whites arrived in the area, Bdote was still a nucleus of Sioux life.

As the Sioux flourished in Minnesota, they continued to grow and diversify into three major dialect groups: the Dakota, Nakota, and Lakota. All three of these Sioux groups were part of a larger common social and political order called the Oceti Sákowin, or Seven Council Fires. Within the Seven Council Fires, the three dialect groups were represented in bands. The Dakota bands lived farthest to the east, in southern Minnesota. They were called the Mdewakanton, Sisseton, Wahpeton, and Wahpekute bands. The Nakota bands—Yankton and Yanktonai—lived just west of the Dakota along the Red River of the North. The Lakota were all originally in the Teton band and lived just west of the Nakota. These bands communicated with one another and shared many elements of culture, but they were not one homogeneous tribe. Europeans called them Sioux because they first learned about them through the Ojibwe, who called them *naadowesiwag,* a species of snake.

The "siw" root morphed into the word *Sioux.* That has left many Dakota, Nakota, and Lakota unhappy with the term Sioux, although it has persisted simply because Oceti Sákowin is hard for some people to say, and the Seven Council Fires has changed so much that it no longer reflects the composition of Dakota, Nakota, and Lakota groups today.

PAHA SAPA: LAKOTA JUGGERNAUT
Once the Lakota started migrating farther west onto the Plains, their transformation accelerated. They were slowly pulled west by the lure of excellent hunting on the prairies. And they were pushed west as well by powerful enemies in the Assiniboine, Cree, and especially the Ojibwe. That conflict lasted for more than 100 years. As the Sioux moved onto the prairies, the distinctions between the eastern Dakota and the western Lakota became ever more pronounced.

LAKOTA-PAWNEE WARFARE The Lakota, more numerous and with large horse herds, brutally dispossessed the Pawnee in decades of conflict in the northern Plains.

By the 1800s, the western Lakota made it to the Black Hills. They called it Paha Sapa, "the heart of everything that is." Many Lakota even abandoned the idea that Bdote was their original spiritual home. They picked up the Sun Dance as a religious ceremony and abandoned farming in favor of the hunt. The Lakota were surrounded by hostile tribes. They still fought the Assiniboine and Cree to their north, but they also fought the Pawnee to the south and the Blackfeet and Crow tribes to the west. They grew in numbers, but dared not venture farther than the Black Hills until another momentous change again transformed the tribe.

Long before the Lakota made it to the Black Hills, the Pueblo Indians in New Mexico united and rose up against the Spanish. When they did, they flung the gates open to the corrals, dispersing the Spanish horse herds onto the southern Plains. The horses multiplied, and eventually the Comanche and Arikara captured mustangs; the great horse culture of the Plains was born. The Lakota acquired horses late, after 1770, but they took to riding like no other tribe. Horsemanship

LAKOTA VILLAGE The Lakota were entirely mobile—lodges, supplies, food stores, and people. An entire camp from the oldest to the youngest could be ready for travel in minutes should hunting or war necessitate a move.

uncorked the military power of the Lakota. Their access to 60 million buffalo (more than the human population of the United States and Canada in 1800) and the horse enabled a Lakota population explosion.

The Lakota spread out throughout what is now North Dakota, South Dakota, Nebraska, and parts of Wyoming and Montana, conquering other tribes to expand their territory twentyfold. As the population grew, the Lakota diversified into seven more bands: Brulé, Oglala, Sans Arc, Hunkpapa, Miniconjou, Two Kettles, and Sihásapa (also called Blackfoot Sioux, not to be confused with the Algonquian-speaking Blackfeet tribe they often fought). Only the Ojibwe and Cree could compare in terms of population and territory expansion.

Of all tribes, only the Lakota successfully challenged the U.S. Army and defeated it in the field, as they did in Red Cloud's War, forcing the U.S. government to concede terms dictated by tribal leaders. But in the late 1800s, they also suffered some of the last, most horrific massacres of Indians by the U.S. Army. ∎

RAIDERS OF THE SOUTHWEST
MILITARY ECONOMY IN MOTION

Indians waged war for many reasons. Sometimes they fought for territory. Exclusive access to land meant exclusive access to resources—food, furs, and commodities for trade. This fueled the Beaver Wars and other conflicts between tribes. Sometimes they fought for political objectives—to cement alliances. Sometimes they fought for war captives or for vengeance. If a family member was killed in battle, many eastern tribes believed that his soul was offended and required redress on the battlefield so he could be released into the spirit world. The widely misunderstood scalp dances of many tribes served this purpose.

In the Southwest, another reason overshadowed all these: raiding for plunder.

CANYON DE CHELLY
The Navajo farmed, raided, and defended Canyon de Chelly beginning in about 1400. It was a bastion of their economy and their military strength.

Tribes across the continent raided one another, swooping in swiftly to fight or to take prisoners. Captives were adopted into conquering tribes or sold into slavery. Raids were an effective tactic for disrupting an enemy or seizing initiative. Additionally, raids did not tie up men in long military campaigns, which were always difficult for Indians who were full-time providers (farmers, hunters, fishermen) in addition to being warriors.

In the Southwest, though, economics motivated raids. More nomadic tribes frequently raided the stationary pueblos. The stone and adobe villages never moved, and were full of corn, woven mats, tanned hides, and other items of great value. It was worth the risk to take what was not easily made at home. All tribes transformed in reaction. The pueblos rose taller, with more formidable walls for defense. They were sited not just for proximity to fertile fields and water sources, as early pueblos were, but on high mesas for best defense. Raiders had to gather larger war parties, cleverly plan attacks, and develop sophisticated military strategies. It was worth the effort, because successful raiders could feed their families for months. Unsuccessful defenders could lose food supplies for an entire year. The entire economy for all people required relentless military strategizing from both attackers and defenders.

RISE OF THE NAVAJO AND APACHE

For centuries, Athabascan Indians had been slowly moving south from Alaska into the Southwest, arriving as early as the year 1200 and continuing to arrive in groups sporadically as late as 1400. They were hunters and gatherers, skilled with bows, adaptable to different environments. They struggled with cyclical droughts and conflict with other tribes as they moved into occupied territory.

In the Southwest, they came to stay. By the year 1400, they found the Pueblos and actively traded with them. Over time, language and cultural differences between Athabascan groups became more pronounced, and they diverged into the Apache and Navajo people. The Navajo farmed corn acquired in trade with the Pueblos, but continued to hunt and forage, settling between the four sacred mountains that bound the Navajo

NAVAJO BLANKET Textiles like this have been highly prized by the Spanish and by collectors ever since.

homeland today. The Apache spread through the rugged mountains of what is now Arizona, New Mexico, and Mexico. They were more nomadic than the Navajo and often had territorial disputes. Eventually the Apache and Navajo, who really had little to offer in trade with the Pueblos, found raiding to be a far more successful way to feed their families.

The arrival of the Spanish, who brought with them sheep and horses, further changed the tribes. First contact for most tribes happened with the Coronado expedition in the 1540s, but was sustained after Juan de Oñate arrived in 1598. The Apache soon acquired horses, initially killing them for food, but eventually seeing their value for transportation and war. The size and range of raiding parties increased.

The Navajo acquired horses too, but through successful raiding also stole and built some of the largest sheep herds in North America. Soon the Navajo and Apache were expanding their territories through the Southwest and east into the Plains. After the Pueblo Revolt in 1680, thousands of Spanish horses were released into the wild, and the feral herds grew until eventually all of the Plains tribes had horses. That transformed many of the Plains tribes into successful raiders on horseback, just like the Navajo and Apache. The Comanche began raiding the Pueblos and even the Navajo. Life became more dangerous for everyone. Raiding continued and intensified until the end of the U.S. Indian wars. ■

CHACO CANYON: NATURAL PROTECTION FROM RAIDERS

Chaco Canyon, a nine-mile stretch near where the Chaco and San Juan Rivers converge in New Mexico, holds the largest pre-Columbian ruin north of Mexico. Its early occupants, the Anasazi, were ancestors of the Hopi and Pueblo. From 900 to 1150, the canyon was a major economic hub. With many residents and a location difficult for strangers to penetrate, it was well defended from enemy raids. It sheltered massive sandstone structures

and more than 70 satellite communities. At Chaco, the Anasazi built 15 large sandstone kivas, or ritual chambers, each big enough for 400 people, plus more than 100 smaller ones. Chetro Ketl, one of the buildings, took 50 million sandstone blocks and 5,000 trees to construct. Many buildings were multistory, with more than 100 rooms. From 1130 to 1180, there was a debilitating drought. Crop failures and the depletion of animal and tree resources stressed

food production for the large population at Chaco. The size of the settlements there made it an alluring target for enemy raids, too. As villagers foraged farther and farther from the security of the main city center, attacks intensified. Eventually, the population dispersed for easier access to food. That gave rise to the Hopi and Pueblo communities that flourish today, where the people still tell histories of their ancestral occupation of Chaco Canyon.

FEATHERS AND TRIBAL WAR REGALIA

WARRIOR SPIRIT ON DISPLAY

Wearing eagle feathers is a distinctive Native American war custom. Every one of the more than 500 tribes in North America has some variation of this practice.

Indians consider the eagle a sacred bird, related to the thunderbird, a messenger for prayers, and a spiritual force in its own right. In war, no other creature is as venerated. Ceremonially, eagle wings, feathers, and whistles made from eagle bones were broadly used across Indian country and remain so today.

In most of the Plains and Great Lakes regions, a warrior had to earn his feathers. That could be done by killing an enemy, wounding an enemy, being wounded by an enemy, or scalping an enemy. Across the Plains, a feather could also be earned by counting coup—touching an enemy warrior in battle without killing him.

Accomplished warriors displayed their military honors in battle. Most commonly, this was done with anywhere from one to four eagle feathers tied to the top of a man's head. But more accomplished warriors often wore elaborate feather war bonnets. Many feathers meant that someone was an exceptionally skilled veteran. The dog soldier hat—a feather war bonnet with numerous feathers protruding in all directions instead of two neat rows—could strike fear in enemies even from a great distance. Many Plains tribes also had warrior societies with unique colors, insignia, or methods of feather display to celebrate ferocity and comradeship. Warriors sometimes attached their feathers to weapons and shields as well, all in the display of military prowess, but also with a belief that the eagle would protect them in battle.

Warriors had many other tools for war, with regalia to display them. Eagle whistles were used to call spirits to aid warriors in battle and to signal to allies at the start of an attack. Bone breastplates protected warriors spiritually and physically, as did hide shields. Tribal war leaders did not have command and control powers—nobody had to follow orders. Warriors followed inspiring examples, and war regalia, especially earned feathers, inspired them.

FROM FATHER TO SON

If a warrior earned enough feathers to make a feather war bonnet, dog soldier hat, or feathered otter-skin turban, others could not appropriate his honors as their own. They had to earn their own feathers. For most tribes, the honors of ceremonial leadership or civil chieftainship originally were entirely separate from the pursuits of war. This changed over time. Warriors wore their feathers for war, but they also wore them for council. When an accomplished warrior spoke, his head covered in feathers, his sway as a man of power on the warpath carried weight in politics.

> "THE EAGLE FLIES HIGHER THAN ALL OTHER BIRDS, CARRYING OUR PRAYERS TO THE GREAT SPIRIT."
>
> ANNA GIBBS (RED LAKE OJIBWE)

Most tribes had a lineal inheritance for civil chieftainship. But increasingly, civil chiefs had to demonstrate aptitude in war or lose influence, and many proven warriors rose to positions of civil chieftainship because they had so much influence. As a result, accomplished leaders often bequeathed their positions and war regalia to their sons, including feather war bonnets. Eventually this eroded the importance of earning each feather, but it also made feather war bonnets into chief bonnets in many places.

Many tribes today continue to use feathers as sacred symbols of leadership and warrior status, although customs have changed over time. It is no longer the case that someone would be chastised or questioned for wearing an eagle feather not earned in battle; many people receive feathers for important service to their people and they are still considered to be earned. Display of feathers has become stylized in modern powwow regalia, but reverence for the feathers and respect for those who wear them remains. ■

LAKOTA WARRIOR The Lakota, like most Plains tribes,
displayed eagle feathers to represent their accomplishments in battle.

Scouts in the War for the West

FIGHTING WITH THE ENEMY'S ENEMY

Native Americans have served in every U.S. war from the Revolution to the present. For many Indians, serving was an opportunity to earn money and respect in the larger world outside their communities. They also loved their homeland and, if they had to defend America to defend their homes, it was an easy decision, even though Americans had fought most tribes. Serving in the U.S. armed forces was also a way to maintain warrior customs. Joseph Medicine Crow, a Crow Indian who served in World War II, completed his tribe's four ritual acts of war while in the U.S. Army—killing an enemy, disarming an enemy in battle, counting coup, and stealing the enemy's horses. It made him the last true Plains Indian war chief.

In the 1800s, though, many Indians served as scouts for the U.S. Army for another reason—to destroy their enemies. Throughout the history of colonization, more powerful groups have strategically pitted conquered groups against one another. The British used Irishmen to suppress Irish resistance. They bought off Scottish nobles and sent them into the field against William Wallace. In North America, they employed the Yamasee against the Tuscarora. The Americans perfected the tactic in their many wars against the tribes in the West.

The approach succeeded in large part because the Plains tribes fought each other in brutal campaigns for territory, plunder, and ritual vengeance. When America went to war against a Plains tribe, there was always another tribe eager to join the fray against ancient enemies. The Pawnee and Crow scouted for the U.S. Army against the Lakota. The Osage scouted when the United States fought the Cheyenne. The Apache scouted for the United States when the army fought other Apache. Ancient divisions ruptured with new force.

WINNING THE WEST

The position of Indian scout had a special history and devastating impact. Although Indians had long scouted for Europeans and then Americans, those scouts weren't considered soldiers until an army designation of Indian Scout was formally created in 1866. The Osage responded to the call in 1868, leading General George Armstrong Custer to the Cheyenne and Arapaho camp at Washita River and participating in a brutal massacre of Black Kettle's band. Famous scouts included the Pawnee warrior Luther H. North, and Crow scouts Curley and White Swan. In 1916, Indian Scouts led General John J. Pershing's troops in pursuit of Pancho Villa deep into Mexico. Indian Scouts had a special unit insignia of crossed arrows. The Indian Scouts were deactivated in 1947.

Sometimes Indian Scouts were the deciding factor in

WASHITA RIVER
Osage warriors served as some of the first Indian Scouts for the U.S. Army, leading Custer to Black Kettle's band at Washita River for one of the worst Indian massacres in U.S. history.

crushing tribal resistance. Apache leaders Geronimo and Naiche, for example, eluded American pursuit for years. At the high point of the conflict, a fifth of the U.S. Army was deployed against the Apache. Geronimo and Naiche stealthily raided in both the United States and Mexico, covering incredible distances by horse, hiding in remote mountainous areas and offering stiff resistance. Unable to force a confrontation in the field, the U.S. Army turned to rival Apache groups to find men adept enough to track Geronimo and Naiche. In a short time, these scouts located the Apache resistance. Then, serving the war effort not only with their tracking

skills, but also with their diplomatic abilities, they persuaded the Apache to abandon the fight and parley with U.S. Army officers. Geronimo, Naiche, and their followers surrendered in 1886, ending the longest Indian war in American history.

Although some would cast Indian Scouts as men who betrayed their native brothers, for those who served, the role was entirely different. They were fighting ancient enemies, ending conflicts, winning political favor, and leveraging it into direct benefits for their people. They were also serving their native nations and their new American nation honorably, and maintaining the warrior traditions of their people. ∎

CHEROKEE BLOOD LAW

LAND SALES BRING DEADLY REVENGE

The Cherokee were never afraid of a fight, but they knew what they were up against when it came to the Europeans. Instead of battling the French and English intruders, they accommodated them, developing plantation-style economies and in some cases, even owning black slaves. It worked for a while. The English and Cherokee formed an alliance that usually served both sides well. The eventual rise of the United States, however, tore the Cherokee off their land and also tore the Cherokee people apart.

BLOOD LAW IN GEORGIA

The Cherokee had an ancient cultural code, known as Cherokee blood law: If someone was killed in battle or by murder, the kin of the deceased had to remove the spiritual offense caused to their departed relative. They did this by avenging the loss or through ancient ceremonies. As the Cherokee developed ever more formalized political customs, Cherokee blood law became formalized, too. By the time Americans tried to evict the tribe from Georgia, the Cherokee considered it a capital offense not just to commit murder but also to sell Cherokee land.

In 1830, Americans were pushing deep into Cherokee land to settle or to prospect for gold. Major Ridge was an accomplished but controversial Cherokee diplomat, deeply respected by both tribal and white leaders in Georgia. He forged an alliance that helped Andrew Jackson to defeat the traditionalist Red Stick Creek in 1814 and to fight the Seminole in 1818. When the Americans wanted the Cherokee to leave Georgia for good, Ridge again advocated accommodation. Along with two other Cherokee leaders, Charles Hicks and James Vann, he urged his tribe to sign a new treaty that would give the Cherokee homeland to the Americans. Ridge was already richer than most white plantation owners in the South, and his ability to survive the move with his wealth intact was assured.

The Cherokee were deeply divided. Most refused to move, felt betrayed by the request, and boycotted the negotiations. But Ridge strongly felt that the people would be killed and stripped of all their land if he did not negotiate for a new home. He signed the Treaty of New Echota in 1835, knowing it would alienate and infuriate many of his people. A tiny fraction of the tribal leadership signed with him. Most Cherokee, including their principal chief, John Ross, did not sign.

Ridge moved to Oklahoma in 1837, long before others in his tribe were forced onto the Trail of Tears, the long, deadly walk to Oklahoma. Ross and other Cherokee leaders questioned the terms and the timing of the treaty, acquiring 15,000 Cherokee signatures on a petition of protest. Ross could not persuade the U.S. Senate to nullify the treaty. It was ratified by a one-vote margin, and the Cherokee were evicted.

JOHN ROSS

John Ross, who was only one-eighth Cherokee by blood and seven-eighths Scottish, nonetheless rose to prominence in the Cherokee nation. He was committed to land rights and political development. The Cherokee were in the midst of momentous change when Ross started his political career in 1816. They developed a modern democratic governance structure, including a bicameral legislature and supreme court. Ross did not do all of that himself, but was named president of the Cherokee national committee in 1818. He was an avid student of Major Ridge and other Cherokee diplomats who often accommodated the U.S. government, but his passion for land issues and the plight of common Cherokee citizens earned the respect of tribal elders. In 1828, he was elected as principal chief of the Cherokee.

No sooner did Ross assume his position than Andrew Jackson, who Ross had fought with both in the War of 1812 and against the Red Stick Creeks at the Battle of Horseshoe Bend in 1814, turned on the Cherokee and advocated their removal from the Southeast. Ross pushed hard against removal. His dedication won the support of most Cherokee people, but cost him his friendship with Ridge, who was the first Cherokee executed under the Cherokee blood law after removal to Oklahoma. The blood law killings and reprisals nearly tore the Cherokee nation apart. The Civil War further divided the Ross and Ridge factions, but in the end Ross held the people together, navigated the turbulent waters and helped heal his nation.

BLOOD LAW IN OKLAHOMA

In 1839, the Cherokee survivors of the Trail of Tears invoked the Cherokee blood law. Major Ridge, his son, and his nephew were assassinated. In reprisal, Ridge family members killed the assassins. Reprisal murders went back and forth for decades. John Ross was likely not complaining when Ridge was killed, although there is no evidence that he orchestrated the killing. As the killings continued, Ross tried to avoid further bloodshed. But the people had suffered so severely in the Trail of Tears and mourned the loss of their homeland so painfully that he had little immediate effect. His position was complicated by the fact that he was trying to uphold Cherokee land rights in Georgia, arguing that Ridge had no authority to sign the treaty for the entire Cherokee nation, but now needed people to step away from their ancient belief in the Cherokee blood law to make peace.

STAND WATIE
Stand Watie was a brigadier general in the Confederate Army and the principal chief of the Cherokee for four years. He was part of the Major Ridge faction, and sometimes bitterly opposed to John Ross.

Tensions continued through the Civil War. Stand Watie, a Cherokee who signed the Treaty of New Echota in 1835 along with Ridge, successfully deposed Ross. He committed the Cherokee to siding with the Confederacy and raised troops for segregated Confederate units. Union soldiers captured Ross and brought him to Philadelphia, where he remained for the duration of the war. He returned to Oklahoma afterward and resumed his position as principal chief. With time, the Cherokee blood law killings subsided, but the ripples influence tribal divisions even today. ■

HORSE RAIDS AND WARS

TRANSFORMING TRIBAL WAR CULTURE

All cultures change over time. In the Native American experience, many cultural changes were involuntary, the results of forced assimilation. But some were willingly accepted, especially the warmly welcomed introduction of the Spanish horse, which transformed tribes across the Southwest, Great Plains, Great Basin, and even the Great Lakes and Northwest coast. Methods for hunting, travel, and war evolved rapidly. The tribes that got horses in greater numbers or before their enemies ascended in the harsh environment of tribal conflict.

The Pueblo Revolt in 1680 dispersed the Spanish horse herds from their settlements into the wilds of the Southwest. The animals reproduced and spread so quickly that within decades millions of horses roamed all across the Southwest, Great Basin, and Plains. The Apache and Navajo got the horse

THE PREHISTORIC NORTH AMERICAN HORSE MIGRATION

When the Spanish brought horses to North America in the 1500s, it was not an introduction of the species to a new place so much as a reintroduction to its original home. From 45,000 to 11,000 years ago, periodic ice ages deposited a huge percentage of the Earth's water into massive glaciers, which connected the continents of Asia and North America. While the land masses were connected, prehistoric horses and camels, which then existed only in North America, migrated across the land bridge and populated Asia, the Middle East, Europe, and eventually Africa.

The animals transformed civilizations across those continents, enabling incredible innovations in travel and warfare. Ironically, those innovations equipped Europeans for their eventual colonization of North America. Meanwhile, the horse and camel went extinct in North America, leaving only a fossil record.

The climate and the human landscape across the planet totally transformed over time, but when horses were returned to North America thousands of years after their ancestors had died out, they found a fertile home and proliferated. Again, these animals transformed the landscape, the tribal cultures, and the nature of relationships among human groups.

early, which led them to dominance in war and raiding. Previously those tribes had been at the mercy of Pueblo traders who lived in fortified villages. Now the Pueblos were at the mercy of the raiders on horseback. Even the Spanish army offered little protection or ability to pursue what had quickly become some of the best light cavalry in the world. And that was just the beginning.

RISE OF THE COMANCHE

As the feral horse herds multiplied, they moved out of the Southwest into Colorado and Texas. The Shoshone took to horses quickly, and one small band of Shoshone used them with such remarkable skill in war against the Ute that the Ute word for "enemy" was applied to the entire band. The name stuck: *Comanche*.

The Comanche seemed unstoppable on the warpath. From 1700 to 1840, they exploded onto the southern Plains. Soon they eclipsed the main body of Shoshone in numbers, horses, territory, and reputation in war. Within a few decades, the Comanche controlled territory that included much of the present-day states of New Mexico, Texas, Oklahoma, Kansas, and Colorado. Famous Comanche leaders such as Iron Jacket, Peta Nocona, Quanah Parker, Buffalo Hump, and Santa Anna helped build the tribe and lead armed resistance against Spanish, Mexican, and American settlers and armies.

A dozen bands of Comanche, all independent, feeling no need to develop a national tribal identity, flourished in their homeland, known as Comancheria. They traveled hundreds of miles to raid, taking thousands of captives from other tribes, Mexico, and white settlements in Texas. Most captives were adopted into the tribe. White women, such as Cynthia Parker, who was captured in 1836, married Comanche men and had children. At the high point of Comanche power, more than 45,000 Comanche were in control of millions of acres of land with access to more than two million horses. They raided, took captives, and rustled cattle with impunity. They hunted buffalo with great skill, and the herds remained their primary source of food.

The Comanche fought every tribe on the southern Plains and every European power that came. Over time, they forged

GERONIMO Accomplished raiders Geronimo and Naiche led
the Apache in the longest military resistance to American colonization.

alliances too, especially with the Kiowa. They traded with Americans and Mexicans alike, but anyone who resisted them was usually crushed. And anyone who seemed weak was likely to be raided.

WARRIORS OF THE NORTHERN PLAINS
While the Apache and Navajo rose with the horse in the Southwest and the Comanche rode the southern Plains, the northern Plains trembled under hooves, too. There the horse empowered many tribes. Being the first to get horses mattered, but who could keep their horses mattered more in a new dynamic of mounted raids and cavalry campaigns.

The Arikara were among the first on the northern Plains to get horses, but they traded some to their neighbors. Between the trading and the ongoing dispersal of feral mustangs, the Arikara's early entry did not translate into military dominance. The region's Crow, Blackfeet, Cheyenne,

> "HE CARRIES SEVEN SCARS FROM AS MANY BULLET WOUNDS. THERE ARE FOUR BACK OF THE FORESHOULDER, ONE THROUGH A HOOF, AND ONE ON EITHER HIND LEG."
>
> JOHN RIVERS, ON A U.S. ARMY HORSE THAT SURVIVED LITTLE BIGHORN

Nez Perce, and especially the Lakota used horses to great effect. They abandoned the ancient practice of chasing buffalo off cliffs to kill them. Instead, with skilled lance and bow work at high speed, they chased down their prey, skills equally useful in raiding and war.

With better hunting because of horses came better food and a growing population. War captives further accelerated growth of the stronger tribes. Everyone knew horses were key to leveraging growth in numbers and a better standard of living. Tribes now afforded the greatest honors not to those who could kill the best or the most enemies, but rather to those who could steal the most horses. The compounding effect of horse raiding on the economy, culture, and military might made horse raiding the order of the day. Tribes that once spent most of their time hunting now spent less than half their time hunting and the rest warring, raiding, and building empires. ■

APACHE MARKSMAN After the Apache applied their equestrian skills to raids and war, few could stand in their way.

HOPI FARMER Agricultural tribes were often targets of
raids, which worsened after their enemies got horses.

NATION BUILDING: WARS OF CONQUEST

INTO THE WEST
As thousands of white prospectors, settlers, and migrants spilled into the West, their aspirations of gain and nation building required equal losses from the original inhabitants of the land.

SUBJUGATING THE TRIBES

Native nations faced their greatest existential crisis yet after the American nation was formed. The original 13 colonies dramatically increased their population, expanded their territory, and built a new economy—all at the expense of the tribes whose land and resources were the primary incentives for all the taking and growing. This was the fundamental dynamic in the wars of conquest. The rise of the American nation and all the prosperity and opportunity that it created were mirrored by an equally dramatic story of loss for the first people of the land.

Although many Americans have viewed that development as an unavoidable process—whether tragic, wonderful, or both—the nation made no effort to avoid it. A new philosophy underpinned the new nation: Manifest Destiny. Many Americans truly believed it was the God-given right and unavoidable fate of the American nation to spread from Atlantic to Pacific and beyond and to subjugate or destroy those who had called the land their home for millennia. These are stories of conquest and resistance—the invasion of Hawaii, Indian removal to Oklahoma, the Black Hawk War, Red Cloud's War, the Seminole Wars, and the Invasion of the Black Hills. Many died on all sides of the conflicts, and no group would be the same again.

> **"THE HUNTER STATE, THO MAINTAIN'D BY WARLIKE SPIRITS, PRESENTS BUT A FEEBLE RESISTANCE TO THE MORE DENSE, COMPACT, AND POWERFUL POPULATION OF CIVILIZED MAN."**
>
> JAMES MONROE

land attracted thousands of white colonists west as settlers in native homelands. The discovery of gold, new industries, coal, and vast timber resources brought many more. They came across the Oregon Trail and countless other paths, eventually developing railroads to haul people and freight across the continent.

There was a sense of unbridled purpose. Nothing would get in their way. Forests would be cut. Mountains would be flattened. In their place, wagon roads, railroads, and highways carved the landscape. Sixty million buffalo were exterminated and replaced by 108 million cattle.

Indians were obstacles, too, and the Americans made it perfectly clear how they would deal with them. The Office of Indian Affairs—the federal bureaucracy that handled Indians—was part of the Department of War. If Indians were peaceful and cooperative, the army would relocate them to Oklahoma.

ONE NATION RISES

Manifest Destiny was an article of American faith and a powerful guiding force for many. The agricultural potential of the

---

1804	1813	1830	1835
Tlingit warriors clash with the private army of the Russian-American Company in the Battle of Sitka.	**Tecumseh dies in the Battle of the Thames, shattering the multitribal resistance he led.**	**Indian Removal Act paves the way for removal of tribes from the Southeast and ignites the 1832 Black Hawk War.**	**Andrew Jackson sends the army into Florida and meets resistance organized by Osceola in the Second Seminole War.**

MANIFEST DESTINY Many Americans believed that it was the nation's destiny to expand from sea to shining sea. Any obstacles would be destroyed—from buffalo herds to Indians.

If they resisted, the army would crush them and then move the survivors to Oklahoma. Either way, Indians were army business. Some tribes avoided relocation, but it was always in spite of rather than because of the army and Manifest Destiny.

The nature of conflict changed during this time as well. There had been many horrible conflicts before. The first contacts between tribes and Europeans were marked by perpetual misunderstanding and frequent fighting; some of those were truly devastating for Europeans or the tribes or both. The wars between empires were different—multiple players had competing agendas and alliances, where skill at diplomacy was as important as battlefield strategy. The wars between the tribes were different, too—ranging from ancient conflicts to divide-and-conquer strategies engineered by powerful European nations. But now the primary driver for conflict was conquest. America intended to conquer and subjugate the tribes and take their land. Much was at stake for the Indians, and the wars of conquest inspired unforgettable and sometimes incredibly effective resistance.

MANY NATIONS FALL

In the wars of conquest, tribes were fighting for their lives and lifeways like never before. They had to develop new strategies and tactics on and off the battlefield. The results were usually tragic either way, but the choices the tribes made let them have some effect on their own destinies.

Some chose accommodation. Queen Lili'uokalani capitulated the Kingdom of Hawaii when U.S. Marines invaded, rather than lose thousands of her people in a bloodbath with a predictable result. The unraveling of indigenous governance in Hawaii was heartbreaking, eclipsed only by the suffering endured by the people in the colonial era that followed. The

1836
A raid on Fort Parker in Texas begins the four-decade-long Comanche Wars.

1862
U.S.-Dakota War results in the largest mass execution in American history and ignites the wars with the Plains tribes.

1868
After defeating the U.S. Army in Red Cloud's War, tribal leaders dictate terms for the Treaty of Fort Laramie.

1893
The U.S. Marines invade Hawaii and depose Queen Lili'uokalani, toppling the Kingdom of Hawaii.

> "OTHER NATIONS HAVE TRIED TO
> CHECK . . . THE FULFILLMENT OF OUR
> MANIFEST DESTINY TO OVERSPREAD THE
> CONTINENT ALLOTTED BY PROVIDENCE
> FOR THE FREE DEVELOPMENT OF OUR
> YEARLY MULTIPLYING MILLIONS."
>
> JOHN L. O'SULLIVAN

Cherokee and Chickasaw refused to fight the Americans, choosing to negotiate for better outcomes. Internal divisions plagued the Cherokee in particular, and they, like most tribes in the Southeast, marched on trails of tears to Oklahoma.

Other tribes fought. The Ho-Chunk rose up against American aggressors in the first major tribal resistance after the War of 1812. Black Hawk led Sac and Fox resistance efforts in 1832. Little Crow led the Dakota in a bloody clash in 1862. One by one, they were subjugated, with devastating consequences for their tribes' landholdings and the prosperity of their peoples.

The Lakota and Cheyenne fought back, too. In Red Cloud's War, repeated tribal successes on the battlefield, including the annihilation of 81 soldiers during the Fetterman Fight, forced the Americans to concede defeat, abandon their forts in Lakota land, and sign the Treaty of Fort Laramie in 1868. When gold was discovered in the Black Hills, George Armstrong Custer led U.S. troops to Little Bighorn for the worst American defeat in the Plains Indian wars. Although they were winning more wars than they lost, the Americans did lose Indian wars; and win or lose, the expense and loss of life was a heavy cost.

Private citizens began a wholesale slaughter of the buffalo in the middle of the 1800s, selling hides and crushing dried bison bones for dinnerware and fertilizer. When it became clear just how much the Plains tribes depended on the buffalo, the U.S. Army enabled and protected the hunters in a dramatic escalation of killing. In the end, 60 million buffalo were massacred, reducing the population to 300 animals by 1890. Undefeated in battle, Crazy Horse and other Lakota leaders came into the forts to surrender. Attacking the food source and starving Indians into submission was even more effective than fighting them had been. ∎

CONTINENTAL CONQUEST The nature of conflict shifted in the 1800s as Americans embarked upon a concerted effort to subjugate the tribes and take their land.

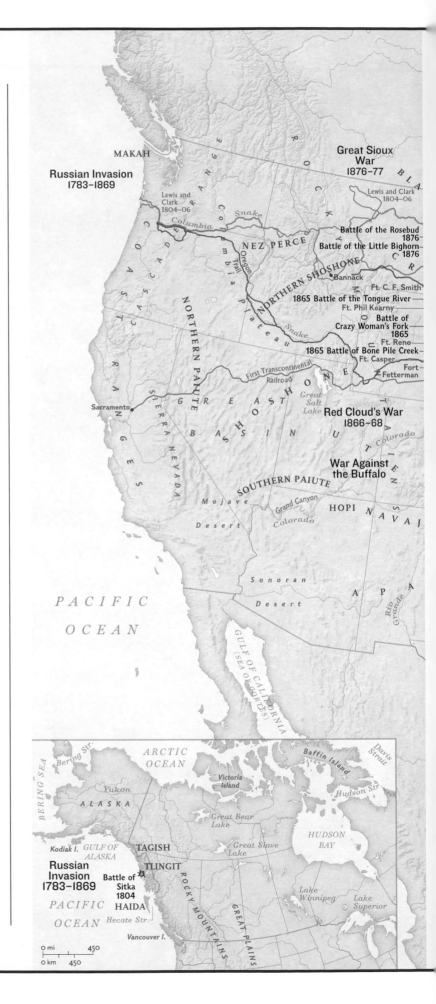

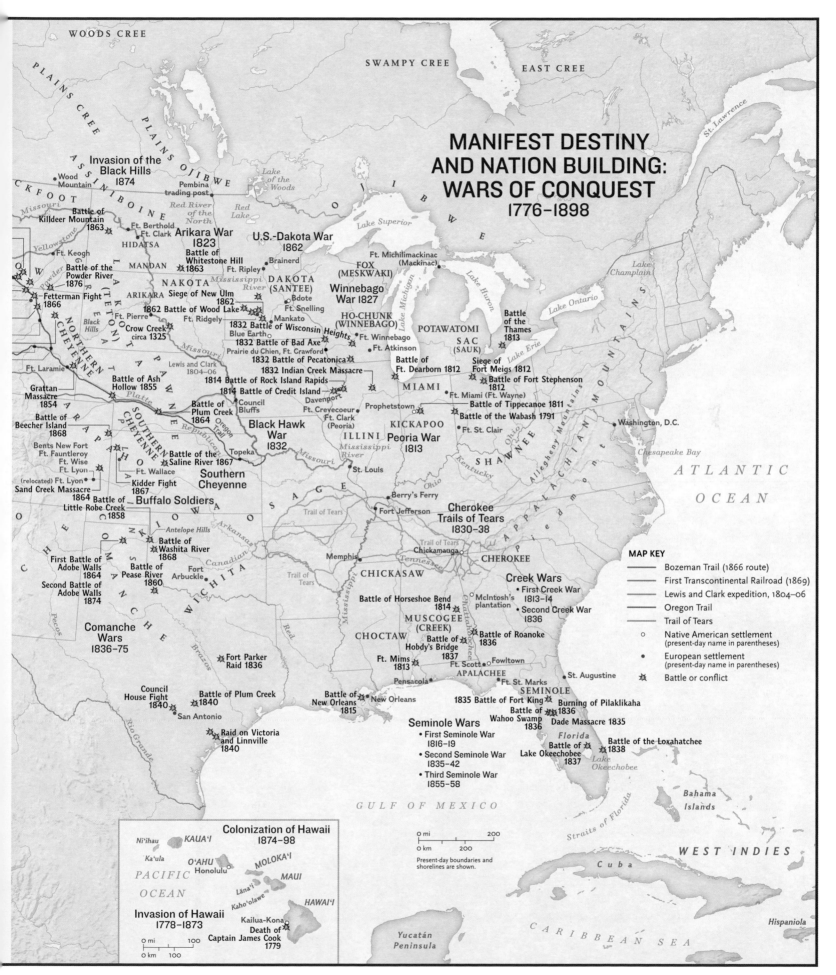

WOODS CREE

PLAINS CREE

PLAINS CREE

SWAMPY CREE

EAST CREE

MANIFEST DESTINY AND NATION BUILDING: WARS OF CONQUEST 1776–1898

Invasion of the Black Hills 1874
Wood Mountain
Pembina trading post
ASSINIBOINE
BLACKFOOT
OJIBWE
Lake of the Woods
Red River of the North
Red Lake
St. Lawrence

Missouri
Battle of Killdeer Mountain 1863
Ft. Berthold
Ft. Clark
HIDATSA
MANDAN
Arikara War 1823
U.S.-Dakota War 1862
Brainerd
Ft. Michilimackinac (Mackinac)
Lake Champlain

Ft. Keogh
Yellowstone
Battle of Whitestone Hill 1863
Ft. Ripley
FOX (MESKWAKI)
Lake

Battle of the Powder River 1876
NAKOTA
Mississippi River
DAKOTA (SANTEE)
Winnebago War 1827
Lake Ontario

Fetterman Fight 1866
ARIKARA
Siege of New Ulm 1862
Bdote
HO-CHUNK (WINNEBAGO)
Battle of the Thames 1813

Powder
LAKOTA (TETON)
Ft. Pierre
1862 Battle of Wood Lake
Ft. Snelling
Mankato
POTAWATOMI
Lake Erie
Battle of Fort Stephenson 1812

Black Hills
Crow Creek circa 1325
Ft. Ridgely
1832 Battle of Wisconsin Heights
SAC (SAUK)
Siege of Fort Meigs 1812

NORTHERN CHEYENNE
Blue Earth
1832 Battle of Bad Axe
Ft. Winnebago
MIAMI
Ft. Miami (Ft. Wayne)

Ft. Laramie
Lewis and Clark 1804–06
Prairie du Chien, Ft. Crawford
Ft. Atkinson
Battle of Ft. Dearborn 1812
Battle of Fort Stephenson 1812

Battle of Ash Hollow 1855
1832 Battle of Pecatonica
Prophetstown
Battle of Tippecanoe 1811
ALLEGHANY MOUNTAINS

Grattan Massacre 1854
Platte
1832 Indian Creek Massacre
Battle of the Wabash 1791

Battle of Beecher Island 1868
SOUTHERN CHEYENNE
1814 Battle of Rock Island Rapids
Davenport
MIAMI
Ft. St. Clair
Washington, D.C.

Bents New Fort Ft. Fauntleroy Ft. Wise
Oregon Trail
1814 Battle of Credit Island
Ft. Creveceour
KICKAPOO
Chesapeake Bay

(relocated) Ft. Lyon
Republica
Battle of Plum Creek 1864
Council Bluffs
Ft. Clark (Peoria)
Peoria War 1813
ATLANTIC

Ft. Lyon
Battle of the Saline River 1867
Black Hawk War 1832
ILLINI
Mississippi River
SHAWNEE
OCEAN

Sand Creek Massacre 1864
Ft. Wallace
Kidder Fight 1867
Topeka
St. Louis
Ohio
Kentucky

Battle of Little Robe Creek 1858
Buffalo Soldiers
IOWA
OSAGE
Berry's Ferry
Ft. Jefferson

Antelope Hills
Arkansas
Trail of Tears
Cherokee Trails of Tears 1830–38

First Battle of Adobe Walls 1864
Battle of Washita River 1868
Canadian
Ft. Arbuckle
Memphis
Trail of Tears
Chickamauga
CHEROKEE

Second Battle of Adobe Walls 1874
Battle of Pease River 1860
WICHITA
Trail of Tears
CHICKASAW
Tennessee
Creek Wars

Comanche Wars 1836–75
Pecos
Red
MUSCOGEE (CREEK)
Battle of Horseshoe Bend 1814
McIntosh's plantation
First Creek War 1813–14
Second Creek War 1836

Fort Parker Raid 1836
Brazos
CHOCTAW
Battle of Hobdy's Bridge 1837
Battle of Roanoke 1836

Council House Fight 1840
Battle of Plum Creek 1840
Ft. Mims 1813
Ft. Scott
Fowltown
APALACHEE

San Antonio
Pensacola
Ft. St. Marks
St. Augustine
SEMINOLE

Rio Grande
Raid on Victoria and Linnville 1840
Battle of New Orleans 1815
New Orleans
1835 Battle of Fort King
Battle of Wahoo Swamp 1836
Burning of Pilaklikaha 1836
Dade Massacre 1835

Seminole Wars
• First Seminole War 1816–19
• Second Seminole War 1835–42
• Third Seminole War 1855–58
Florida
Battle of Lake Okeechobee 1837
Battle of the Loxahatchee 1838
Lake Okeechobee

GULF OF MEXICO

Bahama Islands

Straits of Florida

WEST INDIES

Cuba

CARIBBEAN SEA

Yucatán Peninsula

Hispaniola

MAP KEY

— Bozeman Trail (1866 route)
— First Transcontinental Railroad (1869)
— Lewis and Clark expedition, 1804–06
— Oregon Trail
— Trail of Tears
○ Native American settlement (present-day name in parentheses)
• European settlement (present-day name in parentheses)
✷ Battle or conflict

O mi 200
O km 200
Present-day boundaries and shorelines are shown.

Colonization of Hawaii 1874–98
Ni'ihau
KAUA'I
Ka'ula
O'AHU
Honolulu
MOLOKA'I
LĀNA'I
MAUI
Kaho'olawe
HAWAI'I
PACIFIC OCEAN
Invasion of Hawaii 1778–1873
Kailua-Kona
Death of Captain James Cook 1779
O mi 100
O km 100

TAKING SCALPS
FROM TRIBAL TRADITION TO WHITE BOUNTY

Many tribes took scalps, and the practice was accepted long before European contact. In approximately 1325, there was a major battle at Crow Creek, in present-day South Dakota. The remains of about 500 bodies have been excavated. More than 90 percent had been scalped.

The practice has been widely misunderstood. Tribes considered scalping an honorable act. It was not performed as disrespectful mutilation, but rather to enable an important ceremony. Many tribes believed that if a relative was killed in battle, his or her spirit might be offended and the offense was so great that it could inhibit the victim's departure to the spirit world. The offense could be lifted through religious ceremony, however. The most common ceremony was the scalp dance, which allowed survivors to show their loved ones that they had been avenged, removing any remaining inhibitions for peaceful departure to the spirit world. The scalp was closely associated with the spirit of the person who was scalped, and seen as a symbol of that person's life or even as a home for his spirit.

Indians who practiced scalping usually viewed the person who was scalped with great respect. Often, victorious warriors participated in mourning rituals for both their own family members and for the people they killed and scalped. Some did this by blackening their faces or making food offerings on behalf of the people they killed.

Because this custom was shared across many tribes over a large region, it was considered a great honor to be the foe chosen to be scalped. An Ojibwe warrior once said, "We consider it an honor to have the scalps of our countrymen exhibited in the villages of our enemies, in testimony of our valor." Joseph Nicollet, an early French explorer, observed, "Not to be scalped is a sign of contempt."

SCALPING AND EUROPEANS

Scalping was practiced in Europe and Asia prior to contact with the Americas. Herodotus, among others, noted this as a common practice among the Scythians. The Visigoths have also been described as practicing scalping. There were differences between the European and Native American practices, however. The early European warriors usually took scalps to provide evidence for a kill. In complex military campaigns with mercenaries or punitive campaigns with people paid by the kill, the custom evolved to allow fighters to prove they were owed payment—quite different from the ancient Native American practice.

When the French and British began colonizing North America, they immediately observed the tribal practice of scalping. Samuel de Champlain watched a scalp dance as early as 1603. As the British embarked on punitive and genocidal campaigns against tribes in the Chesapeake and the Northeast, then England and France fought horrendous

MANIFEST DESTINY

Every square inch of North America was home to some Native American. However, from the papal bulls to the Doctrine of Discovery, Spain, France, England, and other European nations never saw indigenous land tenure or use as ownership. They believed that Indians had rights of occupancy only, not ownership. Without obtaining any permission from the first peoples of North America, they fought one another over rights to colonize the land and the people who were there first. After the American Revolution, the new American nation adopted the beliefs and practices of the colonial empire they had revolted against. The government paid war veterans in land grants to tribal territory it had never obtained, setting the stage for repeated conflicts. The Office of Indian Affairs was created in the Department of War, with full knowledge that its mission was to systematically dispossess the tribes. The Americans felt that trampling the Indians was not only unavoidable, but also their God-given right. The 19th-century political writer John L. O'Sullivan summed up the sentiment: "Other nations have tried to check . . . the fulfillment of our manifest destiny to overspread the continent allotted by Providence for the free development of our yearly multiplying millions." That perspective shaped Indian policy for much of the country's history.

wars with one another through native proxies, the two European powers seized upon the native custom of scalping and transformed it. They paid Indians to scalp one another and also their European enemies. The effects were profound.

SCALPING Many tribes considered a scalp the embodiment of the spirit of a slain enemy, often taken to release to the spirit world a relative killed in battle.

In 1703, the Massachusetts Bay Colony offered a cash bounty for native scalps. The New York Scalp Act of 1747 further formalized the practice in that colony. There were six major wars in New England before the French and Indian War, and scalp bounties played heavily in each. Even after military objectives were accomplished, bounties remained prevalent and sometimes were the motive for conflict, as in the John Lovewell scalp raids in Massachusetts in 1724 and 1725. During the French and Indian War, both France and England paid for Indian and white scalps. England offered 40 pounds for a man's scalp and 20 pounds for a woman's. In 1756, Pennsylvania offered 130 pieces of eight for a male scalp and 50 pieces of eight for a female one.

The practice of scalping for bounty and also for sport became part of American military tradition, too. Patriots scalped Indians frequently during the Sullivan expedition against the Iroquois in the Revolutionary War. Union and Confederate soldiers scalped one another with no Indian involvement during the Civil War. And the practice continued for decades afterward during the punitive raids and wars for the West. ■

INVASION OF HAWAII

COOPERATION, COLLUSION, AND CONSPIRACY

The Hawaiian Islands are among the most geographically isolated and distinctive places on Earth. Although there are deserts and snow-capped mountains, most of the islands are lush, verdant natural food factories. The ancient Hawaiians arrived from elsewhere in Polynesia about the year 300, and kept coming in periodic waves of migration until about the year 1000. They fought one another, but never in debilitating colonial campaigns or depopulating levels of conflict. In the end, there was plenty of food for everyone, and little other incentive to wage war beyond ritual collisions and conflicts between those who wanted to rule.

It is possible that the Chinese and various European explorers made it to Hawaii before British Captain James Cook's famous expedition in 1778, but Cook's arrival changed Hawaiian history. That began sustained European contact with

DEATH OF CAPTAIN JAMES COOK The Hawaiians responded to Cook's kidnapping of their king by killing and disemboweling the British explorer.

Hawaii, and the British, French, and American governments immediately saw the potential of Hawaii as a colony.

The Native Hawaiians felt the sting of contact right away. Cook's sailors arrived during the makahiki season, a ritual time of feasting and friendship. War was taboo. In liaisons with Hawaiian women, British sailors spread venereal disease and tuberculosis.

ALI'I NUI Hawaii's highest-ranking elites, the ali'i nui, had the special privilege of wearing these brightly colored feather capes.

BRITISH BLUNDERS

Cook soon learned the hard way that the Hawaiians were peaceful but not submissive. In 1779, he returned to Hawaii, but grew frustrated when Hawaiians stole one of his small ships. Cook kidnapped the monarch on the Big Island, Kalaniʻōpuʻu-a-Kaiamamao. The Hawaiian king did not realize that Cook intended to capture and ransom him as he walked with Cook to the landing. A crowd of Native Hawaiians figured out the plot, though, and blocked Cook. The captain tried to force the king onto his ship; the Hawaiians attacked with clubs and shark tooth knives. The British were overwhelmed and Cook was killed. His body was treated with high respect in the Hawaiian custom, disemboweled and deboned. The bones were distributed to chiefs so they could absorb the mana of a great war leader.

Cook's death did not, however, head off the deaths of many more natives from European disease. By 1831, only about 130,000 Hawaiians were left from a precontact population of more than a million. In 1850, a fifth of the remaining Hawaiian population died from measles.

King Kamehameha the Great rose to power during the time of epidemics. He openly traded with the British, acquired guns, and used the new technology to leverage his efforts to unite the islands by conquest. Successful, he created the Kingdom of Hawaii in 1810. He constructed highways around the Big Island of Hawaii, and reinforced and formalized the ancient kapu system of taboos and land divisions to maintain harmony and cultural continuity. In spite of Kamehameha's outreach to the British as a trading partner, the relationship was always strained. The British did not have the power or will to subjugate the islands by force, and instead pursued a diplomatic path to colonization. They supported Kamehameha. It was easier for them to gain influence through his efforts than it was to do so by conquering everyone.

In 1819, Kamehameha died and his son, Liholiho, became Kamehameha II. In 1820, British missionaries came to Hawaii and worked with great success to engineer cultural change. Liholiho abolished the ancient kapu system and offered no protest as the missionaries banned central cultural practices such as hula and even surfing. The missionaries brought good and bad. They undermined the ancient culture, but they also developed an alphabet for the Hawaiian language in 1826, and schools for the ali'i elites in 1837. Soon, the Hawaiians had one of the world's highest literacy rates.

DESTABILIZING HAWAIIAN SOVEREIGNTY

Hawaiian monarchs responded to British demands to accept their Protestant missionaries and prohibit French Catholic missionaries. The Hawaiians expelled the Catholics, and in 1839, that brought the wrath of the French monarchy down on Hawaii. To avoid a military invasion, King Kamehameha III gave a land grant to the French to establish Catholic missions at Honolulu. He also paid restitution to the French government to keep the peace. Kamehameha III developed a new constitution for the Kingdom of Hawaii and tried to accommodate foreigners, while keeping them as distant as possible. That was almost impossible. France and England, already in the midst of major military and trade wars across the globe, set Hawaii as a new battleground for empire.

In 1843, Lord George Paulet brought the British Navy to Honolulu and threatened to attack. King Kamehameha III, desperate to avoid bloodshed, capitulated. The British soon realized that without the Hawaiian monarchy on their side, the islands would descend into disorder, allowing the French to expand their influence. Richard Darton Thomas, a British Navy officer, reinstated the Hawaiian monarchy, and the English continued to work with and to manipulate the Hawaiian monarchs.

King Kamehameha V died in 1872 and that was the end of that dynasty. Hawaiian nobles were elected to fill the vacancy, but the Kingdom of Hawaii was more threatened than ever when America finally moved to colonize the islands. ∎

COLONIZATION OF HAWAII: THE KINGDOM'S LAST QUEEN

LILI'UOKALANI, THE BAYONET CONSTITUTION, AND THE OVERTHROW

I n the late 1800s, French and British colonial power was waning as America ascended. In Hawaii, British and American missionaries and plantation owners slowly supplanted Native Hawaiian ownership of the land.

Native Hawaiian monarchs used to operate under their ancient kapu system; land divisions were governed by territories under the supervision of ali'i, or royal elites. This system worked for the Hawaiians, but the Europeans disrupted it. Hawaiian monarchs sought to avoid conflict and appease foreign military powers. They did so with generous land

QUEEN LILI'UOKALANI
The queen refused to let a drop of Hawaiian blood be spilled as she defended the land and people from American betrayal and invasion.

grants and sales. By the time the results became evident, there was no way to undo the damage. White missionaries and plantation owners had legal title to vast tracts. They converted the land from food production to sugarcane plantations and brought in Chinese laborers.

The accommodation by the Hawaiian monarchs eroded Hawaiian identity. Land, business, and education authority slowly transferred from Native Hawaiians to British and American Protestant missionaries, settlers, and plantation owners who colluded to wrest control of Hawaii from the

"WE NEED HAWAII JUST AS MUCH AND A GOOD DEAL
MORE THAN WE DID CALIFORNIA. IT IS MANIFEST DESTINY."

WILLIAM McKINLEY

original inhabitants. By 1885, all Native Hawaiian children had to attend English language schools. From 1896 to 1983, the Hawaiian language (originally supported by missionary work in Hawaiian literacy) was outlawed in schools.

Great Britain and the United States deployed troops to Hawaii in 1874, waiting for an opportunity to intervene if the monarchy did not cooperate. The British and Americans did not fight with one another then, as the subjects of both nations just wanted to keep the land and resources transferring from the Hawaiians to their control. There were spoils enough for both foreign nations.

In 1875, the Americans made a clever series of arrangements to bring Hawaii into their primary influence. It began with the Treaty of Reciprocity, which treated Hawaiian sugar the same as American sugar in U.S. trade. This was the age of protectionism, and removing heavy tariffs on Hawaiian sugar for sale in the United States created a favored status. The business boomed. Most of the profit went to white businessmen and plantation owners, but Hawaiian monarchs, who still had significant landholdings, benefited just enough to keep them willing to enable the change.

SUGAR BUSINESS EXERTS POWER

The Hawaiian monarchs still had the interests of their people in mind and the power to do something when needed. In 1881, King Kalakaua was traveling abroad and his sister, Lili'uokalani, was in charge of governmental affairs in Hawaii. A smallpox outbreak erupted, spread from Chinese sugarcane workers. Lili'uokalani closed the port and quarantined the infected crew. The sugar business exploded in outrage, demanding that the monarchy be stripped of its power so the industry would remain a top priority.

In 1887, King Kalakaua was forced to sign the Bayonet Constitution. It stripped him of the power to veto legislation or issue executive orders. Business interests were in control of most government functions. The monarchy seemed little more than a figurehead.

American trade protectionism reached a new pitch in 1890, and the 1875 treaty that gave Hawaiian sugar the same trade status as American sugar was threatened. In 1891, the king died, and Lili'uokalani became queen. She wanted to restore the monarchy to proper power and former glory so she could advance the needs of her people. She worked on a new constitution. Two months later, a tariff war resulted in revocation of the 1875 treaty. Tariffs of 50 percent on foreign imports were applied to Hawaiian sugar. The business was in danger of collapse. Now the sugar magnates needed Hawaii to become part of the United States to protect their economic interests. U.S. policy makers were supportive, but needed the residents of Hawaii to petition the U.S. government. The queen blocked the way.

In 1893, U.S. Marines landed in Honolulu. The queen, unwilling to spill Hawaiian blood, surrendered, hoping to petition for reinstatement of the monarchy. She was arrested in 1895, but pardoned and released as a citizen in 1896. Hawaii became a territory in 1898 and a state in 1959. The queen died in 1917, and for days the people observed strange natural phenomena—huge volcanic eruptions and ocean waters turning red from the sudden appearance of millions of red fish. ∎

HONOLULU **The flag of the Kingdom of Hawaii still flies over a fort in Honolulu in 1853, early in the colonial era.**

RUSSIAN INVASION
BATTLE FOR THE NORTHWEST

W hile the French, Spanish, and English Empires came to North America looking for slaves, gold, and land, the Russians wanted fur. In 1795, the Russian-American Company established a presence in the Northwest and conducted trade with many native communities. Russians soon spread to the coastal communities of present-day Alaska, British Columbia, Washington, Oregon, and California not for exploration, but for colonization—with missionaries, military forces, conscripted labor, and brutal retaliation for any kind of resistance. Their colonies lasted for generations, and the chain of devastating impacts reverberates today.

In 1804, Tlingit resistance to Russian subjugation, conscripted labor practices, and forced marriages culminated in the Battle of Sitka. The Tlingit repelled the Russian advance, but they could not sustain the war and soon came under Russian control. That era lasted until after Russia sold its landholdings to the United States in 1867 and withdrew in 1869.

RACE TO COLONIZE THE ARCTIC
The indigenous peoples from the Arctic to the Northwest were independent and geographically isolated from one another. They never mounted a resistance effort across numerous groups the way Tecumseh, Pontiac, or some of the Plains tribes were able to do. But Europeans tested their warmth and hospitality, and there was both a military collision and a colonial effort that changed everyone involved.

SITKA Tlingit Indians like this one (above) called Sitka (left) home long before the Russians arrived. The island village was an economic center for them and a focal point for intense conflict as they defended their land and lifeways.

Europeans from several nations came to the Northwest and the Arctic to exploit resources such as furs and whales, and they sought a passage across North America. The early British expeditions of Martin Frobisher brought military conflict to some of the Inuit people. The Russians made a more concerted effort to control and colonize Aleuts in Alaska, massacring villages, raping women, relocating communities, and pressuring the native people to harvest sea otters to extinction in some areas.

The French spent less time in the Arctic than the Russians and British, but they also wanted to find a Northwest Passage and to open trade routes to the Arctic from the Great Lakes. They sent Joseph La France, the son of an Ojibwe woman and a French fur trader, to advance their goals. He aspired to a lofty position in the French fur trade, but in 1739 was denied a license by New France because he had violated Indian liquor laws. La France then sold his services to the British. He spent three years building relationships, acquiring birchbark canoes, stockpiling furs, and planning a route to the British forts in Hudson Bay.

In 1742, he made the connection to Hudson Bay with a small armada of birchbark canoes full of beaver furs. La France's successful mission inspired the British, Danish, and Russians to further trade and exploration of the Arctic. Even today Greenland remains part of the Danish Commonwealth. The Russians dominated European empire building on the Arctic west coast and Northwest.

> "LIVE CAREFULLY—WHAT YOU DO WILL COME BACK TO YOU. TAKE CARE OF OTHERS—YOU CAN NOT LIVE WITHOUT THEM. HONOR YOUR ELDERS—THEY SHOW YOU THE WAY IN LIFE."
>
> LaVonne Rae Andrews (Tlingit)

THE RUSSIAN-AMERICAN COMPANY

The Russian emperors knew they needed an economic driver for their aspirations in America. They followed a familiar path when they focused on the fur trade, empowering Grigory Shelekhov to explore, trade, and claim lands in North America in the 1780s. Rather than government agents and the full might of the navy, the Russians used independent companies with their own security forces to represent the empire. It was a structural difference that reduced Russian government risk and expense in empire building, but also let a small number of individuals make their own rules for dealing with indigenous peoples. It was a lethal recipe. Shelekhov established the Shelekhov-Golikov Company and navigated, mapped, and colonized significant parts of the Alaskan coast. At Kodiak Island, where the indigenous population resisted, his forces killed hundreds of natives.

From 1783 to 1786, Shelekhov established the first Russian colonies, forts, and trading posts in North America. As it matured and grew, his company morphed into the Russian-American Company, an independent organization that had the power to colonize, kill, trade, settle, and control Russian America on its own behalf, not just on behalf of the Russian Empire. Between 1799 and 1867, the Russian-American Company did exactly that, establishing 14 forts in North America, including on the Aleutian Islands. The company ran an armada of 72 ships on numerous trips back and forth between Alaska and Russia. Sitka, an ancient Tlingit village site, became a thriving Russian port.

The Russian-American Company systematically dispossessed the indigenous peoples of Alaska. The Russians wanted furs, a conscripted labor force to process them, and enough land to run their empire. They saw conversion of the natives

MAKAH **Russians traded with and colonized the Makah of present-day Washington, who were adept basket makers, whalers, and fur trappers.**

as part of a path to their pacification. They established Russian Orthodox missions, and brutally suppressed resistance. Although the fur trade declined and Russia sold its interests in Alaska to the United States in 1867, the company endured for many years. Many of the indigenous peoples of Alaska today still follow the Russian Orthodox faith, and many have the blood of Russian traders and company men running through their veins.

BATTLE OF SITKA

Sitka is an auspicious place. Recent archaeological excavations have revealed human use of the area for 11,000 years. The high ground on the bay there is not just a beautiful site for a tribal village or a trading post. It also has a commanding view of the water—the key to its military importance. The view also made the location perfectly suited for spotting whales and shipping. Sitka was prized by the Tlingit for its spiritual importance and practical use and by the Russians for its close proximity to the Tlingit, whom they wanted to exploit for labor and furs.

The Battle of Sitka was the last clash between Alaskan Natives and Europeans, and it changed the indigenous Tlingit in many ways. The Tlingit had occupied the Alaska Panhandle for countless generations. They fought sporadically with and raided other tribes and sometimes other Tlingit clans and villages, but their prosperity and autonomy were never seriously challenged until the Russian-American Company arrived in 1795. The Tlingit, especially those living at Sitka, endured several years of Russian efforts to coerce their labor. Alexander Baranov, who ran Russian operations at Sitka, exerted tight and uncompromising control over the natives there. He forced numerous Tlingit women to marry his fur traders, and when they resisted, they were raped. This was a pervasive pattern in Russian treatment of the Tlingit, not just at Sitka under Baranov, although he had a special reputation for the practice.

In 1802, the Tlingit could endure no more. They attacked a small force of 20 Russians and more than 100 of their Aleut allies, killing all of them. Some British traders supplied the Tlingit with gunpowder. Although the Tlingit courted an

alliance, a supply of guns was the limit of the help they received. Most of the British, French, Spanish, and American merchants who traveled the Inside Passage for trade and exploration were not willing to support the Tlingit with troops, supplies, or refuge. The Tlingit were on their own to fight the Russians.

In October 1804, Baranov came back to Sitka from Kodiak with a substantial force. The Tlingit awaited the Russians in a hastily constructed but heavily reinforced wooden fort. As the Russians landed, the Tlingit warriors trapped them in a pincer movement and then closed ranks, displacing the Russian lines, and repelling the entire deployment. Baranov was seriously wounded in the melee. After defeat on the beach, the Russians retreated to their ships. They spent three days engineering an intensive naval bombardment of the tribal fort. The Tlingit had no desire to endure a pounding from Russian cannon and secretly evacuated Sitka, moving the entire tribal population to a different area. They were ready for a protracted conflict.

The Russians redoubled their efforts to hold Sitka. Because the Tlingit had abandoned Sitka, the Russians moved their American base from Kodiak to Sitka, reinforced the buildings, and determined to starve the Tlingit out of the valuable trade. They showed little interest in diplomacy with the Tlingit for many years. The Tlingit felt the impact of fewer European trade goods, but also the benefit of a reprieve from colonization, brutality, and rape. The Russians eventually reestablished trade with the Tlingit, but not trust. They hired some tribal members to work the docks and skin furs. As a whole, though, the tribe for generations was denied access to the ancestral village site, the many sacred sites nearby, and the vast natural resources in the bay.

The Russians continued to expand their domain, with permanent trade posts across tribal villages all along the Alaska, British Columbia, Washington, and Oregon coasts. They even established posts in California, primarily to pursue the sea otter trade, but also to hunt whales. Every tribe on the coast needed a strategy to deal with the Russians. Their eventual retreat from colonial efforts in America did not provide a reprieve from colonization. No sooner did the Russian Empire retreat than the Americans arrived, and there was no escaping the coming wave of colonization. ■

HAIDA **The Haida of British Columbia had a highly developed social and religious structure, revolving around a deep appreciation of spirits in the land, water, and air, like this carved and painted thunderbird.**

PEORIA WAR
POTAWATOMI AND ILLINOIS RESISTANCE

Tecumseh, whose name meant shooting star, was a human meteor who united tribes in resistance to American expansion. His rise, his challenges after the attack on Prophetstown, and his dramatic fall at the Battle of the Thames in 1813 receive attention from historians, and rightly so. But Tecumseh was just one of hundreds of tribal chiefs and war leaders who made the resistance possible.

In present-day Indiana and Illinois, some of Tecumseh's supporters started the fight before him and carried it on long after he was gone. In the Potawatomi villages along the Yellow River, Main Poc was a magnet for warriors ready to make a stand. Black Partridge also rallied the Potawatomi across the southern Great Lakes in dramatic confrontations with American forces. Sac and Fox chief Black Hawk made a name for himself in the Battle of Credit Island and other clashes. The Sac and Fox were less devoted to Tecumseh than were the Potawatomi, but just as effective on the battlefield. More than a dozen other Algonquian tribes formed the Illinois alliance. These were the remnants of the great Miami alliance led by Little Turtle during the Old Northwest War and included some of that conflict's prominent war chiefs.

America was intent on westward expansion. It was widely believed to be the nation's destiny, and any tribe that owned land and intended to defend it was sure to feel the sting of American musket balls and bayonets. Tecumseh was the meteor that landed in the way of expansion. But before and after Tecumseh, the epic struggle for the land claimed many lives and remained the preeminent fight of the time.

BATTLE OF FORT DEARBORN In 1812, as Americans abandoned the fort in present-day Chicago, Black Partridge's Potawatomi warriors ambushed the caravan.

Great Lakes Guerrilla War

Little Turtle died on the eve of the War of 1812. He was a powerful Miami chief who led the most successful resistance to American expansion to date in the Old Northwest War, including the dramatic success of the Battle of the Wabash (St. Clair's Defeat). At the conclusion of that conflict, he advocated peace. Many times the Miami, Shawnee, and other tribes were on the verge of renewed conflict and Little Turtle's gravitas swayed the people to peace. His passing allowed frustrated warriors to rally against the Americans in a way not seen for decades.

Tecumseh had already been building an alliance. The American attack on Prophetstown, also known as the Battle of Tippecanoe, sparked deep tribal resistance. The Americans continued to squat on unceded tribal lands in Indiana. The rest of North America was already occupied by other Indians. For the tribes in Indiana and Illinois, it was fight or die.

The Potawatomi were a large tribe, with villages in Michigan, Indiana, Illinois, and Wisconsin. Many Potawatomi had fought with Pontiac against the British, with Little Turtle against the Americans, and then with Tecumseh, who allied with the British in the War of 1812. The tribal surge propelled the British to early victories in the Great Lakes. Fort Mackinac fell in June 1812 and Fort Dearborn, in present-day Chicago, sat vulnerable on America's western frontier, surrounded by Potawatomi villages.

U.S. troops at Fort Dearborn were ordered to retreat to Fort Wayne. There were only 66 soldiers and militia, with a few dozen civilians. As they formed a caravan to retreat, the Potawatomi offered to escort them in return for payment. The Americans instead destroyed unneeded provisions, distrustful of Potawatomi motives. As the caravan departed the fort, Black Partridge led the Potawatomi warriors in a clever attack. Feinting over the top of a dune, tribal forces seemed to melt away as the soldiers charged the dune, before realizing it was a ruse. The Potawatomi flanked the Americans, dividing the soldiers from the militia and civilians, enveloping both groups, and killing or capturing everyone. They burned the fort, confiscated the provisions, and ransomed most hostages. Tribes controlled the western Great Lakes.

The War of 1812 was complex, with major battles near Washington, D.C.; New Orleans; and throughout the Great Lakes. Although the Potawatomi held their own,

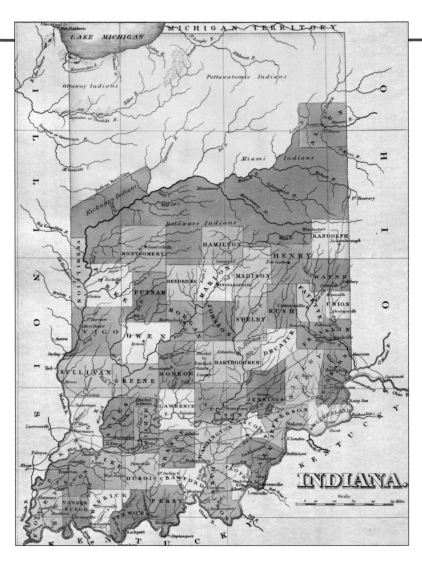

INDIANA IN 1826 This early map shows the tribal territories of several tribes as they were enveloped by the white counties and municipalities in Indiana.

British support oscillated, and the tribes went from overwhelming superiority to isolated pockets of resistance several times as America and Britain shifted priorities and troop deployments.

Tecumseh fell at the Battle of the Thames in 1813, largely because of British failure to reinforce his lines. It took the heart out of tribal resistance in Ohio, Kentucky, and much of Indiana. In 1813, the Americans sent Colonel William Russell in punitive raids against Potawatomi and Kickapoo villages in Illinois. In 1814, the United States built Fort Clark in Peoria, and it became a staging ground for further action against the tribes.

The Americans also built a fort at Prairie du Chien, Wisconsin, in 1814, but the Sac and Fox helped the British take it almost immediately, then repelled two American attempts to retake it in the Battle of Rock Island Rapids and again in the Battle of Credit Island. Each time, the Sac and Fox mustered more than 500 warriors and deployed them against smaller American detachments with devastating effect. ■

BATTLE OF FORT KING In 1835, at the start of the Second Seminole War,
Osceola ambushed and killed General Wiley Thompson, shooting him 14 times.

SEMINOLE WARS
AMERICA'S LONGEST INDIAN CAMPAIGN

The Seminole fought longer than any other tribe in the Southeast, from 1816 until 1858. Wild Cat, Billy Bowlegs, Osceola, and countless other Seminole leaders rallied their warriors to battle for their individual lives and the life of their native nation. The fighting spirit of the Seminole warriors propelled them through 41 years of conflict, but each of the three major Seminole Wars had a distinct group of leaders, challenges, and outcomes. Through it all, the language and identity of the Seminole people united them, while at the same time that identity evolved and changed. Nobody was the same after the wars.

FIRST SEMINOLE WAR, 1816–19

The First Seminole War did not even start in Seminole territory. During the War of 1812, the Creek descended into their own civil war. Many of the traditionalist Red Stick Creek joined Tecumseh and fought against the Americans. Some of the southern Creek towns sided with the Americans against the British. Tensions led to escalating raids, and then a major attack by the Red Sticks on Fort Mims, Alabama. The Red Sticks killed or captured about 500 White Stick Creeks, American soldiers, and civilians. That brought the wrath of the U.S. military down on the Red Stick Creeks, who were later crushed by Andrew Jackson at the Battle of Horseshoe Bend. That battle resulted in 1,000 Red Stick Creek casualties and effectively ended the Creek civil war.

The U.S. Army then sent punitive expeditions against the Creek towns in Alabama. The Red Stick Creek were in a vulnerable and disadvantaged defensive position. They fled. Most ran south into Seminole territory. The Creek and Seminole languages were mutually intelligible, and the Seminole had a long history of offering refuge to escapees from slavery and colonialism to their north. The Seminole population tripled with the influx of Creeks.

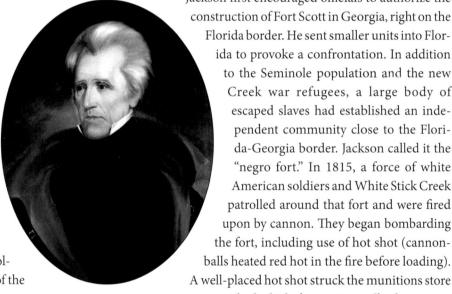

ANDREW JACKSON **The general's renown for defeating the British in the Battle of New Orleans at the end of the War of 1812 was soon eclipsed by his fame as an Indian fighter against the Creek and Seminole.**

General Jackson was not content to see the Creeks escape into Florida, which was not yet part of the United States. Most of the region was unceded Indian land, and the Spanish claimed exclusive colonial rights there. America was embroiled in a war with the British at the time and hoping to avoid escalation of U.S.-Spanish conflict. Jackson, however, saw an opportunity to continue punitive military assaults on the Creek and simultaneously expand American domain at the expense of the Spanish and of Florida's tribal populations, including the Seminole and Miccosukee (an offshoot of the main body of Seminole).

Jackson first encouraged officials to authorize the construction of Fort Scott in Georgia, right on the Florida border. He sent smaller units into Florida to provoke a confrontation. In addition to the Seminole population and the new Creek war refugees, a large body of escaped slaves had established an independent community close to the Florida-Georgia border. Jackson called it the "negro fort." In 1815, a force of white American soldiers and White Stick Creek patrolled around that fort and were fired upon by cannon. They began bombarding the fort, including use of hot shot (cannonballs heated red hot in the fire before loading). A well-placed hot shot struck the munitions store inside the little fort, setting off a destructive explosion that was heard more than 100 miles away in Pensacola. It was so powerful that it instantly killed 250 black defenders.

In 1817, Jackson sent 100 soldiers and 150 Creek loyalists against the Miccosukee village at Fowltown, in what is now Decatur County, Georgia. The first foray was repelled, but the second broke through. They massacred many civilians, burned the village, and ignited a massive resistance across the Miccosukee and Seminole villages. Tribal forces ambushed an American patrol and killed four dozen. Now Jackson had the rationale he needed for his war. The U.S. government ordered the invasion of Florida.

Jackson marched into Florida with 3,000 soldiers and militia plus 1,500 White Stick Creeks. They killed two British agents and took Fort Marks with little resistance from the Spanish or their Indian allies. Then they embarked upon a scorched-earth campaign against the Seminole and Miccosukee. The Indians ran for shelter in the swamps, but their lodges and food supplies were destroyed. Jackson marched on Pensacola, and the Spanish fort there was surrendered after an artillery bombardment.

The Spanish had light garrisons at St. Augustine, St. Marks, and Pensacola before Jackson invaded. They were in no position to fight it out, so they sold Florida to the United States before Jackson could march on St. Augustine. Spain and the United States signed the Adams-Onís Treaty in 1819 to effect the land transfer. America took possession of Florida in 1821. The Seminole saw several of their villages burned, but suffered very few casualties. The First Seminole War gave America legal pretext for colonizing Florida. It also, however, ignited rather than crushed the fighting spirit of the Seminole.

SECOND SEMINOLE WAR, 1835–1842

In 1823, the U.S. government pressed the Seminole to concentrate their villages on a large reservation in central Florida that included about 25 percent of the state's acreage. The British and Spanish had given up their claims and any hopes to challenge American

BILLY BOWLEGS **The Seminole war chief, a cunning tactician, was a perpetual threat and frustration to American forces during the Second and Third Seminole Wars.**

sovereignty there. America and Spain would fight wars over territory in the Southwest, but in Florida, the Seminole were on their own. They were undaunted by the First Seminole War, but wary of American military power. Some of the Seminole chiefs agreed to the Treaty of Moultrie Creek, which established the new reservation. Others refused to cede land. Regardless of the treaty, nearly all the people stayed put exactly where they were.

In 1829, the Seminoles' military nemesis, Andrew Jackson, became president of the United States. He launched a ferocious new Indian policy, designed to kill all Indians or move them west of the Mississippi River. In 1832, his delegates came to Florida with a message to move by peaceful means or be moved by military force. A small group of Seminole chiefs agreed to parley and sign the Treaty of Payne's Landing. They did not represent all of the Seminole population, but that was of little consequence to the U.S. government. The Americans viewed the land cession as binding on the entire tribe. A few Seminoles relocated to Oklahoma in 1832, but most carried on village life in Florida unaware that any agreement had even been made. When they learned the contents of the treaty, they repudiated the agreement. The U.S. Senate haggled over the treaty for two years, but ratified it in 1834 with every intention of forcing the Seminole out of Florida.

Enforcing the new treaty would surely mean resistance from the Seminole. It was the

BILLY BOWLEGS

For his entire life, Billy Bowlegs was immersed in conflict. He was just a small child during the First Seminole War, but his band was at the center of fighting. By the start of the Second Seminole War, Bowlegs had two wives and several children. He signed the Treaty of Payne's Landing, not fully understanding its terms. He later repudiated the treaty and rallied his warriors when U.S. troops came to force relocation. He fought with Osceola and Wild Cat in that war. By the time it ended, Bowlegs was the principal chief of the

largest Seminole band left in Florida. He sometimes engaged in diplomacy with the Americans, but preferred to avoid contact. Hundreds of troops remained in Florida with orders to move the Seminole to Oklahoma.

As white settlers and soldiers continued to encroach on tribal lands, Bowlegs feared that his entire band would be captured. He rallied his warriors and prevented an American attack with a simple show of force at the start of the Third Seminole War. Bowlegs was ready for conflict, but halted war preparations when

Wild Cat, another Seminole chief, arrived in his village. Wild Cat was a prominent chief who moved with his band to Oklahoma at the end of the Second Seminole War. The U.S. government brought him back to Florida to persuade Bowlegs to leave Florida for good. The effort paid off, as Bowlegs agreed to cease hostilities and take his band to Oklahoma. Unlike Osceola and some of the other Seminole chiefs, Bowlegs embraced slavery and kept black slaves. When he moved to Oklahoma, he brought 50 slaves with him.

BURNING OF PILAKLIKAHA **Soldiers from Fort Scott, led by General Abraham Eustis, massacred a Miccosukee village at the start of the Second Seminole War. Warriors ambushed U.S. troops afterward, killing four dozen.**

practice of the day in U.S. Indian policy, and the Americans were ready. The stage was set for renewed conflict. In 1835, Jackson ordered the U.S. Army into Florida to see the Seminole relocated.

Osceola rallied his warriors. The Seminole always operated as many independent bands, but they needed to come together. More and more warriors answered his call for resistance. About 4,000 Seminole and several hundred allied black runaway slaves mustered a force of about 1,000 to 1,500 warriors against America's professional army deployment of 9,000 troops.

Seminole snipers killed a soldier in 1835, one of the first casualties of the conflict. The Indians stole cattle, and a couple Seminole were caught with the cattle and whipped by white civilians until Seminole reinforcements arrived and killed those inflicting the whipping. U.S. troops braced for a major attack, but it never came.

Osceola then planned a careful ambush of U.S. troops under Major Francis L. Dade, killing all but one of the 110 soldiers in his command. Osceola's warriors then spread out in a series of smaller coordinated attacks. They burned the Cape Florida lighthouse, dozens of plantations and farms, and numerous isolated settlements. The U.S. Army, unable to respond to so many simultaneous calls for aid and encumbered by huge supply trains and by illness among the ranks, abandoned several forts.

In 1836, Osceola played a deft hand as a large force of 2,500 soldiers descended on one of the primary Seminole settlements in the Battle of Wahoo Swamp. His warriors made excellent use of terrain cover and small flanking moves to dislodge the American lines. In spite of being outnumbered, they drove off the soldiers. Among the American casualties, ironically, was the first Native American graduate from West Point, David Moniac.

Despite the overwhelming odds, for two years the Seminole harassed, harried, and raided the invading army and nearby white settlements. They thus successfully protected their families while avoiding a head-on battle. Thomas Jesup assumed command of American forces after Wahoo Swamp, and sent numerous smaller patrols, trying to isolate and overwhelm Seminole groups. This strategy slowly withered the resistance. Some prominent chiefs surrendered with their entire bands.

Osceola was still undefeated, but weary from conflict. He came to parley under a flag of truce in 1837, assuming the United States was ready to offer terms amenable to both sides. Instead he was captured and imprisoned along with Chiefs Wild Cat and John Horse. Wild Cat and John Horse escaped, but Osceola was sick and unable to flee. He died in prison a few months later, in early 1838.

The Seminole fought on. At the Battle of Lake Okeechobee, Wild Cat led Seminole warriors against Zachary Taylor's 800-man force, killing 26 and wounding 112. After the Battle of Loxahatchee, a band of 500 Seminole proposed a truce and the establishment of a new reservation at Lake Okeechobee. The U.S. government rejected the offer and Jesup captured all 500 Seminole there while they waited for a response to their request.

By 1842, most of the fighting was over. A group of 3,800 Seminole surrendered. They were forcibly relocated to Indian Territory. Other bands were rounded up in subsequent campaigns over the next few years.

More than 40,000 Americans had served in the Seminole Wars to that point. About 400 of them were killed in action. The conflict had cost the government $40 million—an immense amount in those days. And although most Seminole Indians had moved to Oklahoma, some remained in Florida. Billy Bowlegs, Sam Jones, and other tribal leaders were determined to stay.

> "I WILL MAKE THE WHITE MAN RED WITH BLOOD; AND THEN BLACKEN HIM IN THE SUN AND RAIN . . . AND THE BUZZARD LIVE UPON HIS FLESH."
>
> OSCEOLA, SEMINOLE WAR CHIEF

THIRD SEMINOLE WAR, 1855–58

As U.S. troops continued to hunt for Seminoles hiding out in the wilds of Florida, they eventually stumbled across Billy Bowlegs's band in 1855. When a small patrol located the band's main village, Bowlegs decided that his people would try to wipe out the patrol to avoid being rounded up for deportation to Oklahoma. He attacked with about 40 warriors, killing or routing most of the patrol, but the survivors alerted command. Soon 700 U.S. troops were hunting for Seminoles in earnest. The Indians tried to use Osceola's hit-and-run tactics, but were so vastly outnumbered that they had no way to force peace on their own terms. Whittled down, constantly harassed and harried, the Seminole quit fighting in 1858. Bowlegs agreed to move to Oklahoma with his band. Two other bands of Seminole and Miccosukee stayed in Florida, concealed in the Everglades. ■

OSCEOLA

Osceola, raised as a Red Stick Creek, moved to Florida as a child with other refugees of the Creek civil war. He grew into a war leader of the Seminole.

The Seminole had long offered refuge not only to Indians from other tribes, but also to runaway slaves who were absorbed into the tribe. Some of the Creek refugees were slave owners, and continued to own those slaves even after coming to Florida. Osceola, however, repudiated slavery. When he fought the Americans, Osceola wanted warriors of every color to join in the common Seminole defense, and they did.

Osceola also advocated for tribal blood law at the outbreak of the Second Seminole War—and sanctioned killings to punish lawbreakers. The chiefs agreed in council that anyone who sold Seminole land was committing a capital offense. Seminole chief Charley Emathla, however, thought the odds did not favor the Seminole in the war. He sold his band's cattle to raise money to move his people to Oklahoma. Osceola confronted him on the road back to his village and killed him. He grabbed the wad of cash and scattered it across Emathla's body.

In the field, Osceola made brilliant use of his often outnumbered forces. He refused to engage major troop deployments in open battle, instead waging guerrilla campaigns. After he died, Osceola was decapitated by an army doctor, Frederick Weedon, who made a death mask and embalmed Osceola's head, which was later displayed at a museum.

OSCEOLA One of the greatest Seminole war chiefs, Osceola carried out
daring raids and devastating attacks on U.S. forces in the Second Seminole War.

ARIKARA WAR
BLOOD AND FIRE IN THE PALISADES

The Arikara, or Ree, are a Caddoan tribe closely related to the Pawnee. Unlike most other tribes on the Plains, they relied primarily on agriculture to support themselves, rather than hunting. Unlike the nomadic hunters, the Arikara stayed by their cornfields, occasionally sending out extended-duration hunting parties to supplement their crops. That lifestyle choice came with advantages and disadvantages. Their food supply was constant and balanced, and their population grew rapidly. But their fixed village sites were predictable and thus vulnerable to enemy attacks. To protect themselves, the Arikara built elaborate wooden palisades around their villages. They also fenced some of their cornfields to prevent enemy raiders from trampling the crops and to buffer potential attacks.

The densely populated villages of the Arikara were highly vulnerable to disease once whites reached the Missouri River. In 1795, traders counted 30 large Arikara villages on the Missouri River, near present-day Pierre, South Dakota. In 1804, when Lewis and Clark came to Arikara lands, there were only 18 villages. By the outbreak of the Arikara War in 1823, only two medium-size villages were left. The rapid decline of the Arikara population was due primarily to smallpox and other European diseases.

The Lakota were also hard on the Arikara. The Arikara actually obtained horses before the Lakota, but the potential advantage they had in war was never realized. They used the horses to farm, travel, and hunt, rather than to attack other tribes.

In contrast, once the Lakota acquired horses, they became the best raiders on the northern Plains. The Arikara were constant targets. The Lakota were numerous and quickly becoming more so. Their attacks taxed the Arikara population, bringing steady attrition from conflict casualties and from capture of Arikara children in raids.

The Arikara relationship with the Americans began in 1803, but it did not start off well. Several of their prominent chiefs accepted an invitation from Lewis and Clark to travel to Washington, D.C., which they did in 1805. Most died from disease on the trip, but the villages were not notified until two years later, when U.S. traders came again, escorting a Mandan chief. The Mandan and Arikara were at war at the time, and the unspoken message was that the Mandan were important to the Americans but the Arikara were not. Tensions ran high.

ARIKARA The Arikara were farmers first and hunters second, meaning they were well fed, but a target for Lakota raiders and American traders.

MELEE AT THE PALISADES

After the Lewis and Clark expedition, American traders and trappers poured into the Missouri River region, traveling by horse and keelboat. In 1823, a large entourage of 90 traders, trappers, and boatmen came to the Arikara villages. During the exchanges at the trader encampment, a white trapper killed an Arikara chief's son. It is hard to tell if this was a belligerent act or an accident, but the chief did not take it well.

The Arikara sallied out of their palisaded village, taking the traders by surprise and killing 15 of them. The rest fled in their keelboats back to Fort Atkinson, Wisconsin. Colonel Henry Leavenworth marched on the Arikara

MANDAN ATTACK The Mandan and Arikara were ancient enemies, as seen in this image of an attack on the Arikara. After disease and Lakota raids reduced the Arikara, though, they reached out to their old foes for a protective alliance.

villages with a force of 230 soldiers. The traders, fully aware of Lakota-Arikara hostilities, invited the Lakota to the assault. More than 750 Lakota warriors converged on the villages, arriving ahead of the main U.S. troop deployment. They started the assault immediately. The Arikara came out from their palisades and engaged in a spirited fight with the Lakota—muskets, then arrows, and finally lances, war clubs, and knives. Leavenworth and his troops showed up when the assault was already well under way. The Arikara retreated behind their palisades and assumed defensive positions as the fighting dragged on all day. Casualties mounted, and Leavenworth reported 50 Arikara killed in action.

Toward nightfall, the Arikara, internally divided as to the best course of action, agreed to parley with the Americans. Leavenworth persuaded them to agree to a truce with no punishments or damage to their village. Fearing a trick, the Arikara slipped away in the night and retreated up the river. Leavenworth pulled his troops back to Fort Atkinson.

The traders disregarded the agreement from the night before and burned the Arikara village and crops. The Arikara could not afford another loss like that. They abandoned the village site for the next ten years.

The Arikara's reduced numbers and sedentary lifestyle forced them to look for accommodation with the Americans before most Plains tribes. They moved their villages north, to the vicinity of Fort Clark, North Dakota, on the Knife River. Sustained contact with whites meant that the Arikara continued to suffer from disease, with new smallpox epidemics reported in the 1830s. Repeated Lakota attacks nearly wiped the tribe out in the 1870s. The once mighty Arikara reached out to their former enemies, the Mandan, as well as the Hidatsa for alliance and mutual protection. The people, who became known as the Three Affiliated Tribes, eventually settled at Fort Berthold, North Dakota. The Arikara proudly scouted for the U.S. Army when the campaigns against the Lakota began in the 1870s. ■

WINNEBAGO WAR

HO-CHUNK RESISTANCE IN THE WISCONSIN WOODS

The Ho-Chunk, also known as Winnebago, avoided entanglements in most wars between Great Britain and France and then between Great Britain and the United States. They made peace with the Americans and several other tribes at a major treaty conference in Prairie du Chien, Wisconsin, in 1825. They ceded no land in that agreement, which drew lines between tribal territories and set the stage for American land acquisitions.

The Ho-Chunk, unlike most tribes, mined metals. During the fur trade era, they dug and sold lead for musket balls. It was a lucrative business, and they soon found themselves encroached upon by many white lead prospectors hoping to edge them out of their land and profit from the mines. The Ho-Chunk tolerated many abuses to keep the peace, but by 1826, their patience was at an end. The chiefs tried to diplomatically protect their land and counsel their warriors toward peace, but tensions were growing.

In 1826, Ho-Chunk warriors killed a French-Canadian settler and his family in the middle of sugar bush season. The U.S. Army responded, arresting two Ho-Chunk warriors, who soon escaped from Fort Crawford. Hoping to avert an escalating crisis, some Ho-Chunk chiefs surrendered six of their men who had nothing to do with the attacks. Troops from Fort Snelling, Minnesota, came to reinforce military posts in Wisconsin. The Ho-Chunk chiefs sent two more men, who were indicted for murder and transferred to Fort Snelling.

At Fort Snelling, Ojibwe chief Hole in the Day and his brother Strong Ground came to parley with Lawrence Taliaferro, the Indian agent there. Dakota warriors attacked their party, killing one Ojibwe and mortally wounding the daughter of the chief. U.S. soldiers lined up 30 Dakota and turned four of them over to the Ojibwe for punishment. The Ojibwe executed and scalped them in front of the fort, then U.S. soldiers

LITTLE ELK Ho-Chunk (Winnebago) chief Little Elk allied with the British against the Americans in the War of 1812.

threw their bodies over a cliff. Two more Dakota were surrendered at the fort and treated the same way. Afterward, the Dakota told the Ho-Chunk that the government planned to turn their two imprisoned warriors over to the Ojibwe as well.

That rumor had an effect. Ho-Chunk women had been sexually assaulted by U.S. riverboat crews, and the government and army were doing nothing to stop the white miners from encroaching on tribal land. The Ho-Chunk chiefs broke off diplomatic relations and boycotted a treaty conference.

OUTBREAK

Red Bird, Sun, and Little Buffalo then approached Prairie du Chien to carry out a plan of resistance. The Ho-Chunk warriors attacked the home of farmer Registre Gagnier, killing Gagnier and his hired hand, and scalping his daughter alive. Gagnier's wife escaped and called for aid. It didn't take long for U.S. troops to mobilize.

Red Bird rallied his men, leading 150 Ho-Chunk warriors and a few Dakota allies in a daring attack on U.S. keelboat crews near the mouth of the Bad Axe River. They killed two Americans and wounded four, suffering several casualties of their own. It was the first major Indian attack since the War of 1812, and it sent white settlers into a panic. They flooded into towns and army forts, prompting an equally wide military response.

Red Bird was unsuccessful in recruiting Potawatomi, Dakota, or even other Ho-Chunk villages to join his alliance. Lewis Cass, governor of the Michigan Territory, came to Prairie du Chien to raise a militia. Soon there were 1,500 troops from Fort Snelling and across the region assembled at Fort Crawford.

As U.S. troops marched on the Ho-Chunk, one of the chiefs intervened in daring diplomatic fashion. Waukon Decorah blocked the march and forced a parley with U.S. Army officers. He was determined to avoid destruction of Ho-Chunk villages. Decorah said that Red Bird acted alone, without the backing of other Ho-Chunk chiefs, and should be treated as a criminal rather than as a leader of the tribe engaged in war. Decorah captured Red Bird and surrendered him to American authorities.

General Henry Atkinson promised to push out the miners squatting on Ho-Chunk land, but that never happened. At least 10,000 more white settlers poured into the Ho-Chunk mining region over the next three years. Even Henry Dodge, an American military officer and commander of the Wisconsin militia, set up a camp to mine and said the army could never make him leave. He settled there with his slaves and started mining. Eventually, he led U.S. troops in the Black Hawk War, becoming territorial governor of Wisconsin and then a U.S. senator.

The U.S. Army built Fort Winnebago and staffed two other forts in Wisconsin. Red Bird died in prison awaiting trial in 1828. Two other tribal members, convicted of murder, were pardoned by President John Quincy Adams in 1828 to avoid further conflict, but also to ransom them for land. The Ho-Chunk agreed to a land sale to avoid the executions and further bloodshed. In his State of the Union address that year, Adams laid out plans for a new policy called Indian removal, avidly enforced by his successor, Andrew Jackson. ■

HO-CHUNK CAMP The Ho-Chunk moved constantly during the Winnebago War.
This photo of a Ho-Chunk harvest camp from several years later gives a glimpse of that life.

CHEROKEE TRAILS OF TEARS

After their first contact with the British, the Cherokee openly embraced many European ideas. They developed a new government structure, shifting their matrilineal clan-based chief system into a representative council. They farmed like Europeans and kept black slaves to work large plantations like their British neighbors. After the Revolutionary War, the Cherokee continued to accommodate white power. They were one of the first tribes to acquire U.S. citizenship, enabled by treaty in 1817, more than 100 years before most Indians became citizens through the Indian Citizenship Act in 1924. Along with the Chickasaw, Choctaw, Creek, and Seminole, the Cherokee were called one of the Five Civilized Tribes.

At the start of the removal era, the Cherokee controlled a diminished but still impressive territory in the heart of the Southeast. Gold was discovered in Georgia in 1828, compounding the pressure on the government to confiscate tribal land there for white use. Americans wanted it all, and eventually they got their way, engineered through the Indian Removal Act in 1830.

Cherokee leader Major Ridge, who represented a minority of the tribe, agreed in 1835 to the Treaty of New Echota, which sold their homeland and required relocation to Oklahoma. He was later assassinated for his part in Cherokee removal. John Ross, the principal Cherokee chief, fought relocation. He organized a petition signed by 15,000 Cherokees repudiating the Treaty of New Echota. Nonetheless, the U.S. Senate ratified the treaty in 1836. Andrew Jackson ignored U.S. Supreme Court rulings in favor of the Cherokee, even saying about the Chief Justice, "John Marshall has made his decision, now let him enforce it."

REMOVAL

Some Cherokee hid in the mountains in North Carolina. About 2,000 Cherokee, led by Major Ridge, moved to Oklahoma on their own terms ahead of the main body of Cherokee. Others sought refuge with white friends across the south and even in Mexico. But most were rounded up by the U.S. Army and forced into a concentration camp in Tennessee before they were marched to Oklahoma in the winter of 1838, a journey

of more than 1,000 miles. The army chose the worst time of the year and some of the least expeditious routes imaginable to avoid having Indians walk through or near white towns. The Cherokee were divided into 13 groups and followed at least three major routes to Oklahoma. John Ross led the last group.

The weather, disease, and poor food rations combined to take a heavy toll on the travelers. White citizens and soldiers often made things worse. At Berry's Ferry, Kentucky, white ferry crews charged the Cherokee a dollar each to be ferried

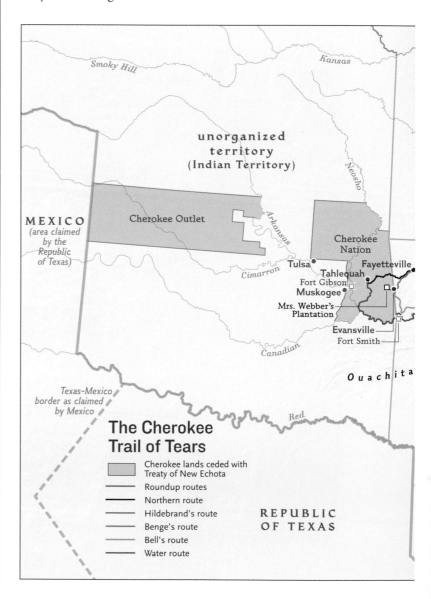

The Cherokee Trail of Tears

- Cherokee lands ceded with Treaty of New Echota
- Roundup routes
- Northern route
- Hildebrand's route
- Benge's route
- Bell's route
- Water route

across the river instead of the normal rate of 12 cents. Many Cherokee died from exposure waiting to cross the river. Several Cherokee were murdered by civilians along the route. It was a brutally cold winter, with ice as thick as 12 inches on some of the rivers. The Indians had to cut through the ice to water their horses and collect drinking water. The pre-removal Cherokee population was 16,543. Anywhere from 2,000 to 6,000 people died along the Trail of Tears.

One U.S. soldier remarked, "I fought through the War Between the States and have seen many men shot, but the Cherokee Removal was the cruelest work I ever knew." In the end, the Cherokee

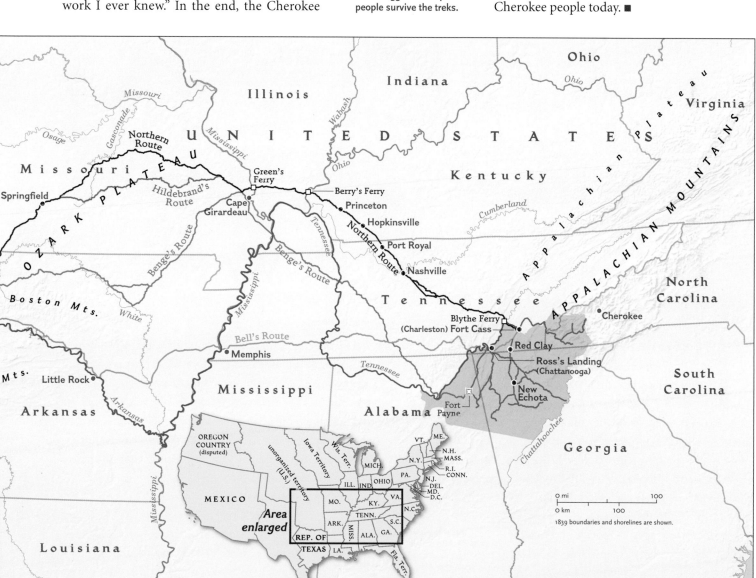

MANY TRAILS Cherokee chiefs struggled to help their people survive the treks.

diaspora took most of the tribe to Oklahoma. White settlers in the Southeast had a feeding frenzy on the spoils of war left behind. The Georgia Assembly distributed tribal land to white citizens via special land patents.

The survivors of the trails of tears tore at each other in Oklahoma. Major Ridge and several others were assassinated for selling tribal land. The people grappled with the loss of land and life, the legacy of slavery, and the onset of poverty. The Cherokee nation rebuilt itself, but always in spite of the U.S. government rather than because of it, and the bitter legacy of 1838 still burns in the minds of the Cherokee people today. ■

1839 boundaries and shorelines are shown.

SECOND CREEK WAR
FIGHTING ENCROACHMENT IN 1836

The First Creek War, which took place during the War of 1812, deeply divided the Creek nation. American loyalist Creeks from the lower Creek towns, known as the White Sticks, fought against British-allied Creeks from the upper towns, known as the Red Sticks. The Red Sticks were crushed at the Battle of Horseshoe Bend in 1814 and the tribe fractured. The White Sticks stayed in Georgia and Alabama, where they received no reward from the Americans for their loyalty. Instead, the United States quickly moved to dispossess them. Many of the Red Sticks escaped to Florida and fought against the U.S. Army in the Seminole Wars.

Despite those disruptions, there were still about 20,000 Creeks in Alabama, living in both the upper and lower towns. Among the many prominent Creek chiefs of the time was Opothle Yahola, who was from the upper towns and fought the Americans during the First Creek War and the first two Seminole Wars. Afterward, he vowed to fight no more, and kept that promise. Yahola owned a 2,000-acre plantation and kept black slaves. He was moderately effective as a diplomat for Creek causes, but ultimately cooperated with removal.

Politics among the Creek was complicated. Like the Cherokee, the Creek adopted a tribal blood law, making it a capital offense to sell Creek land. In 1821, some of the Creek chiefs signed a major land cession treaty, which ceded a large swath of the tribe's land east of the Mississippi

CREEK HOMESTEAD The Creek lived on lush farmland along Alabama's rivers, property that white settlers coveted. Most lost their homes to military force and to fraudulent deals by land speculators.

River. The treaty was repudiated by other Creek chiefs. There was a standoff, but the U.S. government was not willing to wait. In 1825, William McIntosh and other Creek leaders, mainly from the lower towns, were willing to relocate and so signed another land cession, the Treaty of Indian Springs. They were soon known as the Treaty Party, and found themselves in direct conflict with the National Party, which wanted to keep Creek land in Alabama and Georgia and stay politically united.

CREEK BLOOD LAW

William McIntosh's leadership of the Treaty Party earned him the respect of the American government and the enmity of many of his own people. In 1825, Creek chief Menawa led 150 warriors to McIntosh's plantation to enforce the tribal blood law. They killed him and another cooperative chief, burning their homes to the ground.

Opothle Yahola tried to improve upon the 1825 treaty, with limited success. The Treaty of Washington, signed in 1826, did get the Creek better financial terms, but essentially affirmed the land cession. Many bands of Creek were preparing to move to Oklahoma. But there were so many people that relocation was proving exceptionally challenging both inside and outside the Creek towns.

In 1832, Alabama ramped up pressure on the Creek by asserting state law over the tribe. A subsequent treaty, the Treaty of Cusseta, signed that year, imposed allotment on the Creek. That meant that instead of controlling their land as a tribe, each individual Creek Indian was given a small piece of the tribe's land as a private holding, or allotment. The tribe itself could own land only in Oklahoma. Creek tribal members faced a tough decision. They could sell their allotments and move to Oklahoma as bona fide members of the tribe, or they could stay in Alabama on their allotments as American citizens with no connection to any tribe.

White land speculators descended on the Creeks. Through thousands of transactions, most of the Creeks were swindled out of their land. Francis Scott Key, the lawyer who wrote the national anthem, was sent by Andrew Jackson to investigate. He reported pervasive land fraud.

In 1834, Yahola tried to purchase land for

OPOTHLE YAHOLA **The Creek chief fought the Americans in the First Creek War and the Seminole Wars, but ultimately led 8,000 of his people to Oklahoma.**

his people in Texas, then under Mexican control, and even paid $20,000. American officials blocked the attempt.

BLOOD ON THE PLANTATIONS

The Creek knew there was little hope that armed resistance could preserve their right to stay in Alabama. Most of them, including Opothle Yahola's band, cooperated with the painful move to Oklahoma. Yahola led 8,000 Creeks to Indian Territory. Chief Menawa, who so avidly enforced the tribal blood law, died on the Creek trail of tears.

But some Creek were ready instead to die fighting. In 1836, Creek chief Jim Henry led Yuchi and Hitchiti band Creek warriors in a series of carefully timed raids and attacks. The town of Roanoke, Georgia, was evacuated out of fear of Indian attack as the Creek swooped down on several plantations and farms along the Chattahoochee River, killing some civilians. Henry waited for a few days until the small garrison at Roanoke relaxed their guard. Then he struck with an overwhelming force of hundreds of warriors. His attack came in the form of a three-pronged assault at 2 a.m. The warriors killed 14 guards, and the rest ran. The Creek burned Roanoke to the ground.

The Creek continued to attack smaller plantations and settlements for the next month, then ambushed a large militia force, inflicting 22 casualties and forcing the militia into a hasty fighting retreat. Secretary of War Lewis Cass dispatched General Winfield Scott to crush the Creek and force relocation.

Many of the remaining Creek were not interested in waiting for the American attack. There were 14,500 tribe members on the trail to Oklahoma by the time the soldiers arrived. At the Battle of Hobdy's Bridge, U.S. forces routed a Creek town, but took no captives. The war faded to its end as the Creek dodged a genocidal campaign by an overwhelmingly larger force.

In Oklahoma, ancient divisions in the Creek nation persisted. In the U.S. Civil War, some allied with the Confederacy. A minority, led by Yahola, allied with the Union. Fleeing conflict in Oklahoma in 1863, Yahola led a contingent of Creeks to a refugee center in Kansas, where he died before the end of the war. ∎

BATTLE OF THE BAD AXE RIVER Sac and Fox warriors pressed U.S. soldiers away
from the river to let their families cross, only to watch Dakota warriors ambush them.

BLACK HAWK WAR

TRIBAL GENIUS IN GUERRILLA BATTLES

The Fox Indians fought 200 years of pressure on their land and lifeways. The tribe, which occupied villages in Michigan's Upper Peninsula around the time the French first arrived in the Great Lakes, took part in debilitating cyclical warfare with the much larger Dakota and Ojibwe tribes. Over time, the Fox moved south to the Green Bay area of Wisconsin, where conflict with the French nearly depopulated the tribe in the 1700s. They sought refuge with the Sac (Sauk), and the two peoples freely mingled. Even though many language and leadership distinctions remained evident, the tribes came to be known as a single entity in the late British period, the Sac and Fox.

Conspicuous among the Sac and Fox leadership in 1812 was an accomplished Sac warrior named Black Hawk. His success fighting earned Black Hawk status and respect, which translated into a good deal of civil authority. Even though he was not born a hereditary chief, many of his people came to see him as the equivalent.

THE PRELUDE

Black Hawk was 45 years old when the War of 1812 broke out. The Sac and Fox lived in several villages on the Mississippi River near the present-day border of Wisconsin, Illinois, and Iowa. Black Hawk had closely watched the march of American settlement across the Ohio River Valley and southern Great Lakes, and saw where America was heading next. He rallied his warriors and allied with the British. Black Hawk distinguished himself in that war by leading a sizable band of Sac and Fox warriors in at least eight major battles, including those at Forts Meigs, Stephenson, and Johnson.

The War of 1812 slowed American expansion, but its conclusion uncorked the new nation's westward push. Tecumseh fell. The British retreated to Canada. The Americans started building Fort Snelling in Minnesota in 1819, and the Mississippi River carried regular traffic by keelboat through Sac and Fox territory. There was a flurry of treaty

> ## "WHITES WERE IN THE HABIT OF SAYING ONE THING TO THE INDIANS AND PUTTING ANOTHER THING DOWN ON PAPER."
>
> BLACK HAWK

activity with many tribes. The Winnebago War in 1827, although not especially bloody, resulted in more than 10,000 new white settlers mining and homesteading along the edge of Sac and Fox lands.

A few Sac and Fox delegates had signed a treaty at St. Louis in 1804 and another in 1825. Most Sac and Fox chiefs had no idea what the treaties said, had not attended the treaty councils, and likely would never have agreed to the terms if they had. The treaties asked the Sac and Fox to cede all lands east of the Mississippi River for a small payment of cash and goods. In 1829, some Sac and Fox chiefs, including one named Keokuk, visited with American authorities and came to really understand for the first time the onerous terms of the 1804 treaty. They also realized that the United States intended to enforce the 1804 and 1825 agreements.

Keokuk, who was taken on an extensive tour of eastern American cities, felt that resisting the Americans was futile and urged accommodation. Black Hawk was so upset with the treaty and with Keokuk that it caused a permanent rift in the tribe. Black Hawk was not spoiling for a fight, but he wasn't giving up tribal land east of the Mississippi, either.

THE WAR

In 1832, General Edmund P. Gaines was charged with ensuring that Black Hawk's band stayed west of the Mississippi River. Keokuk supported the American troops arrayed against Black Hawk. They soon marched on Black Hawk's village, prepared to attack if necessary to drive the people farther west. They were surprised to find the village empty. Black Hawk was on the move.

Black Hawk led his band east across the Mississippi, traveling into Illinois and Wisconsin. Gaines was tracking him, but fell ill and tasked Brigadier General Henry Atkinson to parley with Black Hawk. The Potawatomi and Ho-Chunk were not interested in fighting the Americans. The Menominee and Dakota still preferred to fight the Sac and Fox.

COMANCHE WARRIOR At the height of their power, the Comanche commanded a military
and trade empire that covered 240,000 square miles, governed by the lance and bow.

COMANCHE WARS
CAPTIVES AND BLOODBATHS ON THE SOUTHERN PLAINS

For more than 150 years the Comanche dominated the southern Plains, controlling territory of 240,000 square miles in what is now Colorado, Kansas, Oklahoma, Texas, New Mexico, and Mexico, a land known as Comancheria. The Comanche were not one united political group, but rather several independent bands that were allied with the Kiowa, Kiowa Apache, and Wichita.

From 1836 to 1875, the Comanche fought against Spain, Mexico, the independent Republic of Texas, the United States, and several Indian tribes. The conflict consumed white settlements and American politics for four decades, producing some of the largest Indian battles in American history, some of the most unforgettable captivity narratives, and some of the most storied tribal warriors and chiefs, including Buffalo Hump, Peta Nocona, Iron Jacket, and Quanah Parker.

The Plains was contested ground long before European contact. With no mountains and few large bodies of water, there were no natural territorial boundaries other than those enforced by military might. Buffalo, antelope, and deer abounded, but hunting them was a challenge. The Pueblo Revolt of 1680 changed that. The horses released from Spanish corrals transformed the Plains tribes, and the Comanche were among the first to benefit. The Comanche then were an offshoot of the larger Shoshone tribe, but with horses, they became some of the most effective riders and raiders in the world and established their own tribal identity.

By 1706, the Comanche were traveling hundreds of miles into Mexico to raid Spanish settlements, bringing back cloth, tools, horses, and human captives. They raided their native neighbors, too. Among the Comanche, a captive was a prisoner used for barter or ransom—a financial instrument. But if a captive was adopted, he or she became a member of the band with full rights like any other Comanche. Most captives were eventually adopted, helping the Comanche population grow. The Kiowa formed a diplomatic and military alliance with the Comanche in 1790, and both tribes benefited from a protected mutual border. The Kiowa and Comanche raided the Pueblos, the Apache, the Spanish, and as soon as they moved into Texas, white settlers, too.

FORT PARKER RAID

In the 1830s, the Comanche held firm control of their territory, forcing other tribes, Mexicans, and Americans to gain permission for trade or travel. To the Comanche, whose destiny was manifest was entirely a matter of perspective.

On the eastern edge of Comanche territory, white settlers were arriving in Texas, and they soon came into conflict with the mighty Comanche. In 1833, John Parker came to Texas with his family—his brother Daniel and his sons Benjamin, Silas, and James, plus women and children. They built a private fort with 12-foot walls and two blockhouses. They allowed Texas Rangers to use it, inspiring the ire of the previously tolerant tribes nearby. In May 1836, Comanche, Kiowa, Caddo, and Wichita warriors attacked. Rachel Plummer recalled Benjamin Parker yelling, "Run little Rachel, for your life and your unborn child, run now and fast!" Warriors

CYNTHIA PARKER

Cynthia Ann Parker came to Texas as a child, one of a very large family. She was around nine years old when Comanches raided Fort Parker in 1836, killing five of her relatives. The Indians captured her and adopted her into the tribe. She lived with the Comanche for 24 years.

When Parker came of age, she married Peta Nocona, an accomplished warrior and chief. They had three children together, two boys and a girl. In 1860, Texas Rangers attacked her village while most of the warriors were away. Her husband was shot three times but was still alive when the Rangers identified him. Rather than taking the chief captive, they executed him. The rest of the Comanche on the Pease River also faced wholesale slaughter, including many women and children.

Cynthia, well tanned and dressed in traditional Comanche attire, was taken for a Comanche. As the Rangers descended on her, she ripped her dress open, exposing her bare white breasts, and screamed, "Americano!" She had picked up a few Spanish words through the course of Comanche trade experiences but couldn't recall any English. The effort worked. The Rangers took her alive and soon determined who she was. Her daughter Prairie Rose was taken along with her, and died a few years later. Heartbroken over her loss and the possible fates of her sons who were still in Comancheria, she quit eating and died in 1871.

BATTLE OF PLUM CREEK In 1840, a party of Comanche raiders, some wearing top hats and carrying luxury goods taken during the Great Raid at Victoria and Linnville, fought a running battle with Texas Rangers and their Tonkawa allies.

killed five men. They also captured two women and three children, most of whom were ransomed back to the Parkers over the next few years. Most of the other women and children escaped.

John Richard Parker, who was captured during the raid at the age of five, was ransomed back six years later in 1842. He could not tolerate life in the white world and ran back to the Comanche, where he lived for years. During a raid in Mexico in which John Richard fought as a Comanche warrior, he

succumbed to smallpox. The raiding party left him behind to recover under the care of a Mexican woman. He survived and married his caretaker, living largely in Mexico until he died in 1915.

BETRAYAL AT THE COUNCIL HOUSE

In 1840, thousands of whites—farmers, cattle ranchers, prospectors—were streaming into Texas, then an independent republic. But Comancheria remained impenetrable. With

Hump stayed away, warning the others that whites could not be trusted, even at a sacred peace council.

Comanche chief Muguara paid no heed, leading a delegation to San Antonio. He wanted to negotiate for peace and for recognition of Comancheria's boundaries. The delegation brought and released one white captive as a token of goodwill. Muguara, expecting no trouble, had women and children in his party. A peace conference was inviolable to the Comanche and everyone they knew.

The conference did not go well. The Texans wanted all white captives returned and did not understand that Muguara could not compel Peta Nocona and Buffalo Hump to surrender their captives. Armed Texans crowded into the council house, surrounding the confused chiefs who were sitting on the floor, telling them they would all be held prisoner. As the Comanche rose to their feet, a shot was fired and a general slaughter commenced. The Texans killed 12 chiefs. The rest of the Comanche party grabbed weapons for defense and a battle raged through the streets of San Antonio. Twenty-three more Comanches were shot in the streets, mainly women and children. Another 29 Comanches were captured.

The Comanche were furious. Not only had they suffered a terrible loss, but the settlers had proven they had no honor

30,000 Comanche and vast herds of horses, they could raid hundreds of miles in all directions from their main territory. No settlers felt safe, and the raid on Fort Parker proved their fears well founded.

The Comanche were 12 distinct groups of Indians in 35 bands. Militarily and politically, they often cooperated with one another, but none commanded the others. The eastern bands of Comanche held 17 white captives. Texas officials asked the Comanche to attend a peace council at San Antonio, already a bustling town. Chiefs Peta Nocona and Buffalo

QUANAH PARKER

Quanah Parker was the grandson of the great Comanche chief Iron Jacket and the son of Peta Nocona. His mother, Cynthia Ann Parker, was a white woman captured during the Fort Parker Raid as a child. Quanah, born circa 1850, was raised by his parents until age 10, when the Battle of Pease River devastated his village. His father was killed. His mother was recaptured by Texas Rangers. Fleeing for their lives, Quanah and his younger brother, Pecos, followed a faint trail across the short prairie grass for many, many miles. They eventually joined another group of Comanche, who were astounded at the tracking ability of such young boys and their fortitude to survive the fight.

As a teenager, Quanah assumed his father's position as chief. In 1874, he led Comanche warriors at the Second Battle of Adobe Walls in the Texas Panhandle. The following year, the army destroyed 1,500 Comanche horses after a raid, and the Comanche agreed to a peace conference. Quanah eventually settled on the reservation in Oklahoma, where he built a large home for his eight wives and 25 children. He later helped found the Native American Church, which combined pre-Columbian use of peyote with Christianity. He remarked of his religion, "The White Man goes into his church house and talks about Jesus, but the Indian goes into his tipi and talks to Jesus."

and could never be trusted, even in a peace council. Three of the remaining captives held by the eastern bands were adopted and treated as Comanches—no harm befell them. The other 13 white captives were killed.

THE GREAT RAID, PLUM CREEK, AND ANTELOPE HILLS

Buffalo Hump seized the initiative in August 1840. The attack at the council house in San Antonio had so inflamed the Comanche that as many as 1,000 warriors responded to his call for an unprecedented series of raids. Buffalo Hump's force thundered across Texas to the Gulf Coast, attacking the village of Victoria and killing a dozen civilians before descending on Linnville. There the Comanche routed the defenders, who sought refuge on boats in the bay. The Indians plundered until they had loaded all that their horses could carry—more than $300,000 worth of merchandise, linen, and silver bullion. The Great Raid was wildly successful, and the Comanche rode for 200 miles to secure their goods and regroup.

Along the Plum Creek near Lockhart, Texas, the Comanche encountered a band of Texas Rangers. Encumbered by huge herds of mules and horses laden with goods from the Great Raid, they fought a running battle with the Rangers. The Comanche moved uncharacteristically slowly, allowing the Rangers to exact significant casualties and even recover some livestock. But the Comanche were just getting started. So, too, were the Rangers.

KIT CARSON
The frontiersman gained fame fighting the Apache and Navajo before confronting the Comanche.

By 1858, Texas, a U.S. state by this time, was a danger zone for everyone of every race. Whites encroached on Comanche land and shot Indians on sight. The Comanche raided small farms and settlements with ferocious intensity. The U.S. Army pulled troops from Texas to Utah to confront Mormon settlers there. Texas reconstituted the Texas Rangers and sent John Ford, a seasoned Indian fighter, into the field with more than 100 Rangers to punish the Comanche. Ford's Rangers had the most impressive arsenal available—long-range buffalo guns, repeating rifles, and soon-to-be-famous Colt revolvers. Their expedition focused on the Comanche bands around Antelope Hills, Oklahoma. Ford proved his worth as a strategist by first visiting the Tonkawa and Shawnee in Oklahoma and recruiting more than 100 to join him. The Tonkawa in particular had fought the Comanche for decades and were eager for a chance to have the upper hand.

Along the banks of the Little Robe Creek, Ford's force found a small Comanche encampment, consisting of a dozen lodges. The Tonkawa led the attack, catching the Comanche in their sleep. This was the heart of Comancheria and they had never been attacked so far north in their domain. Comanche warriors struggled to protect their fleeing families as the Rangers charged into their midst. Their Colt revolvers proved an unbelievable advantage. They were deadly accurate, with maximum knockdown power, and could fire multiple shots before reloading. All the Comanche warriors were killed, as were most of their wives and children.

WEAPONS OF WAR: LANCE, BOW, AND REPEATING REVOLVERS

The Comanche war arsenal fused practical and spiritual power. Comanche warriors were experts with the lance, used for both buffalo hunting and war. The lance was a personal projection of spiritual identity, adorned with colors obtained through ceremony and eagle feathers earned in battle. It was a powerful weapon that was likely to kill with each use, but it was long and cumbersome in close quarters.

The Comanche bow was a weapon of unparalleled accuracy and force. During the height of Comanche power, warriors lined up and urged white defenders to shoot at them, emptying their single-shot weapons. At medium distance, Comanche bows could fire six times before a musket could be reloaded. Time after time, the Indians wore down their enemies and then came in close with knives and clubs to finish the fight. Comanche warriors demonstrated their archery expertise by throwing a handful of coins in the air and hitting each with an arrow before it landed. The training and arsenal of the Comanche were pervasive.

With weapons like these, massive horse herds, and ruthless cunning on the warpath, the Comanche were nearly invincible for decades. The invention of repeating revolver and rifle technology became the key to conquering the Comanche. During the Antelope Hills expedition, Texas Rangers closed ranks on Comanche warriors in close combat with repeating revolvers and thus devastated the defenders. The Colt nullified the advantages in military technology long enjoyed by the Comanche and soon crushed tribal defenses.

ADOBE WALLS Kit Carson led 372 U.S. infantry in the First Battle of Adobe Walls against a Comanche, Kiowa, and Kiowa Apache force of 3,000 warriors, making it one of the largest engagements in the Comanche Wars.

Ford proceeded along the Little Robe until he found a larger village of as many as 100 lodges. Iron Jacket was chief there. He had a suit of Spanish armor acquired in a raid many years before; in several previous engagements, the armor had saved him from small-arms fire. As he rallied the warriors to defend their village, Iron Jacket rode in front and challenged any enemy to single combat. A Tonkawa sharpshooter took aim with a buffalo gun and killed the chief. Most of the warriors scattered, and it was another one-sided victory for the Rangers.

Peta Nocona, the son of Iron Jacket, arrived with around 150 warriors to reinforce the Comanche along the creek bed before they were overwhelmed. Seeing the devastation caused by the Colt revolvers, Peta Nocona instead challenged the Tonkawa to single combat. One by one, Tonkawa braves faced off against Comanches with feathered lances in horseback duels. It was a regal but bloody spectacle as the Comanches bested their Tonkawa opponents over and over. Ford, frustrated by the Tonkawa losses in single combat, ordered the Tonkawa to attack en masse. His Rangers, however, were unable to distinguish the Tonkawa from the Comanche and give supportive fire, so he bugled for the Indians to retreat, then sent in the Rangers. Peta Nocona spread out his warriors in a running battle over several miles, successfully negating the power of revolver fire in close quarters. Ford retreated to Texas before reinforcements arrived.

The Antelope Hills expedition was the first campaign into the heart of Comancheria. Comanche losses were significant, but more important, their vulnerabilities were exposed. The Comanche were still lords of the southern Plains, but it was the beginning of the end for Comanche dominance.

ADOBE WALLS

The Texans pressed their advantage after the Antelope Hills expedition. In 1864, Kit Carson led 372 soldiers and about 100 Indian allies into the field at the First Battle of Adobe Walls, in the Comanche-controlled Texas Panhandle. They faced a force of 3,000 Comanche, Kiowa, and Kiowa Apache, and used howitzers to cover their retreat before being overwhelmed. The Comanche were on the defensive after Adobe Walls, and some bands negotiated for peace while others fought on. At the Second Battle of Adobe Walls in 1874 Peta Nocona's son Quanah Parker fought a group of buffalo hunters and sustained heavy losses. He too soon saw the need to sue for peace, and the Comanche Wars came to an end. ∎

U.S.-DAKOTA WAR

MINNESOTA GENOCIDE

The U.S.-Dakota War of 1862 forever altered the fate of the Minnesota Dakota, and also changed the course of American history. Between 400 and 800 white civilians and soldiers were killed. Thousands of Dakota died, and thousands more were exiled from Minnesota. Abraham Lincoln ordered the largest mass execution in the history of the United States. Then the U.S. Army, intent on punishing the Dakota, ignited the wars with the western Plains tribes. This is the story of Little Crow, Shakopee, the 38 Slain, Alexander Ramsey, and Henry Sibley. Even today this memorable conflict remains deeply divisive.

American expansion required Indian land. Although some tribes tried accommodation and negotiation and others fought to keep what they had, the end result was always the same—and the loss was always painful. Usually the Indians were forced to surrender not only their land, but also their tribal lifeways, religions, and languages. And even in the more peaceful surrenders, there usually was a loss of dignity and life, making the experience poignant and traumatic. For the Dakota, provocations and accommodations piled up like dry tinder in a fire pit. All that was missing for the inferno to erupt was a spark.

SIEGE OF NEW ULM As Dakota warriors swooped down on the town of New Ulm in 1862, residents fought off several assaults before they evacuated.

"THE SIOUX INDIANS OF MINNESOTA MUST BE EXTERMINATED OR DRIVEN FOREVER BEYOND THE BORDERS OF THE STATE."

ALEXANDER RAMSEY

KINDLING FOR THE FIRE

The initial kindling for the fire was the arrival of the first Americans who planned to stay in Minnesota. They came in 1819, when construction began on Fort Snelling, near present-day St. Paul. Fort Snelling was built on the high ground near the confluence of the Minnesota and Mississippi Rivers. To the Dakota in Minnesota it was Bdote, the birthplace of their people, and the fort was a sacrilege. Southern Minnesota included some of the richest farmland on the continent, and the flurry of economic activity around agriculture, logging, the fur trade, and mining soon brought thousands of whites to Minnesota.

The Dakota were eager to trade with the newcomers, especially for guns. They fought tribes in all directions—the Ojibwe, Cree, and Assiniboine to the north and the Sac and Fox to the south. Their accommodations just provided whites a stable foothold in Minnesota. In 1851, the foothold became a major land cession with two treaties—the Treaty of Mendota (with the Mdewakanton and Wahpekute bands of Dakota) and the Treaty of Traverse Des Sioux (with the Sisseton and Wahpeton bands). Most of southern Minnesota was opened to white settlement. Settlers came by the thousands.

The Dakota were farmers, and watching whites claim their fields to plant the same crops, simply by virtue of the color of their skin, never went over well. Confined to a small strip of their homeland along the Minnesota River, the Dakota had less access to food, and as times grew hard, so too did dispositions. In 1857, Inkpaduta led a small band of Wahpekute in an attack on white settlements along the Iowa border, killing 30 settlers. Inkpaduta's group escaped west and took refuge among the western Lakota. Their willingness to rise up and fight encroachment and land loss did not, however, segue into a larger conflict.

In 1858, Dakota chief Mankato led a delegation to Washington, D.C., and, under tremendous pressure, sold the rest of Dakota lands on the Minnesota River. Just four tribal communities remained there, with very little acreage. The Dakota depended on their annuities from land sales to support them while they tried to make a transition that would enable them to survive.

By 1862, the Dakota had become desperate. The U.S. Civil War was not going well for the Union. Food annuities and treaty payments were delayed by the war. They were also stalled by the government, which hoped to coerce the Dakota into selling their remaining acreage in southern Minnesota. The federal government owed $71,000 to the Dakota, and because it was not forthcoming, traders refused to give Indians food or goods on credit. Store proprietor Andrew Myrick famously said, "If they are hungry, let them eat grass or their own dung."

Some Dakota warriors sold their guns for food. Others ate their dogs and horses. Some even boiled their moccasins, hoping to eke out some nutrition in the form of a bitter, watery soup.

Four Dakota braves approached a farm in Meeker County on August 17. One of them stole eggs from the chicken coop and was chased off the property by the farmer's wife. Humiliated

HENRY H. SIBLEY

Henry H. Sibley worked his way through the Great Lakes to Minnesota as an agent in the fur trade. He set up headquarters at St. Peter's (now Mendota) in Minnesota in 1834, building a private economic empire and political career. He constructed Minnesota's first stone house in 1836, but that was just the beginning. He had a relationship with a Dakota woman, Red Blanket Woman, and had one child with her, although he soon married a white woman and built a larger family.

Minnesota became a territory in 1849, and Sibley was voted in as representative to the territorial legislature. In 1851, with the Treaty of Mendota and the Treaty of Traverse des Sioux, most of southern Minnesota was opened to white settlement. Sibley was deeply involved in the treaty politics, and he and other traders claimed $500,000 of the treaty payments. They said the Dakota had charged huge quantities of goods at their stores. Many of the claims were inflated, and the agreements not well understood by tribal leaders. Sibley and his associates made out handsomely from the treaties. Sibley manipulated the homestead process in the newly acquired Dakota lands and bought what he could not get for free, claiming vast acreage immediately adjacent to the Dakota reservations. In 1858, he was elected the first governor of the new state of Minnesota. In 1862, he was in charge of the army that crushed the Dakota and expelled them from the state.

by his hunger and broom beating, the young man responded to the teasing from his friends by returning to the farm and killing the entire family. The four warriors then returned to their village and informed people what they had done.

Dakota people along the length of the Minnesota River converged on the village of Little Crow, a prominent Dakota chief. They realized they were at a decision point. The chief could turn the warriors over to the government to be prosecuted for murder or he could raise a war party and join the fight. Little Crow had been to Washington and knew what the Dakota were up against. He told his people: "See! The white men are like the locusts when they fly so thick that the whole sky is a snowstorm. You may kill one—two—ten; yes, as many as the leaves in the forest yonder, and their brothers will not miss them. Kill one—two—ten, and ten times ten will come to kill you."

The Dakota debated late into the night. Eventually, many came to the same conclusion. The government's path gave them no hope. The whites would not stop until they owned all the land. Rather than die of starvation, the Dakota chose to die fighting.

OUTBREAK

Little Crow, now at the head of a large Dakota force, attacked the very next day. His warriors first targeted government employees and traders. Andrew Myrick's body was found with his mouth stuffed with grass.

Fort Ridgely was nearby and lightly garrisoned. Little Crow quickly defeated a relief force sent to disrupt the attacks and to cover civilians trying to retreat. Dakota warriors continued to attack with only light resistance across Renville and Brown Counties, killing 200 and capturing 200 more.

At the Upper Sioux Indian Agency, a Dakota man named John Other Day rescued whites and led them to safety at great personal risk. Other Dakota, unwilling to take part in violence, also hid white war refugees. They saved many lives.

Little Crow massed his warriors for a major assault on Fort Ridgely. Twice the warriors tried to breach the fort but were unsuccessful. They turned their attention to an attack on the white settlement at Lake Shetek, then sought other targets of opportunity. White war refugees were fleeing across southern Minnesota, and Alexander Ramsey, the governor, called for aid. Two regiments were recalled from the front lines of the Civil War to come to Minnesota. It would take a while for them to arrive, so in the meantime, Ramsey tapped Henry H. Sibley, a former Minnesota governor, to call up a citizen militia and confront Little Crow in the field.

Dakota warriors laid siege to the town of New Ulm. Twice they made direct assaults, but the defenders held fast. The Dakota warriors moved northwest, and most of the residents fled to the town of Mankato. Soon after, Sibley arrived at Fort Ridgely with the volunteer militia. The Dakota had been attacking with impunity for 11 days. He relieved the fort, which was housing more than 350 civilians.

U.S. troops were ambushed by Red Eagle, Mankato, and around 300 Dakota warriors at Birch Coulee. The Dakota killed 13 soldiers and several civilians, wounded 47, and killed 90 horses in the engagement, losing only two warriors. Sibley eventually brought an artillery battery and relieved the detachment at Birch Coulee. Dakota warriors pressed attacks at Forest City, Hutchinson, and Fort Abercrombie. By this point, white settlers had fled and Sibley was on the move. At Wood Lake on September 23, 1862, the militia won decisively. Little Crow

OJIBWE REACTIONS

When the U.S.-Dakota War began, the Dakota sent runners to many other tribes to seek allies. The Ojibwe and Dakota had been enemies off and on for decades, but they had common concerns with white encroachment and violence. Ojibwe chief Hole in the Day, not looking to kill people but still wanting to manipulate events to his advantage, took white captives and sent runners to Leech Lake and Ottertail Lake, where other Ojibwe also took captives and burned the Indian agency buildings, marching to Crow Wing.

In central Minnesota, far from the active violence in the U.S.-Dakota War, other Ojibwe stopped Hole in the Day from involving their communities in further conflict with the Americans. They protected Fort Ripley, near present-day Brainerd, Minnesota, from possible attack, averting an escalation to crisis. The Ojibwe didn't kill anyone, and in a tense standoff at Fort Ripley, Hole in the Day negotiated new terms with the U.S. government to diffuse the situation.

Governor Alexander Ramsey never forgot how close the Ojibwe had come to joining the conflict. He personally led an entourage with a large military escort to the Old Crossing of the Red Lake River in 1863, demanding a land cession of 20 million acres from the Ojibwe. Ojibwe bands along the Red River at Pembina and Red Lake had to contend with immediate consequences from the U.S.-Dakota War and Hole in the Day's altercation. Leech Lake and the central Minnesota Ojibwe communities also came under pressure for further land cessions in 1863. It was a hard time to be Indian in Minnesota.

knew the tide of the war had turned and told his warriors to gather their families and flee.

Many Dakota escaped. Some made it to Lakota country and took refuge with Sitting Bull's band. Others escaped to Canada. Some Dakota who had stayed out of the fighting formed a peace party and tried to negotiate an end to the conflict and the return of hostages held by other Dakota. White civilians and their politicians, however, were less interested in peace than they were in punishment.

PRAIRIE GENOCIDE

Sibley's men were steadily reinforced while the Dakota fractured. Soldiers and militia constantly tried to round up

MANKATO HANGING After the U.S.-Dakota war, President Abraham Lincoln approved the largest mass execution in American history. Thirty-eight Dakota were hung simultaneously by the neck until dead the day after Christmas, 1862.

Dakota and made no distinction between those who had protected white civilians and those who had killed them. Whites waged retributive violence across the region; it is still unknown how many Dakota died.

Alexander Ramsey engineered a plan to remove all Dakota from Minnesota, whether or not they had been involved in the war. Hundreds of people were chained, and instead of being expeditiously transported to Fort Snelling for temporary internment, they were marched in shackles through the towns that had been attacked in 1862. Some white settlers used pitchforks to run them through. One took an infant from the hands of its mother and dashed its head against the rocks until it was dead.

LITTLE CROW The Dakota chief knew his people were likely to die, but agreed
to lead the war effort so they could die fighting instead of from starvation.

Within a couple of months, more than 2,000 Dakota were imprisoned at Fort Snelling. Adjacent to the fort was a sprawling prisoner of war camp with teepees set up wall to wall. The army separated Dakota men and women. Soldiers, still in uniform and under orders to guard the camp, regularly caroused through instead and systematically raped the Dakota women.

The U.S. government conducted military-style tribunals and convicted 303 Dakota men for murder. Most of the trials lasted less than five minutes. Dakota allies who protected whites were among those convicted. President Abraham Lincoln was soon involved in the process. He wanted to be harsh enough to discourage further resistance and yet not so harsh as to seem cruel in the eyes of white Americans elsewhere. He shortened the list to 100 for execution, and then to 38.

On the day after Christmas 1862, the 38 were simultaneously hanged until dead. A large crowd gathered in Mankato to witness the hanging. The Dakota called the victims the "38 Slain."

The Dakota men who were not hanged were brought to a camp in Davenport, Iowa. Conditions were harsh. At least 120 of them died there. Their families had no news of their fate for years.

The U.S. Army was still active in the field, trying to round up runaway Dakota. They even sortied into Canada and captured Dakota leaders Shakopee and Medicine Bottle, illegally bringing them back to the United States for a hasty trial and hanging.

General John Pope was given command of U.S. military operations, and he attacked Dakota communities in Minnesota and North Dakota. Most of the communities he attacked had no part in the war. At Whitestone Hill and Killdeer Mountain, many innocent Dakota were killed, including children and elders unable to defend themselves or run for safety. The violence cascaded across the Plains, igniting conflict with many Dakota bands and other tribes previously neutral or too far removed to have been engaged in hostilities.

Minnesota's adjutant general, Oscar Malmros, issued a formal bounty on Dakota scalps in July 1863. Soldiers were to be paid $25 per Dakota scalp, and civilians were to be paid $75. That amount was increased to $200 in September. Newspapers across the region reported the taking of many Dakota scalps and the payment of bounties to numerous civilians and soldiers.

The U.S. government also relocated about 2,000 Ho-Chunk (Winnebago) from Blue Earth in southern Minnesota. They had nothing to do with the war either, but they were Indians,

LITTLE CROW'S FATE

After the U.S.-Dakota War, the Dakota scattered. Some fled west and joined Sitting Bull's people. Others, like Little Crow, fled to Canada. In 1863, Little Crow crossed the border into North Dakota. A white farmer named Nathan Lamson shot and killed him. Recognizing the chief's face from a newspaper, Lamson alerted the army, which retrieved the body.

Soldiers scalped Little Crow, dragged his body through the streets of a nearby town for the Fourth of July parade, and then sent it to Brainerd, Minnesota, to be macerated (boiled to remove the flesh). Little Crow's tanned scalp and skeleton were displayed in a traveling exhibit and then at the Minnesota Historical Society. The scalp and skeleton were photographed and printed on postcards for sale to tourists until the 1970s. Nathan Lamson was awarded $500 by special action of the Minnesota Legislature.

In the 1970s, an elderly Dakota man approached David Beaulieu, the first Native American hired to work at the Minnesota Department of Human Rights, and asked him to photograph the remains of Little Crow. Beaulieu thought it a strange request and asked why, only to learn he was talking with Little Crow's grandson, who had tried his entire life to get his grandfather's body returned. They initiated legal action and successfully had the chief's body repatriated for interment.

and in southern Minnesota that was enough. Alexander Ramsey personally guided a military and civilian force north to negotiate with the Ojibwe for cession of a 20-million-acre parcel that spanned Minnesota and North Dakota. The Ojibwe had never fought the Americans either, but in addition to possessing the Red River Valley, which was fertile land well suited for agriculture, they too were Indians in Minnesota.

The U.S. government determined to establish a small reservation far from Minnesota for the Dakota who were interned at Fort Snelling and Davenport. They selected Crow Creek, South Dakota. The Dakota were loaded onto steam barges and brought down the Mississippi River, then up the Missouri to their new home. Close quarters on the boats and the long marches on foot took a toll and many more Dakota died. Food was scarce and the army was still patrolling for Dakota off the reservation. Another 200 Dakota died in the first few months at Crow Creek.

Today, the Dakota are still formally exiled from Minnesota. Some of the Dakota, primarily those who had adopted Christianity and helped protect whites, came back to the four communities set aside for them in 1858. There were around 30,000 Dakota in the region at the start of the U.S.-Dakota War; today there are a little more than 1,000. ■

SOUTHERN CHEYENNE

BLACK KETTLE AND THE WAR FOR THE WEST

As part of the large Algonquian language family, the Cheyenne originally lived on the Atlantic coast. As the Algonquians moved west over the centuries before European contact, the Cheyenne emerged as a distinct group in Minnesota in about 1600. Over the next two hundred years, the Cheyenne slowly moved into the Plains and then the Black Hills. They fought the Lakota there, eventually being pushed farther south. In 1811, the Cheyenne formed a permanent alliance with the Arapaho, which served both tribes well. Together, they controlled a vast stretch of territory in Kansas, Nebraska, Wyoming, and Colorado. They battled the Shoshone off and on; their conflict with the Lakota had waned by the time the Americans descended on all the Plains tribes. The chiefs of all native nations then faced the biggest challenge yet to their way of life and very survival.

WASHITA RIVER George Armstrong Custer led U.S. troops in a brutal and avoidable massacre of the southern Cheyenne on the banks of the Washita River in 1868.

BLACK KETTLE'S STRATEGY OF ACCOMMODATION

When the Americans came, each tribe had to choose a path. Some, like the Ojibwe, walked a fine line between accommodation and conflict to vie for best outcomes. But for most it was a black-and-white choice between fighting and submitting, with loss either way. Black Kettle, who was born around 1803, was experienced enough diplomatically to know what his people were up against. He wanted to protect Cheyenne lives and bargain for the best outcomes with all his remaining diplomatic influence. However, Cheyenne warrior societies like the Dog Soldiers often saw his efforts to accommodate the Americans as weakness.

In 1851, the Cheyenne participated in the first Treaty of Fort Laramie, which defined tribal territories across much of the Plains. The Cheyenne and Arapaho were affirmed in their exclusive possession of acreage in present-day Colorado, Nebraska, Kansas, and Wyoming. For the Americans, defining tribal boundaries was the first step in a broader strategy of dividing and conquering the tribes. For Black Kettle, it offered some leverage to protect his people and borders from encroachment by whites and other tribes.

Black Kettle's ability to avert disaster was soon tested. In 1857, white settlers shot a Cheyenne hunter. In response, some Cheyenne raided a white farm. The U.S. government sent in the cavalry—a punitive expedition led by Colonel Edwin V. Sumner. Although there were few casualties, Sumner's skirmish with Cheyenne warriors that year marked the first official engagement between the Cheyenne and the U.S. Army.

The discovery of gold in the Rocky Mountains led to the Pike's Peak gold rush in 1859. White prospectors flooded Cheyenne territory en route to the mountains. White settlements on the edges of Cheyenne land were growing, and the pressure mounted for the Cheyenne and Arapaho to sell land. Most of the Cheyenne resisted the idea. They had put up with lots of traffic through their lands already; few could see any good reason to relinquish the land they depended on to survive. Black Kettle saw things differently.

In 1861, Black Kettle and five other Cheyenne and Arapaho chiefs signed the Treaty of Fort Wise, which ceded most of the homeland for both tribes and left them with one-thirteenth of their territory as defined in the 1851 treaty. Black Kettle believed this would preserve the peace. He also thought that the annuities and treaty payments would compensate the people for the loss of hunting land. It was a gross miscalculation on both accounts.

The annuities and treaty payments were unexpectedly small and late. The Dog Soldiers refused to come into the new reservation and disavowed the treaty. The U.S. government labeled all Cheyenne and Arapaho off the reservation as hostile and moved to bring them in by force if necessary.

SAND CREEK MASSACRE

In 1864, Colorado Governor John Evans asked Black Kettle to come to Fort Lyon to receive provisions. There were about 800 Cheyenne in his band. The chief camped close to the fort on the bank of the Sand Creek and flew an American flag on the advice of army officers. Most of the men went buffalo hunting. Nobody expected trouble.

Colonel John M. Chivington had command of the Colorado militia, and he minced no words: "Damn any man who sympathizes with Indians! . . . I have come to kill Indians, and believe it is right and honorable to use any means under God's heaven to kill Indians . . . Kill and scalp all, big and little; nits make lice." He disregarded the political efforts of the governor and the officers at the fort and rode on to Black Kettle's camp.

When Chivington ordered the attack, two of his officers refused and held back two companies of the 700-man militia. The rest followed him for one of the most infamous massacres in U.S. Indian history. Anywhere from 100 to 163 Cheyenne and Arapaho were killed, more than two-thirds of them

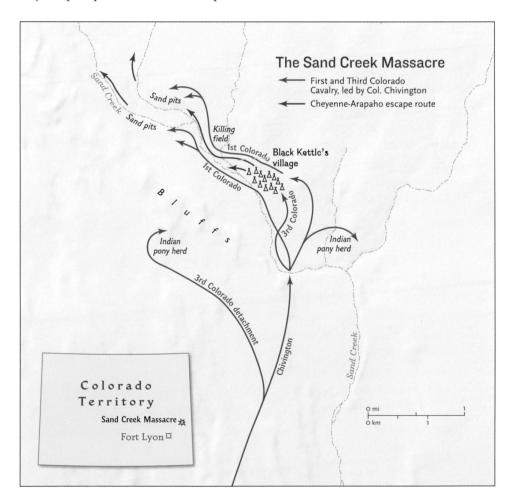

women and children. Eight chiefs and headmen died, as did four of Chivington's soldiers. After routing the camp, the soldiers returned to finish off any wounded Indians. They took turns conducting target practice on two-year-olds. They cut the scrotum off White Antelope to fashion into a tobacco pouch. They cut the genitals off women for hatbands and saddlebows.

Chivington cemented the military resistance of many previously peace-minded chiefs. Roman Nose and several other leaders joined the Dog Soldiers. Soon, the Cheyenne and Arapaho were raiding along the Platte River and into Casper, Wyoming. Black Kettle still refused to raid or wage war.

Congressional investigations verified the human rights abuses by Chivington's militia. The U.S. government offered a new treaty in 1865, the Treaty of the Little Arkansas. It included reparations to survivors of the Sand Creek Massacre and reaffirmed land borders for the Cheyenne and Northern Arapaho. But the treaty was ignored, and then abrogated by Congress two years later. The 1867 Medicine Lodge Treaty forced the Cheyenne and Arapaho to move to a small Oklahoma reservation.

WASHITA RIVER

In 1868, about 6,000 Cheyenne, Arapaho, Lakota, Comanche, Kiowa, and Kiowa Apache Indians camped in several different villages along the Washita River. Black Kettle and his band were camped on the reservation as the army had directed them. Fifteen white settlers had been killed earlier that fall, although nobody could identify who was responsible.

George Armstrong Custer, now in command of the 7th Cavalry, was sent to punish any Indians who raided white settlements. Osage scouts guided his force on the trail of Kiowa who had been raiding the Ute. Some Kiowa rode through Black Kettle's Cheyenne camp. Custer dispatched troops in the middle of the night to four locations around Black Kettle's camp. They attacked at dawn. Black Kettle and his wife were shot in the back, and another 50 to 100 Indians died. Twenty-one soldiers perished in the assault. Warriors from other villages started lining up on hilltops. Custer killed 675 Indian horses and took 53 Indian captives. He ordered a retreat, using the captives as human shields. The Cheyenne wouldn't risk the murder of their kin, and Custer's retreat went unchallenged. ∎

SAND CREEK MASSACRE In 1864, Colonel John M. Chivington led the Colorado militia against Black Kettle's band in one of the most infamous attacks in U.S. history.

BUFFALO SOLDIERS

USING BLACK TROOPS TO FIGHT INDIAN WARS

The U.S. Army established several segregated black military units during the Civil War. They served prominently in the Indian wars and many other American conflicts until disbanded in 1951, when the army integrated all units. The units most active in the Indian wars were formed in 1866—the 10th Cavalry (stationed at Fort Leavenworth, Kansas) and the 9th Cavalry (stationed in New Orleans but redeployed to Texas). The 24th and 25th Infantry regiments were also segregated black units that fought in Native American campaigns.

In 1867, John Randall, a black soldier from the 10th Cavalry, was tasked to escort civilians on the open prairie. His small entourage was attacked by 70 Cheyenne warriors, and all the civilians were killed. Randall was severely wounded, once by gunshot and 11 times by Cheyenne lances. He had only 17 rounds of ammunition, but fought off the war party until reinforcements arrived. He single-handedly killed 13 Cheyenne warriors. The Cheyenne told stories afterward about a soldier "who had fought like a cornered buffalo; who like a buffalo had suffered wound after wound, yet had not died; and who like a buffalo had a thick and shaggy mane of hair." After this, the black soldiers serving in the Indian wars were often called buffalo soldiers and the name stuck, even for soldiers in other American military theaters.

BUFFALO SOLDIERS ON THE PLAINS

On the Plains, the buffalo soldiers saw most of their action in the first few years after the 10th Cavalry was formed. Their first battles were smaller skirmishes, like one in 1867 near Fort Arbuckle, Oklahoma, where two soldiers were killed in an attack by a much larger force of 200 warriors.

The entire 10th Cavalry and elements of the 24th Infantry saw major action in the Battle of the Saline River in 1867. Around 400 Cheyenne attacked the unit, which was in an exposed position. They fought an eight-hour engagement completely surrounded. They kept a box formation to fend off attacks from all sides, running through 2,000 rounds of ammunition and in a sustained fighting retreat for 15 miles before the Cheyenne broke off the attack.

MEDICINE LODGE TREATY In 1867, the success of the buffalo soldiers in fighting the Kiowa, Comanche, Kiowa Apache, Cheyenne, and Arapaho forced the tribes to cede their vast territory.

At the Battle of Beecher Island in 1868, elements of the 9th Cavalry were helping white scouts locate hostile bands when they were ambushed by a party of Lakota, Cheyenne, and Arapaho under the leadership of the legendary Cheyenne warrior Roman Nose. They retreated to a sandbar in the middle of the Arikara Fork of the Republican River (now simply the Arikara River). As hundreds of warriors converged on their location, they killed their horses and used them as breastworks for defense. They dug foxholes and sniped at the Indians with repeating Spencer rifles, inflicting heavy casualties. Two soldiers were dispatched to call for reinforcements, crawling for three miles and then running for help. The 10th Cavalry led a successful relief mission. Six scouts were killed and 21 wounded. Around 30 Indians were killed, including Roman Nose. Throughout 1867 and 1868, the buffalo soldiers fought in William T. Sherman's winter campaign against the Cheyenne, Arapaho, Comanche, and Kiowa.

BUFFALO SOLDIERS IN THE SOUTHWEST

From 1849 to 1886, the U.S. government deployed as many as 7,000 soldiers against the Apache, who were effective guerrilla warriors. Among the units deployed were the buffalo soldiers.

In 1879–80, the 10th Cavalry participated in a major campaign against the Mimbreño Apache, led by a charismatic chief, Victorio. The unit was tasked with covering all water sources to cut off Victorio's retreat. Although their battles were minor, they played a major role in keeping Victorio from reaching his mountain strongholds. Victorio remained on the Mexican border, where Mexican troops eventually overtook his position and killed him and most of his warriors.

In March 1890, elements of the 10th Calvary fought the Apache during the Cherry Creek campaign on the Salt River. Through their many Indian campaigns, 13 enlisted men and 6 officers among the buffalo soldiers won the Medal of Honor.

The U.S. government's use of racially segregated units in the conquest of other people of color raises interesting challenges. It was a stated strategy for the U.S. Army to use one object of conquest against another. Many tribes were used as scouts in campaigns against other tribes. Because these tribes had often fought each other, many saw their service as an opportunity to continue an ancient fight, just with new uniforms and new allies. But the government also wanted to keep oppressed groups oppressed and pitted against one another because any alliance between tribes or across the lines that separated other disaffected and oppressed groups could pose a formidable challenge to the white power structure. The decision to use black to fight Indians was designed to maintain white supremacy. ■

FETTERMAN FIGHT Red Cloud used Crazy Horse to lure soldiers out of Fort
Phil Kearny, then brought his multitribal alliance down on them for a decisive victory.

RED CLOUD'S WAR
CAMPAIGN FOR THE POWDER RIVER

The Lakota valued their individual freedom and the autonomy of their bands. Anyone who tried to assert control over others usually ended up dead or alone. Nobody had ever brought all Lakota together, but Red Cloud accomplished what had been unimaginable.

The Lakota and their allies—the Northern Cheyenne and Arapaho—ranged across the Powder River country of present-day Wyoming and Montana for generations. The country's rolling green hills were some of the least-spoiled land left in America. As whites flooded across the Oregon Trail along the edges of Lakota land, more and more of the traditional Lakota came to the Powder River country. There were rivers there—the Bighorn, Rosebud, Tongue, and Powder—and abundant buffalo. With plenty of water and food, huge horse herds, and many Indians, the land was well defended and the people had few problems providing for themselves.

JOHN BOZEMAN
In 1851, many Lakota, Cheyenne, and Arapaho gathered at Fort Laramie and agreed to a treaty that articulated the boundaries of their tribal domains. For the U.S. government, this was an opportunity to define its divide-and-conquer objectives; soon soldiers would descend on the Southern Cheyenne and other tribes. But for Red Cloud and other Lakota, the treaty was an opportunity to make sure the government left them alone in the Powder River region. For 12 years, they remained unchallenged there, even though violence erupted in other parts of the Lakota and Cheyenne homelands.

The Battle of Ash Hollow in 1855 on the banks of the Platte River in Nebraska foreshadowed a larger conflict with the

RED CLOUD The chief's ability to unite Lakota bands with the Cheyenne and Arapaho was key to his success on the battlefield.

Lakota. Brigadier General William S. Harney led U.S. troops on a punitive expedition against the Brulé Lakota, killing 86 Indians, mainly women and children, and losing 27 soldiers in the process. The U.S.-Dakota War in 1862 ignited a wider conflict with the eastern Dakota and sent many west to seek refuge with their Lakota relatives. Red Cloud watched with trepidation, but the Powder River was still secure.

Then, in 1863, gold was discovered in Bannack, Montana. Gold had already lured thousands of fortune hunters across the Oregon Trail in the California gold rush and other white surges through the Great Basin and the Plains. John Bozeman, a prospector who had struck out in the Pike's Peak gold rush, came to the Powder River country and boldly blazed a trail through the heart of Lakota, Cheyenne, and Arapaho lands. Many Indians wanted to exact tribute from travelers rather then cut them off, but Red Cloud suspected that once the door opened, it would be hard to close again.

DODGE EXPEDITION
In 1864, after Colorado militia massacred and mutilated the Cheyenne and Arapaho at Sand Creek, those tribes divided. Some people went south, while others sought out their Lakota allies and executed often successful reprisal attacks along the Platte River. The U.S. Army rushed to the defense of the settlements. In 1865, General Grenville M. Dodge led an expedition into the Powder River region.

The Lakota and Cheyenne avoided a direct conflict with the soldiers. Dodge had Pawnee, Osage, and Ho-Chunk scouts, who located an Arapaho village and brought Dodge's force within striking distance. In the Battle of the Tongue River, 70 Pawnee, Ho-Chunk, and Omaha scouts and 200 U.S. Cavalry attacked and routed the Arapaho village of 500. Warriors

covered the retreat of the main village, inflicting seven casualties on Dodge's force. Dodge
killed 63 Arapaho, mainly women and children, and captured another 18.

Although Dodge had been charged with punishing hostile
tribes and securing peace in the region, he had trouble achiev-
ing any objectives beyond the massacre in the Battle of the
Tongue River. Pawnee scouts and U.S. soldiers clashed with
the Cheyenne at the Battle of Crazy Woman's Fork. Then on
August 16, 1865, they rode on a Cheyenne camp on the Powder River. Cheyenne warriors mistook the Pawnee scouts for
Cheyenne at first and were unprepared for the assault. The
entire Cheyenne party of 27 was annihilated.

Dodge had the attention of Red Cloud. In the Battle of
Bone Pile Creek, Red Cloud attacked an army wagon train,
inflicting casualties and halting the advance of the column.
He and Cheyenne chief Dull Knife parleyed with the army
officers the next day and agreed to allow passage in return for
payment. Communication broke down,
however, and Red Cloud resumed his attacks.
He inflicted casualties in quick strikes and
retreats at Alkali Creek, Dry Creek, and the
Little Powder River, wearing down military resolve in a war
of attrition and harassment.

THE FETTERMAN FIGHT

In June 1866, Red Cloud came to Fort Laramie to make peace.
He wanted the 1851 Treaty of Fort Laramie honored. If that
could be done, there would be no need to fight. He was willing
to make concessions and even allow some white traffic across
the Lakota homeland in return for payment. U.S. officials met
with Red Cloud in a series of councils. Red Cloud felt that they
were making progress when suddenly Colonel Henry B. Carrington arrived at Fort Laramie with 1,300 soldiers and a massive supply train. He was under orders to occupy the Powder
River and build a string of forts to protect the Bozeman Trail.

The U.S. government had been negotiating in bad faith. Red Cloud and Young Man Afraid of His Horses left the council.

A few Lakota stayed and agreed to let Carrington through in return for compensation. President Andrew Johnson declared in his State of the Union speech that the Cheyenne and Lakota had "unconditionally submitted to our authority." He could not have been more wrong.

Red Cloud knew fighting was a high-risk strategy. Most tribes that fought were crushed—killed, subjugated, and forced to cede their land. There was no precedent for tribes defeating the Americans in long campaigns. The Lakota, Cheyenne, and Arapaho, though, had advantages in the field. They knew the terrain, were acclimated to the place, were superb horsemen, were truly brave, shot six arrows in the time it took to reload one musket, and were likely to have superior numbers if they chose the battles. But the army also had advantages. The Indians were effective fighters at distances of 100 yards or less, but soldiers with Springfield muskets or Spencer rifles could be effective fighting up to 300 yards away. The families of the U.S. soldiers were far from conflict zones. And their command structure had none of the blessings or shortcomings of the complicated relationship-based alliances among tribal bands and warrior societies. Assaulting forts was futile, but in the open, guerrilla tactics or a head-on engagement with superior numbers made the tribes truly formidable. To defeat the U.S. Army, Red Cloud had to control the time and place of engagement.

In 1866, Red Cloud struck unpredictably and with precision. At Fort Reno, he started a campaign against the forts Carrington was sent to build. His warriors stole 175 horses and mules. Two hundred soldiers pursued the Lakota, who killed two soldiers and six civilians. The soldiers returned without punishing the Lakota or recovering the livestock.

The chief then focused on hitting supply trains and woodcutting expeditions, isolating the soldiers in their forts and cutting off supplies and communications. In one encounter after another, Red Cloud's warriors picked off six soldiers and 28 civilian fort personnel in the first months of the conflict without substantial Indian casualties.

That's when Captain William J. Fetterman arrived. He was young, ambitious, impulsive, resistant to taking orders, and had little faith in Carrington as his commanding officer. Fetterman was an experienced Civil War veteran, but had never fought Indians. On December 21, 1866, Red Cloud's warriors attacked the woodcutters outside Fort Phil Kearny again. Fetterman was given command of an 80-soldier relief expedition. He spotted Indians as soon as they left the fort. He brought his cavalry in front of his marching infantry troops. He had already forgotten the relief mission for the woodcutters.

Crazy Horse and a small group of other Lakota warriors were on a hill just ahead of Fetterman's cavalry line. They hoisted their breechclouts, exposing themselves front and back, taunting Fetterman and his men and laughing. Fetterman's blood boiled and he ordered an all-out attack, charging in front of his men. Crazy Horse galloped ahead of him, over the hill and down into a ravine. Fetterman pursued, eager to teach the insolent Indians a lesson.

Fetterman heard the war whoops after he was deep into the valley. About 2,000 to 3,000 Cheyenne, Arapaho, and Lakota charged from elevated positions on both flanks. He tried to fight his way forward, but his force was enveloped and overwhelmed. Fetterman and all his men were killed. Only six were shot by rifles. The others died from arrows and lances. It was the worst defeat yet for the U.S. Army in the wars for the West.

THE BAD FACES: RED CLOUD'S WARRIOR SOCIETY

The Lakota were never a singular united political entity, even though they shared a common language, customs, and way of life. They all depended on the buffalo and used horses with uncommon skill and deadly effect in both hunting and war. But they all belonged to distinct bands. Sitting Bull was Hunkpapa. Red Cloud was Oglala.

Within bands, there were further divisions, including sacred warrior societies. One of these was the Bad Faces. Red Cloud had no claim to chieftainship or prominence as a young man. But as a member of the Bad Faces, he saw lots of war. They often raided the Pawnee, Ute, and Crow. Lakota war customs valued skill with a lance, daring in battle, and cleverness in horse thievery. Red Cloud made a name for himself, and in acquiring many horses, was rich by Lakota standards. Soon, he was leading war parties and eventually became *blotahunka*, or "leader," of the Bad Faces. He had no further ambitions, but was not the sole arbiter of his own fate. One day, a brash young Oglala named Bull Bear, in a drunken rage, killed another Lakota who was one of Red Cloud's Bad Faces. Without waiting for a tribal council to decide how to deal with Bull Bear, Red Cloud strode up to the man and shot him in the head. Although it was never his intent, many Oglala outside the Bad Faces started to look to him to lead them all.

RED CLOUD'S PEACE

Red Cloud pulled his warriors back. They moved to their winter camps, tending to families and sending only small raiding and scouting parties around the forts. It was enough, though. The garrison at Fort Phil Kearny struggled with food supplies and the stress of needing to harvest wood but not having sufficient protection. The weather did as much damage as Red Cloud. When spring came, the great chief returned to the warpath. But the army supply train had gotten through, and it made a huge difference. Soldiers who previously fought Red Cloud with Springfield muskets now had breech-loading Spencer repeating rifles. In August 1867, Cheyenne and Arapaho warriors struggled to overwhelm hay cutters near Fort C. F. Smith, repelled by Spencer rifle fire in the Hayfield Fight. At the Wagon Box Fight the next day, Red Cloud, Crazy Horse, and Hump led Lakota warriors against soldiers who took cover behind encircled wagon boxes. The attackers captured numerous horses and mules, but again the Spencer rifles prevented a more devastating outcome for the defenders. Several soldiers were killed, as were perhaps two dozen Indians.

On the far eastern edge of Lakota land, warriors also attacked the Union Pacific Railroad in the Plum Creek Massacre in Nebraska. Red Cloud's attacks had made the Bozeman Trail effectively impassable and now the Oregon Trail and the railroad were threatened. There were already more than 200 American casualties and maybe 100 tribal casualties. The U.S. government sued for peace.

Red Cloud refused to negotiate peace terms until the government abandoned all forts in the Powder River country—Forts Reno, C. F. Smith, and Phil Kearny. Chagrined but powerless to dictate terms, the army left the forts. The Lakota and Cheyenne burned them to the ground. A long line of Lakota, Cheyenne, and Arapaho came to Fort Laramie in 1868 and negotiated a new treaty. Red Cloud gave the orders and U.S. scribes took notes—the tribal alliance would have exclusive control over territory covering most of five current U.S. states. Whites had to obtain written permission to enter. The Bozeman Trail was abandoned. Against all odds, Red Cloud won the war, and his victory turned into a winnable peace.

On the Great Plains, an Indian's word was his bond, and Red Cloud never fought again. But in Washington, words were wind and ink was water—easily forgotten and often altered. The wars for the West were far from over. ■

TREATY OF FORT LARAMIE After Red Cloud's victories in 1868, tribal leaders dictated terms of a new treaty, including exclusive access to the Great Sioux Reservation encompassing most of five U.S. states.

WAR AGAINST THE BUFFALO

THE 60 MILLION SLAIN

According to the Blackfeet, long ago the people needed help. There was never enough food. People suffered throughout the year and especially in the winter. There was a great hunter in the village who had a beautiful daughter. It pained him to see her suffer when he could not provide. One day, she slipped away. She wandered until she came to the base of a great cliff. There she prayed for her people. She waited patiently and then heard a sound like thunder. Looking up, she saw buffalo falling from the sky, landing on the rocks by her feet. One came to her and said she had to go with him. She was scared, but she traveled with the buffalo. The people found the many fallen buffalo, and the great hunter tracked his daughter across the prairie. He found her, but the buffalo charged and trampled him. His daughter was crying for her father when the buffalo spoke: "This is how we feel when you take our lives." But he took pity on the girl and gave her a sliver of his horn to heal her father. She held the buffalo horn to his wounds and sang to him—the song of the buffalo. The Blackfeet always used that song afterward to give thanks to the buffalo for everything they took from them.

No animal dominated the ecosystems and human landscape of North America as completely as did the North American bison. With a historic range across the Canadian Plains in Alberta, Saskatchewan, and Manitoba down to central Mexico and from California to New Jersey, the bison

BUFFALO HUNT As the railroad reached west across the Plains,
people killed buffalo for their hides, the price of their tongues, or even just for fun.

was abundant in nearly every region of the continental United States except the deserts of the Southwest and the extreme coastal areas. They were numerous, too—recent archaeological evidence and other scientific studies have confirmed a population of 60 million bison before 1800.

For the tribes in the Great Basin and Great Plains especially, the bison provided for all critical needs. Its flesh was food. Its organs were medicine. Its intestines were sinew for sewing and bags for hauling water. Its skins were clothes and lodge coverings. Its dung was fuel for fire.

The tribes hunted buffalo with spears, lances, and bows on foot. Some used collaborative hunting techniques to chase herds off cliffs. The entire community would participate in butchering, cutting, and drying meat to get through the long, harsh prairie winters. The Spanish horse changed the relationship between Indians and buffalo. Hunting from horseback was fast and efficient. People traveled more, following the herds. Some tribes became more powerful. More horses meant easier buffalo hunting, and that meant more capacity to provide. The standard of living increased. Because the buffalo was so important and the horse so powerful, tribes started fighting more often, more intensely, and over larger territories. Some tribes, such as the Comanche and Lakota, ascended. Others, like the Arikara, who were farmers first and hunters second, suffered as their neighbors grew in strength. The buffalo became key to survival on the Plains.

EXTERMINATION AND STARVATION

White settlers in the West often wrote about seas of buffalo. Their amazement, though, did not stay their desire to eradicate the species. General Philip Sheridan wanted the buffalo exterminated to starve the Indians into submission. He summed up the sentiment of most whites at the time when he said of buffalo hunters, "These men have done more . . . to settle the vexed Indian question than the entire regular army has done in the last 30 years. They are destroying the Indians' commissary." Colonel Richard Dodge wrote in 1867, "Every buffalo dead is an Indian gone." Like the Indians, wild animals would become a thing of the past, replaced by cattle as a

> ## "FOR THE SAKE OF LASTING PEACE, LET THEM KILL, SKIN, AND SELL UNTIL THE BUFFALOES ARE EXTERMINATED."
>
> GENERAL PHILIP SHERIDAN, 1874

necessary and natural part of America's Manifest Destiny.

Settlers, traders, and professional hunters took a heavy toll on the herds. William "Buffalo Bill" Cody claimed he shot 4,282 buffalo in 18 months between 1867 and 1868. In a shooting contest with William Comstock he killed 68 buffalo in 8 hours, all with his Springfield Model 1863. People hunted from trains, too, and one person reported shooting 120 buffalo in 40 minutes.

Buffalo hides were tanned and sold for two dollars each. Buffalo bones were crushed and used for manufacture of bone china, fertilizer, and sugar processing. Hides were converted to machine belts during industrialization. Millions of the beasts were also killed for no profit at all beyond impoverishing the Indians who depended upon them.

By 1890, just 300 buffalo were left in the United States. A conservation effort began with the Yellowstone herd in 1902, in Alberta, Canada, in 1907, and with the Theodore Roosevelt National Park in North Dakota in 1908. Today there are 360,000 buffalo, mainly on private ranches. The European equivalent of the buffalo—the cow—now numbers 108 million in the United States and Canada. ■

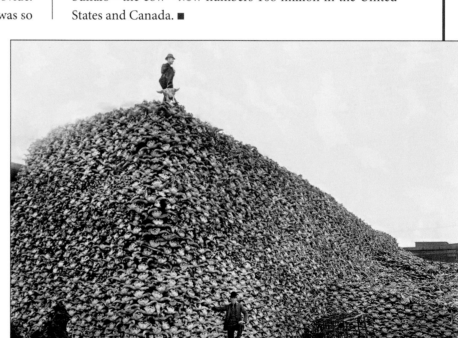

BUFFALO SKULLS Settlers on the Plains earned money picking up buffalo skulls for sale to collectors, like this one in Detroit, Michigan.

MODOC WAR
The Modoc fought for their
lives in the genocidal campaign
unleashed against them in the
Modoc War, 1872–73.

THE LAST STANDS

After everything the tribes had suffered, it was hard to imagine anything worse, but soon there would be a new kind of conflict and dire new consequences. The tribes already had faced terrible experiences with disease and a clash of technologies and cultures in their first contact with Europeans. They had navigated a seismic clash between outside empires as well as shifting dynamics in their wars with one another. They had dealt with American Manifest Destiny and an unprecedented taking of land.

Now, in the wars for survival, the tribes contended with a new array of American strategies designed not just to seize their land but also to subjugate and rule them. At stake was the right of tribes to govern their own communities and chart their own paths forward. This would be a bitter contest, but not without victories and transformative moments. These are the last great stands of the tribes—wicked betrayals, heartless massacres, unforgiving campaigns of dominance, and unexpected pockets of resistance. Great leaders rose to face these challenges—Chief Joseph, Manuelito, Cochise, Captain Jack, Lone Wolf, Louis Riel, and Geronimo. These are their stories—heartbreaking, shocking, and inspiring—in the wars for survival.

> "OUT OF THE INDIAN APPROACH TO LIFE THERE CAME A GREAT FREEDOM, AN INTENSE AND ABSORBING RESPECT FOR LIFE, ENRICHING FAITH IN A SUPREME POWER, AND PRINCIPLES OF TRUTH, HONESTY, GENEROSITY, EQUITY AND BROTHERHOOD."
>
> LUTHER STANDING BEAR

SUBJUGATING THE TRIBES

Government officials and army officers developed myriad strategies for subjugating the tribes. Some were cold and calculated, such as killing tribal chiefs. Leaders were horribly mistreated and died in jails—Osceola, Red Bird, and more. Others nearly perished while incarcerated, but made it home just in time to die, like the great Kiowa chief Lone Wolf. Many were killed in action or shot or hanged when they surrendered, like Captain Jack. Still others were assassinated—Hole in the Day, Crazy Horse, and Sitting Bull most notably.

The government tried to break up the tribes, dividing them to keep them from enough joint strength to resist the American nation. This was the fate for the Ute, Shoshone, Dakota, Lakota, Nez Perce, and Ojibwe. Leaders were often separated from their people, too. Chief Joseph and Geronimo were exiled from their home communities with small fractions of their people.

The destruction of the buffalo was meant to eliminate food sources to starve Indians into submission. During the Red River War this was the most successful tool in bringing the Kiowa, Comanche, Cheyenne, and Arapaho into reservations. The government

---

1848
Gold discovered at Sutter's Mill, California, sparking a surge of white migration west, igniting wars with many tribes.

1846–1866
Narbona, Barboncito, and Manuelito rally the Navajo in the Navajo Wars, ending in Kit Carson's brutal campaign and the Long Walk.

1849–1886
The Apache Wars bring Cochise, Victorio, Juh, Naiche, and Geronimo center stage for one of the longest, most bitter struggles.

1855–1858
The Yakama War breaks out in the Pacific Northwest, leading to the Puget Sound War and Coeur d'Alene War.

isolated small groups as they mopped up pockets of resistance. Many famous Indian fighters made their names in scorched-earth campaigns and Indian massacres, like Kit Carson, who fought the Comanche, Apache, Ute, and Navajo.

Small groups tried to avoid war at all cost, hiding out in remote areas. In the wars for survival, American forces hunted down and forcefully subjugated these previously peaceful groups in the Sheepeater and Bluff Wars. When indigenous people rose up, chafing under oppressive reservation controls, those movements were crushed—Louis Riel's Red River Rebellion, the Yaqui independence movement, even the Ghost Dance. Runaway groups from reservations were rounded up or killed off, as in the Kelley Creek Fight and the roundup after the Bluff War.

Tribes contended with a massive infusion of white people as the government allotted reservation lands and opened

PRAIRIE DU CHIEN In 1825, tribes gathered to declare peace and define boundaries. The site later served as a staging ground for U.S. military campaigns against the tribes.

them to white settlement, sparking the Crazy Snake conflict and the Battle of Sugar Point. For the Five Civilized Tribes, resisting allotment meant that the U.S. government would eliminate their sovereignty. Allotment was imposed and Oklahoma land rushes ensued. Crazy Snake could only delay the consequence. Indians did a lot of the dirty work too, not just as scouts, but also as Indian police, who helped fight the Ute and Paiute in the Bluff War and pulled the trigger that killed Sitting Bull.

There were massacres, too. Some were genocidal, like the Bear River Massacre, Marias River Massacre, and Wounded Knee. And some of those, like Wounded Knee, took on great symbolism. They changed the way natives and whites saw the age of conflict. Although the massacres did not eradicate the tribes, there is no doubt the era changed them, and changed the American nation, too.

1864–1868	1872–1873	1877	1890
Paiute, Bannock, and Shoshone warriors clash with the U.S. Army and militias in the Snake War, causing 1,800 casualties.	The Modoc hold out at the Tule Lake lava beds in fierce fighting during the Modoc War, which almost wipes out the tribe.	Chief Joseph leads his band of Nez Perce on a long fighting flight for freedom, clashing with multiple U.S. Army units.	The refurbished 7th Cavalry inflicts brutal revenge while persecuting the Lakota Ghost Dance at the Wounded Knee Massacre.

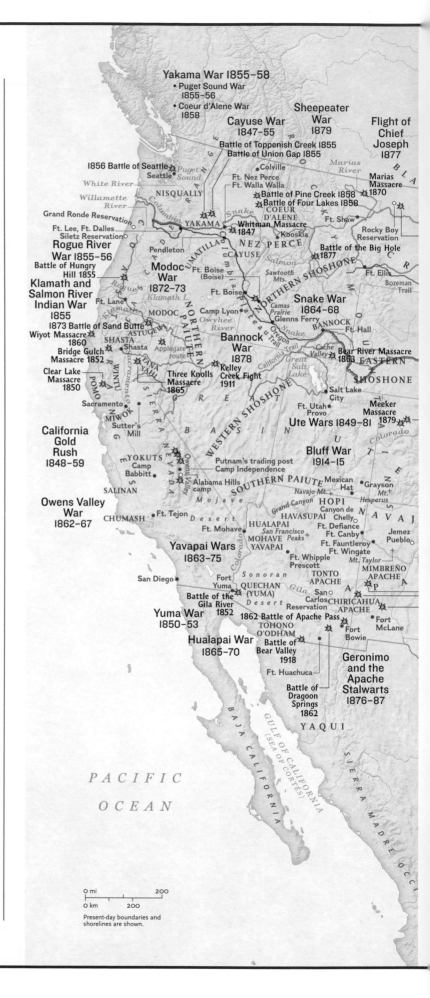

> "WE ARE PERHAPS THE ONLY NATION WHICH TRIED AS A MATTER OF NATIONAL POLICY TO WIPE OUT ITS INDIGENOUS POPULATION. MOREOVER, WE ELEVATED THAT TRAGIC EXPERIENCE INTO A NOBLE CRUSADE."
>
> MARTIN LUTHER KING, JR.

ENDURING FREEDOM OF THE TRIBES

Amid the loss and horror, something truly inspiring happened. In spite of unbelievably overwhelming odds, the tribes often showed incredible resilience. Hole in the Day of Leech Lake, unconquered, had won his war and won the peace too, living a long life, free from white interference after the Battle of Sugar Point. Although compromised and contentious, the tribes kept their native nationhood, their sovereignty, and their warrior spirit. Manuelito worked with great influence to end the Long Walk of the Navajo and to see his people returned to their homeland between the four sacred mountains of the Navajo. And Geronimo, who spent his adult life fighting and 27 years as a prisoner of war, told his nephew that he wished he had never surrendered. Throughout Indian country, ceremony, polity, and community survive to this day.

The wars for survival leave much to ponder. So much of the violence seems so unnecessary. Ultimately, the conflicts destroyed many lives on both sides. They devastated tribes politically, economically, and culturally. They dehumanized everybody they touched, not just the vanquished. Everybody lost. The wars for survival impugned America's honor as a nation. The First Amendment applied only to whites when it came to the religious rights of Native Americans to participate in the Ghost Dance. And if a great nation could not be built with great values—ones that honor all human life—then what does that say about American greatness?

The tribes have yet to recover from the Indian wars. Economically, politically, and culturally, they lost much. But it is amazing to see what they have retained. Although tribes no longer use guns to fight their fellow Americans, their warrior spirit endures, as does their fight for prosperity and freedom. ∎

DIVIDE AND CONQUER As America's dream of dominance from coast to coast was close to being realized, tribes were increasingly isolated from one another and the natural resources they depended upon. Those who resisted were often targeted for severe punishments and even genocidal campaigns.

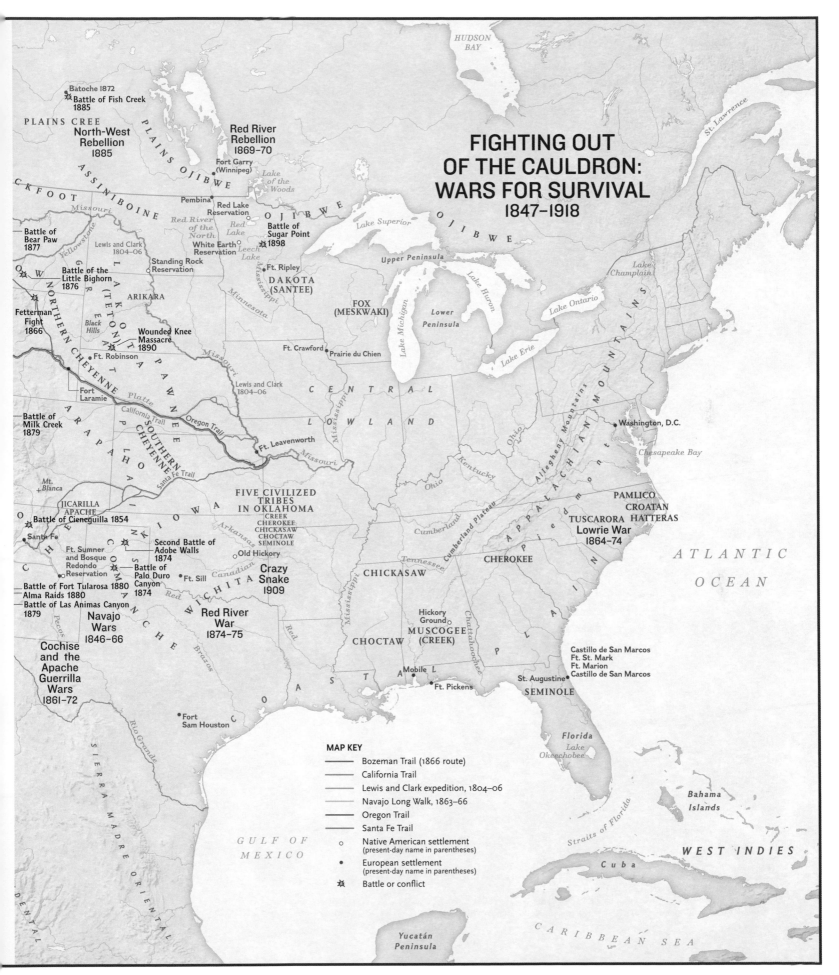

FIGHTING OUT OF THE CAULDRON: WARS FOR SURVIVAL
1847–1918

Batoche 1872
Battle of Fish Creek 1885

PLAINS CREE
North-West Rebellion 1885

PLAINS OJIBWE

Red River Rebellion 1869–70

BLACKFOOT

ASSINIBOINE

Missouri

Fort Garry (Winnipeg)

Pembina

Red Lake Reservation

Red River of the North

OJIBWE

Lake of the Woods

OJIBWE

OJIBWE

Battle of Bear Paw 1877

Lewis and Clark 1804–06

Yellowstone

White Earth Reservation

Red Lake

Leech Lake

Battle of Sugar Point 1898

Lake Superior

St. Lawrence

Lake Champlain

Battle of the Little Bighorn 1876

Standing Rock Reservation

Ft. Ripley

Upper Peninsula

NORTHERN CHEYENNE

ARIKARA

DAKOTA (SANTEE)

Mississippi

Lake Huron

Lake Ontario

Fetterman Fight 1866

LAKOTA (TETON)

Black Hills

PAWNEE

Wounded Knee Massacre 1890

Ft. Robinson

FOX (MESKWAKI)

Minnesota

Lower Peninsula

Lake Michigan

Lake Erie

Missouri

Fort Laramie

Platte

California Trail

Oregon Trail

Ft. Crawford
Prairie du Chien

CENTRAL

LOWLAND

APPALACHIAN MOUNTAINS

SOUTHERN CHEYENNE

ARAPAHO

Battle of Milk Creek 1879

Santa Fe Trail

Ft. Leavenworth

Missouri

Kentucky

Ohio

Ohio

Allegheny Mountains

Washington, D.C.

Chesapeake Bay

Mt. Blanca

JICARILLA APACHE

KIOWA

IOWA

FIVE CIVILIZED TRIBES IN OKLAHOMA
CREEK
CHEROKEE
CHICKASAW
CHOCTAW
SEMINOLE

Arkansas

Cumberland Plateau

Cumberland

Piedmont

PAMLICO
CROATAN
TUSCARORA HATTERAS

Lowrie War 1864–74

Battle of Cieneguilla 1854

Santa Fe

Ft. Sumner and Bosque Redondo Reservation

Second Battle of Adobe Walls 1874

Old Hickory

Canadian

Battle of Palo Duro Canyon 1874

Ft. Sill

Red

Crazy Snake 1909

Tennessee

CHICKASAW

CHEROKEE

PLAIN

ATLANTIC
OCEAN

Battle of Fort Tularosa 1880
Alma Raids 1880
Battle of Las Animas Canyon 1879

COMANCHE

WICHITA

Red River War 1874–75

Red

Hickory Ground

MUSCOGEE (CREEK)

Chattahoochee

Navajo Wars 1846–66

Pecos

Brazos

COMANCHE

CHOCTAW

CO

Castillo de San Marcos
Ft. St. Mark
Ft. Marion
Castillo de San Marcos

Cochise and the Apache Guerrilla Wars 1861–72

A Mobile L

St. Augustine

SEMINOLE

Ft. Pickens

Fort Sam Houston

Rio Grande

SIERRA MADRE ORIENTAL

Rio Grande

COAST

Florida
Lake Okeechobee

Bahama Islands

HUDSON BAY

GULF OF MEXICO

Straits of Florida

WEST INDIES

Cuba

MAP KEY

— Bozeman Trail (1866 route)
— California Trail
— Lewis and Clark expedition, 1804–06
— Navajo Long Walk, 1863–66
— Oregon Trail
— Santa Fe Trail
○ Native American settlement (present-day name in parentheses)
● European settlement (present-day name in parentheses)
✷ Battle or conflict

CARIBBEAN SEA

Yucatán Peninsula

CAYUSE WARRIOR Tensions between Cayuse Indians and white missionaries
led to the killing of 14 whites in the Whitman Massacre, igniting the Cayuse War.

CAYUSE WAR
POISON AND BLOOD

In 1835, Marcus Whitman and Samuel Parker first came to Cayuse country in the Pacific Northwest to negotiate permission to build a mission. Parker promised the Cayuse, "I do not intend to take your lands for nothing . . . there will come every year a big ship, loaded with goods, to be divided among the Indians. Those goods will not be sold, but given to you. The missionaries will bring you plows and hoes, to teach you how to cultivate the land, and they will not sell, but give them to you." In 1838, Whitman returned with his wife, Narcissa Whitman, to establish the mission near what's now Walla Walla, Washington. They were soon followed by many travelers, gold prospectors, and settlers. The Oregon Trail opened in 1842, and the trickle that started with the Whitmans became a flood.

The relationship between the Whitmans and the Cayuse was always tense. The Cayuse were curious and friendly, but the missionaries were private and resented Indians hanging around their house. The Cayuse found the missionaries rude and dishonest. They cut timber all over Cayuse lands to construct buildings, never asking permission or offering compensation. They also encroached on tribal lands in all directions.

Tragedy struck as thousands followed the Whitmans over the Oregon Trail through Cayuse communities. A measles outbreak in 1847 devastated the tribal population, and some Indians held the missionaries responsible for bringing the whites and spreading the disease. Someone at the mission put out poisoned meat for the wolves, and several Cayuse became terribly ill when they ate it. That seemed a forgivable misunderstanding, but one of the missionaries, frustrated with Cayuse tribal members stealing melons from the mission garden, threatened to poison the fruit. When many Cayuse sickened soon after, rumors spread that it was the intentional work of the missionaries.

WHITMAN MASSACRE
On November 29, 1847, several Cayuse warriors descended on the mission, killing the Whitmans and 12 other whites,

> "NEVER DID WE . . . BELIEVE THAT SUCH HEROISM AS THESE INDIANS EXHIBITED COULD EXIST. THEY KNEW THAT TO BE ACCUSED WAS TO BE CONDEMNED."
>
> TRIAL REPORT ON THE WHITMAN KILLINGS

igniting the Cayuse War of 1847–1855. Marcus Whitman was chopped by axes and nearly unrecognizable. Narcissa Whitman was shot. The Cayuse took 54 prisoners.

The Cayuse knew there would be retribution. They ransomed the prisoners in return for a promise of peace and a small payment of blankets and trade items. At first, they hid in remote areas, trying to protect their families from backlash and to outlast any animosity, hoping their brokered peace would last. The Oregon government sent a militia into the field, building Fort Lee and patrolling for hostile Cayuse. Any Indians who came into contact with white soldiers or civilians were in extreme danger. Desperate for supplies and food, some Cayuse raided white farms and settlements.

By 1849, the California gold rush was in full swing, and even more whites poured over the Oregon Trail through Cayuse lands. Both peace and evasion became difficult. In 1850, Cayuse leaders hoped to diffuse animosity and guarantee peace. They turned over five of their tribesmen for the murder of the Whitmans (Tilaukaikt, Tomahas, Klokamas, Isaiachalkis, and Kimasumpkin). A hasty trial was conducted. Kimasumpkin claimed he came at the request of his chief to tell what he knew of the Whitman Massacre, but that the killers had already died and he had played no part in the attack. His words had little effect. The five Cayuse were convicted and immediately executed.

The execution did not end the conflict. Local militiamen, miners, and settlers attacked tribal members. The Cayuse counterattacked and raided periodically until 1855.

That year, U.S. military and political pressure on tribes in the region came to a head, and the Cayuse signed a treaty that relocated them to the Umatilla Reservation in Pendleton, Oregon. They were consolidated there with the Umatilla and Walla Walla as the Confederated Tribes of the Umatilla Indian Reservation. By 1904, the Cayuse had dwindled to 404 people, but the population and culture have since rebounded. ■

CALIFORNIA GOLD RUSH
GENOCIDE ON THE COAST

The California tribes had a wide variety of experiences with colonization prior to the gold rush. The Spanish established a slave-based mission system along the California coast. The Russians raided, traded, and trapped in northern California. Inland tribes, however, had avoided those painful experiences for many decades. In 1821, Mexico won independence from Spain. California, which was still part of Mexico, fell under Mexican governance. That changed little for the mission Indians and even less for the inland tribes. America won the Mexican-American War of 1846–48, then claimed California and the American Southwest through the Treaty of Guadalupe Hidalgo. The inland tribes had ceded no land to any white government, but explorers started to chart the region and search for gold. Even before the discovery of the precious metal there, California's abundant natural resources were obvious to all. Big changes were coming.

HERE COME THE AMERICANS

Soon after Lewis and Clark reported on their 1804–06 expedition to the Pacific, American explorers started arriving in California, even though it was not yet part of the United States. Jedediah Smith made two trips to California between 1826 and 1828, bringing back furs and trade goods via the South Pass through the Rocky Mountains. John C. Frémont and Kit Carson made the trip to California in 1842 and then three more times after. In 1846, they attacked

GOLD RUSH The discovery of gold in California in 1848 brought 300,000 fortune hunters west by 1854. Gold fever led to many atrocities against Indians and the annihilation of entire tribes.

several tribal communities in northern California and Oregon, destroying a village at the Williamson River outlet on Klamath Lake. Frémont later became one of California's first two U.S. senators and was also a presidential contender.

Traffic west on the Oregon Trail accelerated throughout the 1840s, and when California was claimed by the Americans in 1848, even more people came to explore, settle, and prospect. Indians still had not ceded land in California to Spain, Mexico, or the United States, and they outnumbered whites there 10 to 1. Then, in 1848, James W. Marshall discovered gold at Sutter's Mill in Coloma, California. John Sutter was a major early California land baron. He started building his empire when California was still part of Mexico, eventually squatting on 50,000 acres of Nisenan tribal land near Sacramento. Marshall, who discovered the gold, was Sutter's

POMO VILLAGE **The Pomo were systematically dispossessed and enslaved by gold rushers. After sustained mistreatment, they killed some of the rushers and soon had massive force bearing down on them.**

overseer. Sutter kept hundreds of slaves, mainly Miwok Indians.

Within months, white prospectors surged into California. As many as 300,000 gold rushers peppered the territory by 1854 and another 200,000 by 1859, with mining and prospecting operations—Shasta, Feather River, Sacramento River, and every imaginable creek in central California. The peaceful dispositions of the resident tribes just made them easy targets for dispossession or slave labor.

SUBJUGATING THE TRIBES

More than 300,000 fortune seekers showing up uninvited caused chaos. The average age of gold rushers was 22, and in 1850, only 8 percent of the white population in California was female. Although some California tribes numbered in the thousands, most were smaller village-size enclaves of 50 to

500 people. The area was densely populated but loosely organized. The people did not have military traditions or warrior societies like the Plains tribes. They were unprepared for what came next.

California was part of Mexico until 1848. More than 300,000 Americans showed up between 1849 and 1854, and there was yet no government, no police, no army, and no laws. The Compromise of 1850 fast-tracked California to statehood, but for years California was in a condition of anarchy, and the Indians paid a heavy price.

The gold rushers thought nothing of dispossessing or killing Indians to have a chance at riches. There were no negative consequences for killing natives. Entire villages were wiped out. Thousands of native families were forced into slavery. Enslavement of blacks in California was illegal, but there was a special slave code for Indians. In 1850, the newly formed state legislature passed the Act for the Government and Protection of Indians, which ironically stripped Indians of the right to testify in court and legalized the indentured servitude of Indians across the state. More than 4,000 Indian children were sold on the open market, with a premium paid for girls. Rape and murder of Indians became common.

By the time Indians had a chance to react, they were so overwhelmed that they were out of reasonable choices. Many submitted to slavery. Others fled farther inland. Some fought back. Nobody was left alone.

Gold rushers took full advantage of the absence of law enforcement and the placid disposition of the tribes. In 1850, American settlers Charles Stone and Andrew Kelsey enslaved hundreds of Pomo Indians. They used them to work prospecting operations, prepare food, do chores, and for sex. Eventually, the Pomo had enough and killed Stone and Kelsey. A local militia was raised and marched on the Pomo, slaughtering 130 of them at the Clear Lake Massacre.

The population of the Klamath River tribes in northern California was reduced by 75 percent by massacres and disease during the gold rush years. Conflict between Indians and miners led to the Klamath and Salmon River Indian War of 1855. The miners were supported by the U.S. Army, and tribal resistance was crushed.

ATSUGEWI BASKET **Sedentary and peaceful, most of the California tribes were skilled artisans, pottery makers, and basket makers.**

ISHI

◇◇◇◇◇◇◇◇◇◇◇◇◇◇◇◇◇◇◇◇◇◇◇◇◇◇◇◇◇◇◇◇◇◇◇◇

Ishi was the sole surviving member of the Yahi, an offshoot of the larger Yana tribe in California. During the gold rush genocide, most of the Yahi were killed. When Ishi was a small child, he and his family were attacked during the Three Knolls Massacre in 1865. The Yahi were driven into caves and slaughtered. Only 33 Yahi survived. Cattle ranchers killed more than half of those survivors.

With no sanctuary anywhere in the white world, Ishi and his family went into hiding. As most of their kin were killed or died off, Ishi took cover in the woods with his younger sister and mother until 1908. That year, surveyors stumbled upon their small family camp. Ishi and his sister disappeared into the trees. His aged mother was unable to run. It appears that she was knocked around by the surveyors and died shortly after they left. Ishi's sister never returned and her fate is unknown.

For the next four years, until he was 50 years old, Ishi hunted, fished, and gathered, living a solitary life in the Lassen Peak region. In 1911, he emerged from seclusion and made contact with the nonnative world that surrounded him. Alfred Kroeber, an anthropologist at the University of California, Berkeley, latched onto Ishi. He gave him a job as an intern at the university, but his real motive was to study Ishi as a subject—the last Yahi. Ishi died five years later and was the subject of sporadic books and films for the next several decades.

Some tribes were consolidated by treaty in 1855 at the conclusion of the conflict.

California tribes did their best to negotiate for protections. In 1851, they signed 18 separate land cession treaties, hoping that their concessions would translate into protection. The federal government acquired the land. The gold rushers rushed in. Then the state of California formally blocked ratification of the treaties and the Indians were not paid for their land. They lost the land, often received nothing for it, and at the same time had no meaningful protection.

CALIFORNIA GENOCIDE

The newly formed state of California encouraged the annihilation of the tribes. Peter Burnett, the first governor of California, made genocide official policy. The state government paid out more than $25,000 in bounties for Indian scalps during the gold rush years. Bounties were collected at different prices for men, women, and children. Indian killers had to produce scalps from the slain Indians to collect the money. Some miners and bounty hunters killed 50 Indians a day. Local ordinances supported genocide against Indians as well. In 1855, Shasta, California, offered a five-dollar bounty for each severed Indian head produced. In 1863, Honey Lake offered a local bounty on Indians, paid when hunters produced Indian scalps.

In northern California, prospectors and local militia attacked the Yana tribes, including the Yahi, driving tribe members into caves and massacring men, women, elders, and children. After sustained and relentless campaigns against them, the Yahi were exterminated. Ishi, the last Yahi, died in 1916. He was the sole survivor of the genocidal gold rush campaigns directed at his tribe. He eventually came out of the woods and shared his story in the twilight of his life. The Yahi never raided white settlements, committed atrocities or murders, and had no organized resistance movement. They simply had the misfortune of living on land coveted by whites in California during the gold rush years.

In 1852, Wintu Indians killed a miner in self-defense in Trinity County in northern California. The local sheriff, William H. Dixon, gathered a posse of 70 men. Instead of apprehending the person who killed a white man, he led an attack on a completely different Wintu village, killing every single man, woman, and child, except for three small children—more than 150 people died in the Bridge Gulch Massacre.

Genocidal gold rush campaigns were ubiquitous between 1849 and 1855. After that, they waned in frequency but not intensity. In 1860, 188 Wiyot were massacred at Humboldt Bay by a white civilian militia. They timed their attack to take place when the men were away from the villages to hunt. Without resistance, they slaughtered the women, children,

ROCK ART Chumash, Salinan, and Yokuts tribes developed sophisticated social, political, and artistic traditions, as evidenced in these rock art paintings at Carrizo Plain, but the gold rush desecrated many sacred places.

and elders. The attack was so senseless and brutal that a local newspaper reporter described the event without the customary accolades usually printed about Indian massacres in the region. The reporter who wrote the story was forced to leave town.

Many gold rushers derisively referred to Indians in northern and central California as diggers because they gathered roots for food. Some of the gold rush newspaper headlines give a good sense of what was happening: "Good Haul of Diggers," "38 Bucks Killed," "40 Squaws and Children Taken," "Band Exterminated."

GOLD RUSH LEGACY

When the gold rush ended, 24.3 million ounces had been extracted, worth $10 billion. Many areas still feel the ecological damage today. Vast amounts of mercury were used in gold processing. The poison cascaded through the ecosystems and remains in the water in many places. The gold rush populated California with white Americans and depopulated many areas of the state of Indians. The pre–gold rush Indian population in California was estimated as high as a million people. By 1890, it was down to 20,000.

The gold rush remains a celebrated historical event in California. It is taught in schools as the story of brave explorers, prospectors, and businessmen building the great state of California. The San Francisco professional football team is named the 49ers. The great seal for the state of California displays the word "eureka" — "I have found it!" —as its motto. Although California prides itself on being a progressive state in environmental law and educational opportunity, most Californians and other Americans are uneducated about the impact of the gold rush on tribal peoples. America's treatment of the Indian is a story of many different betrayals, misunderstandings, tragedies, and violence. But California saw some of the most pervasive acts of genocide in American history. ∎

YOKUTS FISHERMAN The Yokuts, whose homeland is in central California, struggled during the rush as their self-sufficiency was challenged by land loss and conflict.

YUMA WAR

BLOOD IN THE SAND

The Quechan, or Yuma, Indians held a strategically important territory along the Gila and Colorado Rivers at the present-day Arizona-California border. Although the Quechan villages were widely dispersed and relatively small, with around 250 people each, the people resisted early Spanish efforts to impose slave-labor missions on their communities. They fought the Spanish army in 1781, killing 55 Spaniards and capturing 75. Quechan territory was on the fringe of Spanish control and the empire backed away rather than fight it out. The tribe held unchallenged control over their homeland until the early American period.

When gold was discovered in California in 1848, settlers streamed across Quechan land. The

FORT YUMA After the Quechans killed bounty hunter John J. Glanton and most of his gang, the tribe defeated a California militia sent to punish them, prompting the federal government to intervene by building Fort Yuma.

tribe was clever and powerful enough to establish and command the only ferry crossing of the Colorado River. They made a small fortune in ferry fees. Then, in 1850, John J. Glanton, a famous bounty hunter who was paid by the scalp for Indian kills, came to Quechan territory. Glanton and 12 accomplices attacked the ferry station, killing several Quechan Indians and taking control of the ferry. They started collecting the fees, then killing and robbing both white and native ferry crossers. The Quechan rallied warriors and retook the ferry, killing nine of Glanton's gang.

In response, even though Glanton was a criminal who had murdered whites as well as Indians, the state of California raised a militia to punish the Quechan. It was the state's first formal military operation. Because prospecting was so feverish, the government had to pay soldiers a steep six dollars a day to join the militia. At $113,000, the cost of the operation nearly bankrupted the state. The Quechan conducted a guerrilla war against the militia, keeping the soldiers bewildered and besieged for 30 days. The state eventually called off the expedition because of the expense.

After repeated appeals from California for federal intervention, the U.S. Army sent engineers and 100 men from the 2nd Infantry to build Fort Yuma near Yuma Crossing and to protect all white travelers. The Quechan made peace with the new development, and it seemed that a major conflict had been avoided.

OUTBREAK

The Quechan tolerated the army presence in their land, but the gold rushers posed an entirely different problem. Thousands funneled through Yuma Crossing, and they took whatever they wanted from Indians. The Quechan were overwhelmed and soon became desperate, as the gold rushers took much of their food.

Tensions were rising in both the Quechan and white communities. In an 1851 attack on the Oatman party, a group of Mormons headed across the desert to California, Indians killed six whites and abducted two girls, Mary Ann and Olive Oatman. The captives were sold to the Mohave tribe. Mary Ann died in captivity, and Olive was ransomed back five years later. The Quechan had nothing to do with the attack, but white officials and civilians knew only that the attackers were Indians. The army did not intervene to stop white settler attacks on Indians, including Quechan, in response.

In October 1851, 800 Quechan warriors took up positions near Fort Yuma, and a conflict seemed likely. The Quechan attacked a supply train and killed four soldiers. The garrison at Fort Yuma was low on supplies and severely depleted from desertions as many soldiers ran off

> ### "TO THE HONOR OF THESE SAVAGES LET IT BE SAID, THEY NEVER OFFERED THE LEAST UNCHASTE ABUSE TO ME."
>
> OLIVE OATMAN

OLIVE OATMAN Captured as a teenager, Oatman lived five years with the Mohave, where she received her face tattoos.

to pan for gold. Most of the garrison moved several miles downstream to avoid a direct confrontation against such overwhelming odds. They marched west, attacking the Cahuilla on their way to San Diego. Resupplied and reinforced, they marched back to retake Fort Yuma, which the Quechans had since destroyed.

For the next two years, the U.S. Army garrison at Fort Yuma repeatedly tried to force engagements with the Quechan, but with little success. Every month or so the soldiers would ambush a small party, sometimes inflicting a few casualties, but the Quechan evaded large troop deployments and remained vigilant to avoid a serious attack on their camps. At the Battle of the Gila River in 1852, 150 Quechan and Cocopah clashed with the entire army command, but after firing volleys, they galloped away. Again, there were few casualties.

Aside from the initial attack at Fort Yuma at the start of the war, the Indians had not been the aggressors. Quechan chiefs made several offers to parley and negotiate a peace accord, including during the subsequent Colorado River expedition in 1852. To the credit of Captain Samuel P. Heintzelman, who commanded Fort Yuma, the U.S. Army did not prosecute a slash-and-burn campaign against the Quechan, hoping to preserve enough goodwill to reestablish peaceful relations.

In 1853, the Quechans offered to make a lasting peace. Heintzelman was ready to listen. The Indians had essentially outlasted American aggression, and a treaty that year ended the conflict. The Quechan made land-surrender concessions, but remained along the Colorado River in their original homeland. In 1884, a reservation was formalized for them—the Quechan Tribe of the Fort Yuma Indian Reservation, from which they somewhat expanded their landholdings. The army still occupies Quechan land in the form of the U.S. Army Yuma Proving Ground, located on the reservation. ∎

ROGUE RIVER WAR

FREEDOM FIGHT AMID THE GOLD RUSH

Oregon was immersed in violence from the arrival of the first white Americans. In 1834, the fur trapper Ewing Young arrived, and his party soon murdered several peaceful Indians, burying the bodies at their base camp. The bodies were discovered after Ewing's party left, and local natives retaliated the following year, killing four white trappers. The survivors of that attack murdered an Indian boy in 1837.

Over the next decade, white traffic to Oregon continued, escalating with increased travel on the Oregon Trail by wagon trains full of ranchers, farmers, miners, and other settlers. In 1846, Jesse Applegate cut a new side trail through the Rogue River Valley, diverting some of the travelers on the Oregon Trail route directly through densely occupied native lands. Migration reached a crescendo with the California gold rush and subsequent rushes in Oregon itself.

Isaac Stevens, governor of Washington, wanted to forcefully dispossess the Indians throughout the Northwest to make room for white migrants and settlers. White immigrants supported that goal. The U.S. Army was tasked with protecting whites while also preserving the peace. It proved an impossible task in the face of unrestrained white expansion into tribal land.

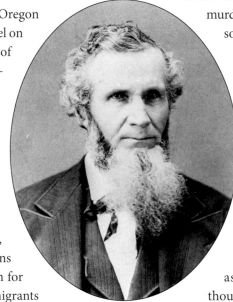

JOEL PALMER At the end of the Rogue River War, Palmer ordered the relocation of most tribes in the region to two reservations at Siletz and Grand Ronde. Some people marched 33 days to reach the new homes.

In 1851, miners and prospectors started hunting for gold in the Rogue River region, building sprawling camps at the site of present-day Jacksonville, Oregon. Indians raided the miner camps, and soon the government responded by stiffening military resolve and pushing for new treaties to gain land cessions and preserve peace. Several tribes, but not all, agreed to the Rogue River Treaty of 1853, which established the Table Rock Indian Reservation across the river from Fort Lane. Despite their many concessions, the Indians continued to be harassed, killed, and encroached upon by white settlers and miners.

ROGUE RIVER IN FLAMES

The Rogue River, or Tututni, Indians were not one unified political group, but rather many different tribes with elements of shared culture—Takelma, Shasta, Shasta Costa, Coquille, Dakubetede, Taltushtuntede, and Yugweeche. They also shared common geography and struggles, especially during the gold rush years, which brought them into a major military confrontation with white miners and settlers. In 1855, as the murder of Rogue River Indians continued unabated, some of the tribes were ready to fight back.

As tension built throughout the region, a small group of Rogue River Indians asked for and were offered military protection from settlers. They set up a camp next to Fort Lane, across the river from their main village. A mob of settlers stormed the camp and murdered 27 women and children. The garrison at the fort did nothing to prevent the attack.

After that, the tribes mobilized. In a series of raids, they killed 27 whites. With the numbers of victims now equal, the tribes asked for a peaceful settlement. By then, though, the white citizenry in the valley was in an uproar. No Indians would be safe for miles around. Because whites had been killed, the army garrison at Fort Lane joined the effort to hunt for hostile Indians.

Indian attacks in the Rogue River War came not as a massive assault, but rather as a series of simultaneous smaller raids and attacks in several places. A band of 23 Takelma were attacked by a settler mob at the start of the conflict. They retreated down the Rogue River, counterattacking whites at Gold Hill and Galice Creek. Other bands of Takelma and other Rogue River tribes rose up, and the conflict spread. White response was equally wide and far more forceful. The tiny Takelma band was ultimately crushed by a large force of 200 militia and armed settlers at Big Bend.

In separate fighting closer to the coast, 30 whites were killed at Gold Beach. At the Battle of Hungry Hill, 200 Indians took refuge at the top of a steep ravine. Only 30 of the band were warriors; the rest were women, children, and elders. They were attacked by 300 soldiers and militia. The ravine offered the band perfect cover as the troops funneled through a narrow opening to climb the hill and engage the Indians. Warriors inflicted 36 casualties on the American force with only a handful of tribal casualties.

By May 27, 1856, the Rogue River tribes were exhausted from running and fighting. Their villages had been largely destroyed, and their food supplies were low. Whites far outnumbered them now, and there was no reasonable way to gain anything by war other than a quick death. They agreed to surrender en masse at Fort Lane.

But the large garrison and the bands of armed miners and settlers spooked the Indians, some of whom believed the arranged surrender was a trick to kill them all. Another battle ensued, and the Indians ran again. A month later they surrendered unconditionally. Several tribes were consolidated on the Siletz Reservation and several more at Grand Ronde. Some endured a 33-day march to their new homes. At both Siletz and Grand Ronde, several tribes were not just consolidated but also politically confederated into those political entities. Those confederations compromised the independence of the tribes, but ancient distinctions and divisions made it hard to preserve tribal languages and also set up the tribes for internal tension and division for generations. ∎

TABLE ROCK This rock formation—after which the Table Rock Indian Reservation is named—rises behind the Rogue River, the site of fighting during the Rogue River War.

YAKAMA WAR

CONTAGION OF VIOLENCE IN THE NORTHWEST

Prospectors who encroached on Yakama land in what is now Washington State infuriated Chief Qualchan to the point of violence. (Yakama is the name of the tribe, but Yakima is the name of the nearby river and city.) In September 1855, Qualchan gathered a party of Yakama warriors from villages along the Columbia and Yakima Rivers, went to the prospector camp, and killed several white men. Hoping to avert a larger conflict, Indian agent Andrew Bolon traveled to Yakama country to parley with the chief. Other Yakamas warned Bolon to avoid direct contact as Qualchan was in no mood to see, much less negotiate with, white people

on his land. Bolon headed back to the Indian Agency, and on the way met another group of Yakamas, led by Qualchan's son Mosheel. He traveled with them for several miles. Unbeknownst to Bolon, throughout their ride the Yakamas debated whether to kill him. When the party halted, Mosheel and three other Yakamas set on Bolon with knives, killing him.

Qualchan knew a war was likely and the Yakama probably would not prevail. He sent word that he would turn his son over to authorities for murder to prevent war, but his efforts came too late. Major Granville O. Haller was given command of an expeditionary force and set out against the Yakama.

YAKAMA CHALLENGE Qualchan sent a beaded spear to the U.S. Army via his wife. The chief meant it as an invitation to council, but the military read it as an act of defiance.

YAKAMA RESISTANCE

Haller's force marched to Yakama territory, but Yakama warriors led by Kamiakin preempted his attack, ambushing and defeating the U.S. Army, forcing the soldiers out of Yakama territory at the Battle of Toppenish Creek. The Yakama War had begun. Panic spread quickly through Washington and Oregon. Some of the neutral bands of Yakama, emboldened by the success at Toppenish, joined the fight.

Brigadier General Gabriel Rains assumed field command of 350 U.S. troops in Washington, soon reinforced by another 350 from Oregon. Qualchan was still trying to repair the damage he had caused and find a way to make peace, but the Americans were not willing and neither was Kamiakin, now the leader of the

YAKAMA LEADERSHIP **After the war, bands were separated so chiefs could not negotiate jointly. Mnainak, shown in 1910, was chief of the Skin village band at Celilo Falls.**

Yakama resistance. The Yakama had built stone breastworks in a fortified defensive position and anticipated being able to hold their stronghold indefinitely, even bringing their families inside the battlements for protection. Rains brought up an artillery battery and made short work of the stone fortifications. Kamiakin did not expect so many soldiers; he ordered the women and children to flee while his warriors delayed and diverted U.S. troops to cover their retreat. The chief engaged a reconnaissance squad and fled on horseback across the Yakima River.

Rains pursued the Yakama, who continued to ambush and skirmish with the soldiers to slow their progress. An Indian scout for the cavalry detachment, Cutmouth John, shot and killed a Yakama warrior—the only tribal casualty of the battle.

The violence soon spread to other tribes. The Oregon governor, George Law Curry, ordered his militia to attack the previously peaceful and neutral Walla Walla, Palouse, Cayuse, and Umatilla. Almost all the eastern Oregon tribes were now fighting the Americans. Leschi, a Nisqually chief in the Puget Sound region, rallied Nisqually, Muckleshoot, Puyallup, and Klickitat warriors to join the growing tribal resistance as well. U.S. troops fought tribes in the Seattle area and in eastern Oregon, as well as the Yakama along the Columbia and Yakima Rivers. Each of those theaters of conflict grew into separate, longer, regional Indian wars.

General John E. Wool came from California to assume command of military operations in the region in November 1855. He was furious with the governor for spreading the contagion of violence. He said, "But for the . . . barbarous

determination of the Oregonians to extermin[ate] its Indians, I would soon put an end to the Indian War. It is these shocking barbarities that gives us more trouble than all else and is constantly increasing the ranks of the hostiles." Washington governor Isaac Stevens tried to persuade U.S. military authorities to dismiss Wool, who resigned in protest before being fired. Stevens said, "The war shall be prosecuted until the last hostile Indian is exterminated."

Although the Yakama War began as a war with the Yakama, the fighting elsewhere in Washington and Oregon demanded most army attention. The Yakama had a reprieve from attacks in their territory and sent warriors to Seattle to assist the other tribes. Army operations intensified in several areas outside Yakama territory—to the west in Puget Sound and to the east in what is now Idaho, with the Coeur d'Alene. Governor Stevens and U.S. military officials inadvertently expanded the breadth and duration of the conflict. Soon U.S. troops occupied Snoqualmie Pass to prevent the Yakama from reinforcing other tribes.

Even though the Yakama were undefeated in major battles during the Yakama War, it became obvious the tribes were in trouble. The Coeur d'Alene and the Puget Sound tribes eventually lost major battles. Yakama chief Kamiakin retreated to British Columbia. Internal struggles in the territorial government of Washington hampered both war and peace efforts as Stevens declared martial law and arrested white citizens he thought were too friendly to Indians. When the fighting in other campaigns ended, the Yakama agreed to a new treaty that established a reservation for them near the city of Yakima. ■

PUGET SOUND WAR

TRIBAL ALLIANCE IN THE NORTHWEST

In 1854, the Treaty of Medicine Creek inflamed tribes in the Northwest, especially the Nisqually. The encroachment of white settlers and the violence regularly directed at tribal people had already stretched many tribes to the breaking point. Leschi, a Nisqually chief, was half Yakama, and at the forefront of an emerging alliance in the Puget Sound region. He refused to sign the treaty or sell Nisqually land. The Yakama War, which started in 1855, sparked a regionwide conflict that engulfed many tribes in what is now Washington and Oregon. Leschi, seizing upon the distraction of U.S. soldiers in the Yakama War, decided to make a move.

BATTLE OF SEATTLE Nisqually chief Leschi led an alliance of warriors from several tribes in a direct assault on Seattle, just three years after Washington Territory was carved out of Oregon.

In 1855, around 150 Nisqually, Muckleshoot, Puyallup, and Klickitat warriors rallied to Leschi's side and advanced on white settlements along the White River. In October 1855, they killed surveyors and then attacked three settler cabins, killing nine more people. A month later, Leschi's warriors clashed with a battalion of U.S. infantry and cavalry at White River. Tribal sharpshooters killed several soldiers who had tried to cross the river and march on Leschi's camp. Ultimately, the army was forced back, unable to penetrate the tribal defenses.

Lieutenant William Slaughter led another infantry unit against Leschi's force at White River at the end of November. Snipers again successfully

"BUT FOR THE . . . BARBAROUS DETERMINATION OF THE OREGONIANS TO EXTERMIN[ATE] ITS INDIANS, I WOULD SOON PUT AN END TO THE INDIAN WAR."

GENERAL JOHN E. WOOL

picked off army soldiers, slowing their advance. While camped at Brannan's Prairie on December 3, 1855, Nisqually snipers killed Slaughter himself, demoralizing the U.S. force, which immediately retreated.

SEATTLE AND LESCHI

Isaac Stevens, the territorial governor of Washington, repeatedly blundered with white civilians and Indians during the conflict. He arrested whites he thought were too friendly to Indians, sparking outrage and conflict with his own courts, and eventually leading him to declare martial law. He encouraged troops from Oregon when they attacked the neutral Walla Walla, Palouse, Cayuse, and Umatilla. The violence also engulfed the Coeur d'Alene. The U.S. Navy attacked Haida and Tlingit fishermen, inspiring raids by those tribes. In January 1856, instead of diffusing tensions, Stevens had inflamed them across the region. A massive multitribal alliance was ready for an all-out attack on Seattle.

Leschi assembled a large force of Nisqually, Puyallup, and Klickitat warriors, reinforced by Walla Walla and Yakama Indians. Two tribal scouts infiltrated defenses for the settlement and signaled the tribal force to commence the attack. Hundreds of frightened civilians fled to blockhouses for protection as warriors stormed the city. They killed two civilians when the naval ship U.S.S. *Decatur,* anchored in the harbor nearby, opened an artillery bombardment, killing 28 Indian attackers. Leschi withdrew his force.

Although Leschi had aborted the attack on Seattle, he remained undefeated in the field. Snoqualmie warriors, allied with the Americans, assaulted Leschi's camp during the winter, inflicting significant casualties in several hours of fighting. Ultimately, the Snoqualmie ran out of ammunition, and again Leschi was controlling the time and place of conflict in the Puget Sound War.

As the U.S. Army began building new forts and sending more troops to the territory, Leschi provided fewer provocations and ultimately tried to broker a peace. Instead of accepting his peaceful overtures, officials arrested him and tried him for murder. Leschi's defense was that he was a lawful combatant in a war with the United States and not a U.S. citizen killing other citizens. He was released because of a hung jury, but rearrested, retried, and hanged. The U.S. Army refused to allow the hanging on military property because it considered him a lawful combatant rather than a criminal. The tribes were forced onto reservations after Leschi's death. More land cessions and then allotment further eroded the land base for most of them. ∎

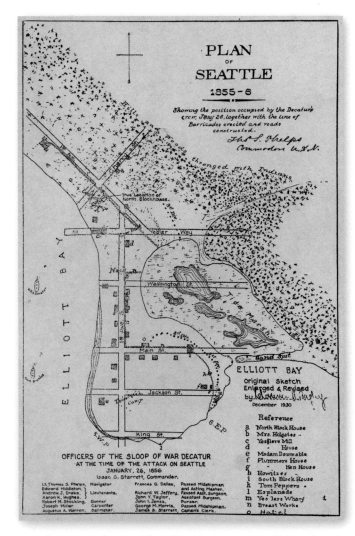

DEFENDING SEATTLE **The military response to the tribal attack came by land and sea, as seen in these naval deployments in Elliott Bay.**

COCHISE AND THE APACHE GUERRILLA WARS
TROUBLE AT APACHE PASS

The Apache had been at war with Spain for generations; when Mexico gained independence in 1821, the Mexicans became the enemy. The Apache were a large group of independent bands. Among those, the Chokonen band of Chiricahua Apache were one of the most resistant to Spanish and Mexican rule and the most successful on the warpath. They fought off their enemies and maintained exclusive control of their lands in the Sonora district, including the jagged Dragoon Mountains. Cochise, born around 1804, grew up in the midst of the fighting. His father was killed by Mexicans, strengthening Cochise's determination and propelling him to leadership of the Chokonen band. Cochise himself was captured by Mexicans in 1848, but was ransomed back for a dozen Mexican captives.

When the United States went to war with Mexico in 1846, Cochise welcomed the idea of white Americans killing his Mexican enemies. He stayed out of the conflict, but occasionally supplied American troops with firewood and other supplies. After the Mexican-American War ended in 1848, the United States tried to assert control over the Southwest, even though the Apache had never surrendered land and remained undefeated in battle. As Americans came to the edges of Chiricahua lands to settle, Cochise left them alone, but tensions were brewing.

FORT BOWIE Built in 1864 Fort Bowie in southeastern Arizona was a staging ground for the epic American campaigns against Cochise and later against Naiche and Geronimo.

In 1861, a raiding party from the Coyotero Apache killed American cattle and kidnapped a rancher's son. Although Cochise had nothing to do with the raid, U.S. Army Lieutenant George Bascom blamed him. The chief came to Bascom's camp at the edge of the Dragoon Mountains to parley and explain his peaceful intentions and innocence, but was arrested. He slashed the army tent with his knife and escaped. Bascom captured some of Cochise's relatives afterward, so Cochise started raiding and captured white Americans to exchange for his family. Bascom, edgy and undiplomatic, panicked and killed his hostages, so Cochise retaliated by killing his. Brutal frontier warfare broke out for another dozen years.

COCHISE The Chiricahua Apache chief led the most unified resistance to American control in the many years of the Apache Wars.

DRAGOON SPRINGS AND APACHE PASS

Cochise worked closely with his father-in-law, Mangas Coloradas, and other Chiricahua chiefs to stage repeated raids on anyone encroaching on Chiricahua lands. They fought Mexico, the United States, and the Confederacy throughout the campaign. Apache raids were so successful that some border towns were completely abandoned, others burned to the ground, and almost all had significant casualties and captives taken from their communities. Hundreds of Mexicans, Americans, and Apaches died in the fighting. U.S. Generals George Crook and then Nelson Miles eventually recruited other Apache to learn how to adapt to war in the rugged and arid Southwest. Until then, the Mexicans and Americans were receiving far more punishment than they inflicted on the Apache.

In 1862, Cochise led 100 Chiricahua against a Confederate supply train carrying Union prisoners at the Battle of Dragoon Springs, killing four and capturing a herd of horses and other livestock. Cochise and Mangas Coloradas led 500 Chiricahua in a prolonged battle with American forces under General James H. Carleton at the Battle of Apache Pass. Carleton essentially stumbled into the Apache stronghold on his way to New Mexico, forcing a rare direct conflict with the Apache, who preferred to raid and run. U.S. forces used a caisson-mounted artillery battery with impressive effect, marking the first time the Apache had experienced artillery fire.

In subsequent battles, the Apache under Cochise held their ground. Encounters grew more frequent, and the Chiricahua pulled some of their villages deeper into the Dragoons. Throughout all the fighting, Cochise kept one lifelong white friend, Tom Jeffords, who had been an army scout. In 1872, Jeffords helped American officials persuade Cochise to sign a peace treaty and relocate to a reservation, with Jeffords serving as Indian agent. Cochise died there of natural causes in 1874. ■

MANGAS COLORADAS

Mangas Coloradas was a Mimbreño Apache chief and father-in-law to both Chiricahua chief Cochise and Mimbreño chief Victorio. He was six feet six inches tall, an imposing figure in both council and war. In 1835, with Mexico offering a national bounty on Apache scalps, Mangas led Apache resistance. He made peace and even signed a peace treaty with the Americans during the Mexican-American War. As America tried to assert dominance over the Southwest, the peace was tested. Unprovoked attacks by miners on tribal camps and villages escalated in 1860, and then were compounded by the Bascom affair in 1861, in which Cochise was captured during a peaceful parley.

Cochise and Mangas allied their bands in 1861, and soon they had Geronimo, Juh, and Victorio fighting along with them in a series of devastating raids. Mangas was shot in the chest in one of those raids, but recovered, and made a serious effort at peace. He traveled to Fort McLane, New Mexico, in 1862. Holding up a white flag of truce, Mangas was invited into the fort by Brigadier General Joseph R. West.

West then told his soldiers, "Men, that old murderer has got away from every soldier command and has left a trail of blood for 500 miles on the old stage line. I want him dead tomorrow morning. Do you understand? I want him dead." Mangas was tied down that night, poked with red-hot bayonets, and tortured for hours. Then the soldiers killed him. They chopped off his head, boiled it, and sent it to the Smithsonian. It has yet to be returned.

OWENS VALLEY WAR
PAIUTE RESISTANCE IN THE MOUNTAINS

Human nature was at the heart of the Indian wars, but Mother Nature triggered the conflict in Owens Valley, California. The winter of 1861–62 was uncommonly harsh, with record snowfall. The brutal weather usually would have been manageable for the Paiute, who had lived in the valley east of the Sierra Nevada for centuries. It came, though, right after a surge in white mining and cattle-ranching activity. Local plants had been grazed down to nothing, then deluged by snow. Wildlife were unable to eat because of the intense cattle grazing, and so migrated out of the valley. The Paiute, who had ceded no land to the miners and ranchers, were on the brink of starvation. Some raided mining camps and ranches for food, killing cattle, and inciting a violent backlash that quickly escalated out of control.

Lieutenant Colonel George S. Evans was given command of three companies of the California Volunteers out of Camp Latham. He marched to Owens Valley at the request of white settlers to provide protection. Owens Valley sits close to the California-Nevada border, and Nevada also began to mobilize troops.

The ranks of local militia and civilian posses also swelled. Settler Charles Anderson gathered one such posse and raided a Paiute camp at Alabama Hills. The Paiute had been concentrating on food raids, but with the lives of their people in danger, they escalated their attacks and shifted focus. The Paiute threatened Putnam's Trading Post and scared the settlers who had congregated there out of fear of reprisals after the Anderson raid. Evans made it to the valley and skirmished with Paiute warriors, who quickly ran away.

At the Battle of Bishop Creek two days later, tribal resistance stiffened and grew. The Paiute continued to hold their own, attacking from elevated positions in guerrilla warfare, with success at the Battle of Mayfield Canyon. Evans depleted his supplies feeding both his troops and the white settlers, who were short of food due to the hard winter. Evans ordered a retreat and advised settlers to herd their cattle out of Owens Valley, leaving the land to the Paiute.

Most settlers and miners heeded his advice. Tribes raided isolated mining camps to chase them out of the valley, too. In 1862, the Paiute agreed to parley and reached a peace agreement in October. The tribes asked for a garrison of soldiers to protect them from settlers, ranchers, and miners. Some Paiute leaders, including Joaquin Jim, refused to sign the peace accord.

Evans focused on building Camp Babbitt, but hostilities flared again. Miners continued to attack Indians and, in response, Indians resumed raiding, killing four miners at Big Pine Creek. The cavalry again went into the field against the Paiute. In spring of 1863, they engaged Paiute warriors at the Battle of Black Rocks, the Battle of Alabama Hills, and the Battle of Big Pine Creek. The Paiute had dictated the time and place of engagements for all conflicts up to this point, but Captain Moses A. McLaughlin, in charge of a detachment of the 2nd Cavalry, soon introduced new tactics, with new results.

KEYESVILLE MASSACRE AND THE FINAL CAMPAIGN
On April 19, 1863, McLaughlin led U.S. troops on a long foray for hostile Indians. He stumbled upon a

SHOSHONE CAMP **Although the Owens Valley War first involved the Paiute, the California 2nd Cavalry soon attacked other tribes, including the Shoshone.**

OWENS VALLEY Home to the Paiute for centuries, Owens Valley was rich in minerals and lush grass, luring miners and ranchers. The Paiute fought back during several years of conflict in the Owens Valley War.

camp of Paiute and Tübatulabal (a Shoshone offshoot) who offered no resistance and did not run. Only a few bands of Paiute had been raiding, and the Indians in the camp felt they had nothing to fear. McLaughlin lined up the men and then, according to his report, "The boys and old men I sent back to their camps, and the others, to the number of thirty-five, for whom no one could vouch, were either shot or sabered. Their only chance for life being their fleetness, but none escaped, though many of them fought well with knives, sticks, stones, and clubs. This extreme punishment, though I regret it, was necessary."

McLaughlin then changed tactics. Instead of chasing the Indians up steep ravines and mountain passes, he sent his units up the mountains at night and attacked tribal camps from higher elevations, chasing the Indians down into the valley, taking advantage of elevation, initiative, and terrain. He emphasized destroying tribal food supplies and taking captives to interrogate for intelligence. With new information, he pressed attacks on the Paiute, but also the Tübatulabal, Kawaiisu, and Shoshone, killing two or three Indians every day during the 1863 spring campaign.

Reeling from the losses, many of the Paiute captives agreed to search out other bands and bring them in to surrender in May 1863. By July, more than 1,000 Paiute had surrendered. Eventually they moved to a new reservation.

Almost overnight, Owens Valley filled back up with white miners and cattlemen. Even though most Paiute had surrendered, Joaquin Jim fought on. His band withered to only 50 by the end of the conflict, but from 1863–67 they were free. The cavalry continued to pursue them even though the overwhelming majority of the tribe was on the reservation by 1863. At engagements at Owens Lake and at Rainy Spring Canyon on March 12, 1867, the resistance was crushed and the war came to an end. ■

BANNOCK FAMILY The Bannock were destitute when first settled at Fort Hall.
In 1878, they left the reservation in search of food, triggering the Bannock War.

BANNOCK WAR
DESPERATION ON THE SNAKE RIVER PLAIN

The Bannock are a band of Northern Paiute who moved deep into Idaho's Snake River Plain in the late 1700s, where they acquired horses from the Shoshone who lived nearby. The Oregon Trail and other westward travel routes brought white cattle ranchers and miners to their lands. They tried to accommodate the arrivals at first, engaging in fur trading and pursuing diplomatic solutions to the problems that came with settlers intent on dispossessing the inhabitants. By 1868, the Bannock signed a treaty that called for their relocation to a new reservation in eastern Idaho, called Fort Hall. By 1869, most Bannock had relocated there.

Fort Hall was a sizable but desolate place. The reservation was 1.8 million acres, a fraction of their original territory. It did not produce enough food for the Bannock. The tribe descended into abject poverty. The people received little help from the U.S. government and chafed under the reservation controls.

In 1877, American officials in Idaho were on alert as the Nez Perce War played out in the region. Their fears extended even to tribal communities like Fort Hall, far removed from the conflict zone. Indian agents and U.S. Army officials tightened controls at Fort Hall, further restricting movement off the reservation and managing most aspects of political and economic life.

Tensions mounted at Fort Hall in 1878. One of the Fort Hall Indians killed two teamsters. The government insisted that tribal leaders bring him to white authorities for punishment even though tribal customs required that the guilty party make restitution through a tribal council. They refused. Soon after that, another murder was treated the same way and the Indian agent took matters into his own hands, sending troops to look for the perpetrators. Between government control and near starvation conditions, many of the Bannock had reached the limits of their tolerance. In June, Chief Buffalo Horn led most of the Bannock off the reservation.

CAMAS PRAIRIE

Buffalo Horn brought the people to Camas Prairie, between present-day Mountain Home and Fairfield, Idaho, and set up camp. He sent men to hunt buffalo, antelope, deer, and small game. An attempt at trade with local cowboys erupted in fighting, and two cowboys were killed.

Brigadier General Oliver O. Howard marched against the Bannock. The cavalry charged into the camp, forcing the Bannock to retreat into the Craters of the Moon lava beds near Camas Prairie. They moved down the Snake River Valley to try to connect with their Paiute cousins.

BANNOCK CHIEFS The Bannock chiefs struggled through the course of the conflict. Both Buffalo Horn and his successor Egan were killed in battle.

The Bannock raided white settlements at Glenns Ferry and King Hill. In July, at Silver City, local militia charged into the Bannock camp, firing rifles and handguns. Two militiamen were killed, as were several Bannock, including Chief Buffalo Horn. In a quick tribal council, the warrior Egan was selected as chief. The Bannock connected with other Paiute groups, but they remained on the run.

CRESCENT CITY AND BUTTER CREEK

As the Bannock moved west, they fought with soldiers and militia at Crescent City and Butter Creek. A neighboring tribe, the Umatilla, were terrified they would be blamed for depredations. They parleyed with the army and sent their warriors against the Bannock. Chief Egan died fighting a mixed force of soldiers, militia, and Umatilla scouts. He was beheaded, and the morale of the Bannock fighters faltered.

The Bannock sued for peace, and many returned to Fort Hall. Another mixed group of 500 Bannock and Paiute were sent to the Malheur Reservation in what is now eastern Oregon and northern Nevada and then onto the Yakama Reservation in Washington. Malheur was closed and the land opened to white settlement. In 1886, many Bannock at Yakama were relocated to the Shoshone-Paiute Reservation at Duck Valley, on the Idaho-Nevada border near Riddle, Idaho. ∎

Coeur d'Alene War

FROM PINE CREEK TO FOUR LAKES

While the Yakama War raged, from 1855 to 1858, conflict spread out from Yakama country throughout the Northwest and Plateau. U.S. troops attacked previously neutral tribes in their effort to crush the Yakama, igniting the Puget Sound War, which included a direct attack on the city of Seattle by a large multitribal force. To the east of Yakama lands, the Coeur d'Alene, Spokane, Palouse (Palus), and Northern Paiute rose up in eastern Washington and Idaho in a regional event often called the Coeur d'Alene War.

HUSH-LOW, PALOUSE.

PALOUSE CHIEF The Palouse were part of the alliance that defeated U.S. troops at the Battle of Pine Creek at the start of the Coeur d'Alene War.

The Coeur d'Alene people tried to isolate themselves from whites during early white settlement of the Plateau. After the Oregon Trail opened in 1842, they avoided conflict and even interaction as much as possible. The gold rush of 1849 brought thousands of new travelers and prospectors to the region. By the time the Yakama War started in 1855, it was clear that isolation would never last. Thousands of squatters came into Coeur d'Alene land, and tribal leaders worried that the newcomers would simply take all their territory and the tribe would have no land and no protection left. They had yet to sign a treaty with the United States or establish a reservation.

The Coeur d'Alene chiefs told American officials that the Snake River was the edge of their territory and anyone who crossed it would be considered hostile to the tribe. They also said they wanted to make a treaty and clearly define their tribal lands to avoid misunderstandings, as well as to protect their territory from further encroachment. Two events precipitated hostilities. First, Isaac Stevens, who was the governor of Washington territory, left for Washington, D.C., in 1857 to serve as the territory's delegate to Congress, before initiating the requested treaty talks. That sparked fear that the whites had no intention of honoring Coeur d'Alene land rights. Second, the trespassers and squatters kept coming to tribal lands. Some of the young warriors intended to enforce the council's decision to consider trespassers as hostile to the tribe and thus subject to attack.

PINE CREEK AND FOUR LAKES

In 1858, a miner was killed near Spokane by unidentified Indians. Many whites had already died in the Puget Sound and Yakama Wars, but this was beyond the range for most of the conflicts in the region. Colonel Edward Steptoe was given command of a cavalry detachment of 159 men. He marched toward the Colville area, worried that the previously helpful Nez Perce and Spokane Indians seemed unwilling to assist his crossing of the Snake River. The Coeur d'Alene viewed the crossing as a hostile act. They assembled warriors, soon aided by the Spokane, Palouse, and even some Yakama Indians. More than 1,000 warriors had gathered

WALLA WALLA TREATY Nez Perce Indians arrive for the Walla Walla Council to negotiate a treaty in May 1855.

when the chiefs invited Steptoe to parley. They gave him a chance to turn his force around and head back to Fort Walla Walla. Steptoe agreed to retreat, but once he had his column moving west, one of the Coeur d'Alene warriors fired at the troops. The soldiers returned fire and the entire tribal force rushed to join the engagement in the Battle of Pine Creek. The Indians so vastly outnumbered Steptoe's detachment that he had to engage in a fighting retreat, eventually escaping in the middle of the night and pulling his forces back to Fort Walla Walla.

General Newman S. Clarke, already preoccupied with fallout from the Yakama War, sent Colonel George Wright back to Coeur d'Alene country with a much larger detachment of 601 cavalry troops, under orders to subjugate and punish the resistance. Wright's detachment was equipped with Springfield Model 1855 rifles, which were accurate up to 500 yards. Most of the Coeur d'Alene, Palouse, Spokane, and Yakama had bows, lances, and some smoothbore muskets accurate up to 100 yards.

In the Battle of Four Lakes, Wright's soldiers clashed with about 500 warriors from the Coeur d'Alene alliance. The new rifles proved incredibly effective as U.S. soldiers assumed covered positions and sniped at warriors from great distances. When the Indians tried to assault in a coup de main, the long-range rifles collapsed their lines before they could come close to the soldiers. The Indians retreated with heavy casualties, then watched in horror as Wright led U.S. troops up the river valley, capturing 800 Indian ponies. Wright kept 100 of the best horses for the army herd and massacred the rest, leaving

their bones to bleach in the sun. The destruction of the horse herds erased a major source of wealth for the tribes, reduced their mobility, and limited their effectiveness in hunting and war.

The army proceeded with a scorched-earth military campaign directed at the Plateau tribes. Villages were looted and most of the food stores destroyed. Warriors tried to rally resistance at the Battle of Spokane Plains, but were again defeated. Wright imposed harsh conditions when the tribes were ready to surrender. They had to allow whites to travel through tribal lands unmolested, surrender land and consolidate on reservations, and also to surrender any resistance leaders. Twenty-three chiefs from the alliance were surrendered, including a prominent Yakama chief named Qualchan. All were hanged.

The Plateau gold rush of 1860–63 brought even more settlers and miners. In 1873, an executive order reduced Coeur d'Alene land to 600,000 acres. Later, in 1894, the tribe was forced to cede a strip to accommodate the Washington and Idaho Railway. The land loss was accompanied by heavy government control, food shortages, and poverty. ∎

JOHN TANNER ("THE FALCON")

Many tribes fought back against America's westward expansion. Throughout the fighting, all parties took captives. Although most Indian captives were sold into slavery, killed, or died of disease, most surviving white captives were adopted into tribes. Some spent their lives in native communities. Some of those were rescued, then stunned the broader white world when they returned to the tribes where they grew up. Once in a great while, a captive grew up to be a bicultural bridge between the white world and the native world.

John Tanner was such a case. Born around 1780 in Virginia, he moved west with his parents during the initial pioneer push into the Ohio River Valley. Captured around age 10 by the Shawnee, Tanner was later adopted by an Ojibwe family and spent decades with them, becoming a monolingual speaker of the tribal language until relearning English late in life. He traveled farther west with the Ojibwe as their territory expanded during their conflict with the Dakota. He spent much of his life on the Plains and in the Great Lakes. Tanner's 30 years with the Ojibwe and other tribes equipped him to become a successful trader, guide, and bridge builder. His memoir, *The Narrative of John Tanner*, is considered a vital source of firsthand information about the Ojibwe and other tribes in the early 1800s.

YAVAPAI WARS
RAIDERS OF THE TONTO BASIN

The Yavapai, although not as famous as the nearby Apache, fought just as hard and nearly as long against Mexican and American intrusions into their Arizona homeland. The Yavapai are part of the Yuman language family, related to the Havasupai and Hualapai, but lived more like the unrelated Apache, relying on hunting rather than farming. The Tonto Apache and Yavapai in particular had a parallel and then intertwined fate through the course of their conflict with the Americans in the Yavapai Wars.

The Yavapai fended off Spanish and Mexican aggressors for centuries. When the California gold rush began, the western Yavapai bands helped the Quechan defend their Colorado River ferry crossing during the Yuma War in 1852. Yavapai-American conflict escalated when gold was discovered on Yavapai land in 1863. Prospectors never asked tribes for permission when invading their land, and the Yavapai would be no exception. The Yavapai, like the Apache, treated American squatters and trespassers as they did the Mexican ones—they attacked them. In 1864, the governor of Arizona declared all Yavapai to be hostile and called for the tribe's removal. U.S. forces in Arizona had their hands full with concurrent Apache conflicts, and for several years the Yavapai held their ground in light skirmishes and raids.

YAVAPAI The Yavapai, who lived near the Mexican border in what is now Arizona, fought just as intensely and nearly as long as the Apache in the wars for the Southwest.

CAMP GRANT MASSACRE
On April 30, 1871, American and Mexican civilians and Tohono O'odham Indians formed a vigilante force of around 100 and attacked an Apache village in the Aravaipa Canyon. Most of the Apache men were hunting, and the attackers slaughtered 144 residents. All but eight of the bodies were identified as women and children. Another 29 children were captured and sold into slavery in Mexico. The attack was so brutal that some participants were charged with murder, but were acquitted. The surviving Apache from that band came to Yavapai country, and the new arrivals both strengthened the Yavapai resistance and added to its ferocity.

A brutal military campaign ensued, with General George Crook commanding American forces against the Yavapai and Apache. Yavapai raids forced the Americans to close the road between Prescott and Fort Mohave. Yavapai warriors also attacked stagecoaches on the La Paz road, killing six travelers in one attack. That sparked more intense, focused American military responses.

SAN CARLOS
The Yavapai and Tonto Apache reeled from sustained losses in a war of attrition they could never win. In 1872, 76 Yavapai were killed when trapped in a cave while Crook's troops dropped boulders and fired repeatedly. In 1875, a large band of Yavapai agreed to move to San Carlos, 180 miles south of their homeland. In 1875, 1,500 Tonto Apache and Yavapai were forced to march to San Carlos in the winter, and nearly half died. San Carlos was inhospitable not only because of weather, but also because it consolidated the Yavapai with the Chiricahua Apache, who unlike the Tonto Apache had warred with the Yavapai. Other Yavapai bands were settled on reservations elsewhere in the region. The Fort McDowell Reservation was established in 1903. In 1910, one Yavapai band was granted land at Camp Verde and another at Middle Verde. The two merged at Camp Verde in 1937. Another band was established at the Yavapai Prescott Indian Reservation in 1935. ∎

CATOCTIN MINE The Yavapai were incessantly encroached
upon by miners (above), a major cause of the raids and war that followed.

BEAR RIVER MASSACRE

SHOSHONE DISASTER IN THE GREAT BASIN

T he Cache Valley on the present-day Idaho-Utah border was home to the Shoshone. The land abounded in game and furbearing animals, attracting, among others, famous mountain men Jim Bridger and Jedediah Smith. The region was late to be occupied by whites due to its remoteness, but the Oregon Trail, California Trail, and Salt Lake City (founded in 1847) were all close enough to set up the valley for a surge in white settlement when circumstances allowed.

By 1856, whites started to settle in Shoshone lands in the Cache Valley. There were no treaties and no permissions. As the settlers pushed aside the Shoshone from their prime village sites and hunting lands, it was only with great restraint that

ORRIN PORTER ROCKWELL **General Patrick E. Connor (mounted), Mormon scout Rockwell (waving his hat), and others who participated were praised for the massacre of the Shoshone at Bear River.**

the chiefs prevented a bloodbath. Conditions for the Shoshone deteriorated over time. In 1862, Utah's territorial superintendent of Indian affairs said, "The Indians have been in great numbers, in a starving and destitute condition."

As poverty, food shortages, and discontent grew, relationships with the people who had moved around them stoked resentment. In 1862, gold was discovered in Montana, and rushers came through the Cache Valley en route to the gold mines. Some accused a Shoshone chief's son of stealing a horse. Although he denied the charge and no evidence or witness was produced, local white settlers hanged the young man.

Shoshone warriors retaliated, killing woodcutters and travelers near Fort Hall. General

Patrick E. Connor marshaled the military response, leading the 3rd California Infantry into the area. He built Fort Douglas near Salt Lake City and patrolled the region, ready to respond to Indian attacks. Idaho, still part of Washington Territory, had been engulfed in wars since 1855, involving the Yakama, Paiute, Shoshone, and a dozen other tribes. Washington territorial militia reinforced Connor's detachment, as did the 2nd Cavalry from California.

Connor sent troops into the Cache to investigate reports of white captives among the Shoshone. They met a group of 20 Shoshone led by Bear Hunter, attacking first and asking questions later. Bear Hunter surrendered after a brief skirmish, promising to see whether anyone could locate white captives. The Shoshone turned over one white boy. The Indians said he was the son of a fur trapper who had been living with them, not a captive.

In December 1862, Connor again sent units into Shoshone lands to investigate reports of stolen livestock. Indians cut the ferry rope, and four of them were captured. Army officers threatened to kill them if the stolen livestock was not produced. Whether the Shoshone had never taken the livestock or had already eaten the cows is not known, but no livestock were returned. The army executed the four men by firing squad. That touched off a series of retaliatory raids by the Shoshone. They killed 2 freight haulers and 15 miners in separate incidents over the next week.

BEAR RIVER

Connor then prepared a punitive expedition against the Shoshone. He wanted to catch the Indians by surprise and inflict maximum casualties. His columns left in the middle of a wicked cold snap, with temperatures at 20 degrees below zero. The infantry marched by day, and the cavalry traveled by night to keep their advance secret. Connor abandoned the battalion's artillery because of the difficulty pulling through snowdrifts.

The Shoshone sent delegates to parley for peace. They felt they had successfully avenged

> "CONNOR IS DETERMINED TO EXTERMINATE THE INDIANS WHO HAVE BEEN KILLING THE EMIGRANTS ON THE ROUTE TO THE GOLD MINES."
>
> GEORGE A. SMITH

the latest execution of their young men, but they had received far more damage than they had caused, so they wanted to avoid further conflict. Because of their diplomatic outreach—and the frigid temperatures—the Shoshone did not expect an attack. On January 29, 1863, however, Connor's units converged on Bear Hunter's winter camp on the Bear River in Idaho. Most of the California 3rd Infantry and 2nd Cavalry were arrayed against the unsuspecting Shoshone. Connor ordered a direct frontal assault as soon as he found the camp, before all of his units had arrived. The first charge was unsuccessful, and most of the army's 21 dead and 46 wounded were hit in the early moments.

Connor regrouped and sent troops around the village to attack from multiple directions. The Shoshone, unable to escape, defended themselves as best they could. The accuracy of army rifle fire and the length of the attack weakened tribal resistance. The Shoshone ran out of ammunition. Many were trying to cast more bullets with lead molds when they were shot. They defended their families with axes and clubs, but the battle turned into a massacre.

Soldiers grabbed infants by the legs and dashed their heads against rocks. They burned all the shelters and raped the women, killing many afterward. Connor's field report indicated 246 Indians killed, 164 captured, and many others wounded. A civilian report after the event tallied 493 dead Indians. Although it is impossible to give a precise count, Connor had reason to understate the nature and number of deaths to avoid potential backlash or discipline.

Connor was hailed as a hero, promoted to brevet major general, and given command of U.S. troops in the Powder River expedition against the Lakota. Some Shoshone survivors converted to Mormonism and stayed in Cache Valley as part of a Mormon farming community. Most of the Cache Valley Shoshone were relocated to Fort Hall. Because they were a very large tribal group divided into many bands, the Shoshone had varied experiences in the treaty period. Today, there are Shoshone on more than a dozen reservations in the Great Basin and Plateau regions. ■

GENERAL PATRICK E. CONNOR
Promoted to brevet major general after the massacre, Connor went on to lead U.S. troops against the Lakota in the Powder River expedition.

SNAKE WAR

WINTER CAMPAIGNS ON THE PLATEAU

The Snake Indians were a loose alliance of several bands of northern Paiute, Bannock, and Shoshone who lived along the Snake River. Some of these bands fought the Americans prior to the Snake War and some fought again afterward in the Bannock War and other conflicts, but from 1864 to 1868, together they offered a formidable resistance and major challenge to America's dominance of the Plateau.

By 1864, the Great Basin and Plateau bristled with American soldiers. Years of conflict with more than a dozen tribes in the region had taught everyone hard lessons. Just because Americans thought it was their Manifest Destiny to spread from sea to sea did not mean that the people who had lived there for centuries before them would surrender their lives, livelihoods, and lands for nothing or without a fight. If the newcomers wanted to take the land against the will of the occupants, someone would have to die. For the tribes, these were impossible times. No strategy would preserve their lands, defend the lives of their loved ones, and protect the prosperity of their people. It was difficult to see the path of least damage when there were so few friends and so many takers.

Governments in California, Oregon, Washington, Idaho, Utah, and Nevada all watched the tribes warily as the first wave of conflict ebbed—the Cayuse War, Rogue River War, Yakama War, Puget Sound War, Coeur d'Alene War, Owens Valley War, and the Bear River Massacre. Some Snake Indians had participated in some of those engagements and campaigns, and all had friends and relatives who had perished fighting the Americans.

Prospectors opened new mines at Boise Basin and Owyhees in 1862 and 1863, escalating encroachment on Snake land and precipitating conflict. The Snake had no reservations, no promises, and no protections. They did not want to sell their land, although they were willing to make a treaty that protected what they had. Because the U.S. government was

SNAKE INDIANS Northern Paiute, Bannock, and Shoshone formed a formidable alliance against encroachment on their lands during the Snake War. The conflict claimed about 1,800 lives, making it one of the deadliest Indian wars.

unwilling to protect tribal land, the tribes raided and retaliated, stealing horses and livestock. Local miner Jeff Standifer raised a posse to fight the Indians. They couldn't force a major battle, but did locate a small band at Salmon River and wiped them out—men, women, and children. With this provocation, the Snake Indians rose up not just to raid and harass whites, but to fight for their lives. Casualties mounted along the Snake River frontier, and settlers across several states and territories pressed for military action.

MILITARY OPERATIONS

In 1865, California pushed other states and territories to provide better protection for stagecoach and foot traffic headed west. Soon, U.S. troops built a new fort, Camp Lyon, on Cow Creek, on what is now the Oregon-Idaho state line. Lieutenant Charles Hobart took charge of missions to scout for hostile Indians, protect white settlers and travelers, and recover horses and livestock taken in raids. The Snake Indians were smart enough to avoid direct clashes with mounted cavalry units, instead effectively raiding white settlements and occasionally engaging the army on their own terms.

The Snake skirmished with Hobart's force in a brief battle at Pilot Rock. Colonel George B. Currey encouraged the use of winter campaigns—a tactic intended to disrupt tribes at their most vulnerable, during the cold months when food was short. General George Crook soon adopted the tactic and employed it throughout the rest of the Snake War

GEORGE B. CURREY Colonel Currey fought the Snake Indians in winter to disrupt them at their most vulnerable.

and his campaigns against other tribes. It was brutally effective.

The Snake continued to raid mining camps, killing 94 Chinese laborers in one attack. The military response stiffened. Major Louis H. Marshall led a new detachment from Fort Boise. Because the Snake attacks until this point had been small raids, army commanders assumed that the Snake were tiny bands of nomadic Indians who lacked the capability to organize a major deployment or formidable defense. Marshall learned the hard way that the limited attacks and raids were an intentional tactic, and that the Snake could fight many kinds of battles.

In May 1866, at the Battle of Three Forks on the Owyhee River, Marshall tracked Snake Indians into the steep 800-foot-deep gorge, exchanging fire with them across the river. His troops struggled with the rugged terrain, lost their artillery trying to cross the river, and were ambushed as they clambered out on the other bank. Casualties were fairly low on both sides, but Marshall was forced into a hasty retreat. The tribal victory inspired a new round of raids—eight in the next month, continuing the attrition of white settlers and stealing another 120 horses and cattle.

The Snake continued to raid across a wide territory. Local posses dared to go on expeditions into Snake country, but usually ran into trouble. At Boulder Creek a local militia was surrounded and almost overwhelmed, relieved by Marshall and a contingent of troops from Camp Lyon only after a six-day siege. The Snake War was not going well for the Americans.

JEDEDIAH SMITH

Jedediah Smith—a fur trader, explorer, cartographer, and author—became the first white American to explore and document the land and peoples of the Great Basin, including the Snake River Valley. Smith initially came to the region as an employee of the American Fur Company in 1821. He was 22 years old.

In 1823, he led a trading cohort that fought the Arikara. Smith lost 13 men but was promoted. In 1824, Smith got another break that helped open paths west. Crow Indians drew

him a map on a buffalo hide. It detailed the South Pass in Wyoming, one of the two passes across the Continental Divide in the Rocky Mountains on the way to California.

Smith traveled across the Plateau and Great Basin after that, eventually receiving credit as discoverer of South Pass. He made two trips to California between 1826 and 1828. He traded thousands of pounds of beaver furs for a small fortune. In Oregon, traders rebuked Smith for attacking the usually friendly Umpqua.

As he continued his trading, Smith fought Indians along the way, attacking Blackfeet in 1829 and Comanches in 1831. But the Comanches were his last fight. He was lanced during battle and died at age 32. Smith's role in opening up the west and the Snake River country in particular was real, if sometimes inflated in romanticized retellings. But more important, in his decade of exploring and fighting, he embodied the ideals—good and bad—of early American settlers.

GENERAL CROOK'S CAMPAIGN

In 1866, experienced Civil War officer and Indian fighter George Crook was tapped to command U.S. military operations against the Snake. Crook immediately prepared a winter campaign, following the advice of George B. Currey. He marched down the California Trail and surprised a large group of Snake Indians at the ferry crossing of the Owyhee River. In a heated engagement, 60 Indians were killed and another 30 captured. This was one of the highest casualty counts for the tribes to date.

Crook went on to attack a Paiute village. He had his cavalry dismount and attack on foot. Once the Indians gave up their concealed positions to engage and advance, his troops fell back, then mounted their horses and caught the Indians in the open. That led to a decisive victory, and the recovery of some stolen horses. For two years, Crook pressed attacks on one village after another, pushing west in an unpredictable zigzag, guided by Indian scouts to targets of opportunity.

Crook skirted death in the winter of 1867. His force attacked the Paiute at Steens Mountain, Oregon, after his Indian scouts found a well-hidden camp. Crook planned to watch the battle from behind his lines, but his horse spooked and ran ahead of his men, straight through the Indian camp. Somehow, he was not hit, reinforcing his reputation among the rank and file.

Crook inflicted heavy casualties on the Paiute again at the Battle of Tearass Plain. Then he pushed into California, where he engaged Paiute, Modoc, and Pit River Shoshone Indians at the Battle of Infernal Caverns. The Snake had built a fortress out of lava rocks in an elevated position, with caverns behind them for cover. U.S. soldiers eventually scaled the cliffs and took the position with 20 casualties. The tribes fared better, but lost their stronghold.

The Snake War was one of the deadliest of the Indian wars. It resulted in about 1,800 combined Indian and white casualties—more than twice the combined casualty count of the Battle of the Little Bighorn. Weary from years of fighting, the Snake eventually agreed to peace talks with Crook. One band at a time, the Snake consented to give up the fight and come into the reservations. It was a hard adjustment for the tribes, who today occupy several reservations across their original homeland. ■

SNAKE RIVER Abounding in fish and wild game, the Snake River Valley was home to many tribes who fiercely protected their land during the Snake War.

LOWRIE WAR
RACIAL ROBIN HOOD

North Carolina's tribes were almost wiped out during the British colonial era. After the Tuscarora War, most of the surviving Tuscarora moved north and joined the Iroquois League. The Yamasee were crushed by the British. The Cherokee and Creek had tried to accommodate Europeans, but became targets for relocation during the American removal era. Throughout this period, there were survivors from several tribes—Cherokee, Tuscarora, Hatteras, Pamlico, and Croatan—who came together along the Lumber River in what is now Robeson Country, North Carolina. They came to be known as the Lumbee.

The Lumbee frequently adopted freed blacks into their community, and today the racial composition of the tribe is mixed Indian, black, and white. Exemplifying this evolving identity was a prominent young Lumbee man named Henry B. Lowrie (also spelled Lowry), who was born in about 1845. He was Tuscarora, white, and black. Although Lowrie was not a slave, life in North Carolina for any person of color before the end of slavery was a challenge. He was from a large family who made a living working as laborers and clerking in local stores.

The Civil War tore North Carolina apart. People of color struggled—fearful of reprisals from white neighbors, but ready to distinguish themselves when opportunities arose. In both Oklahoma and North Carolina, many Cherokee fought for the Confederacy. Some of the Lumbee did, too, although not in independent segregated units. Other Lumbee hid in the brambled swamps of Robeson County to avoid confrontation. Still others saw the Civil War as a chance to fight for the overthrow of race-based oppression.

In 1862–63, a yellow fever outbreak severely affected the population around Fort Fisher, a Confederate fort under construction in Lumbee lands. This led to labor shortages, and soon the Confederacy was doing what it did best—conscripting people of color as an unpaid labor force. Many Lumbee were forced to help build Fort Fisher near Wilmington, North Carolina.

UNION CHAPEL Cherokee, Tuscarora, Hatteras, Pamlico, and Croatan intermarried with blacks and whites in North Carolina to form the Lumbee. Pictured here is a Lumbee group at Union Chapel, North Carolina.

Lowrie became fed up with the heavy-handed practices of southern gentry. He was accused of aiding the Union, and fearing he would be hung, he ran for the swamps. From there he planned to do his part to undermine the Confederate war effort. He killed a white neighbor in 1864, and planned small raids on wealthy plantations. In 1865, in response to Lowrie's growing effect in the region, the Confederate Home Guard captured his father and brother, tied them to stakes, and

executed them. Lowrie reportedly watched the killings from the bushes nearby.

CONTAGION OF VIOLENCE

The murders of Lowrie's relatives inflamed many Lumbee, and soon Lowrie found himself leading a major resistance effort. As the Confederacy started to lose the Civil War, especially when General William T. Sherman's march through the South drew close, the Lowrie gang grew bolder. They focused on killing Confederate conscription officers and forced-labor gang organizers.

Henry led the gang with his brothers Steven and Thomas Lowrie. When Henry was married in 1865, he was arrested at his wedding, but filed through the bars of his jail cell and escaped. Although some viewed Lowrie as a criminal, others saw him as a racial Robin Hood—raiding high-class white southern gentry in support of the oppressed. Among others, Lowrie in 1870 killed John Taylor, presumed head of the local Ku Klux Klan.

In the postwar Reconstruction era, the North Carolina governor tried to crush the Lowrie gang. In 1869, he issued a $12,000 bounty on Henry Lowrie—dead or alive. In 1872, Lowrie robbed $28,000 from the local sheriff's safe, then disappeared. Rumors abounded that he escaped to South America, accidentally shot himself, or stayed in the area. But he was never seen again, and nobody ever collected the bounty on his head. In 1874, Steven Lowrie was killed, ending the Lowrie War. ∎

U.S. military presence. They took it upon themselves to try to acquire land from the Ute, make treaties, and establish reservations. None of those arrangements would ever be considered binding to the U.S. government, and misunderstandings often fueled conflict.

Frustrated by the continual encroachment of Mormon settlers, some Ute raided settlements to discourage squatting and to compensate for the damage to their food resources when the settlers scared off game. Some of the Shoshone bands responded the same way. Raids around Provo in 1850 have sometimes been called the Provo War, claiming at least a dozen lives among the white settlers there, and just as many Ute. A larger regional conflict, usually called the Walker War, caused more casualties on both sides. The Walker War raged from 1850 to 1855 and included raids and engagements at Fountain Green, Nephi, Manti, and Fillmore. John W. Gunnison gathered a militia and pursued the Ute. In a short battle, he and seven militia fighters were killed.

The Mormons tried to establish a reservation for the Indians at Twelve Mile Creek, but it lacked the provisions, protections, and enforcement of a bona fide U.S. government treaty and reservation process. The Mormons claimed the action legitimized their land claims, but raids and conflict continued in 1856. Weary of conflict but frustrated with the growth of the Mormon communities and escalating encroachment, the Ute settled into a troubled truce for several years.

ANTONGA BLACK HAWK WAR

From 1846 to 1890, 70,000 Mormon pioneers poured into Ute lands in the Great Basin. They soon outnumbered the Indians and had the full backing of the U.S. military. That the Mormons came to take tribal land and had no permission or land sale was irrelevant to the newcomers. That their arrival displaced the original inhabitants of the land and

UTE SADDLEBAG The Ute did not rely on horses to the extent the Plains tribes did, but nonetheless horses were cherished parts of the culture, as shown by this decorated saddlebag.

compromised their ability to get food was also of little consequence to them. The Ute were in a difficult position.

With so many whites coming to their land, the Ute had multiple issues: displacement, food shortages, disease, and violence. Smallpox swept through their villages in 1864. The Mormon effort to persuade the Ute to settle at Twelve Mile Creek was abandoned.

A prominent Ute chief named Sanpitch and his son, Antonga Black Hawk, led a major effort to regroup to resist the intrusion of whites in their land. The conflict is often called the Black Hawk War (not to be confused with the Sac and Fox war with the United States in Iowa, Illinois, and Wisconsin in 1832). By the end of that war in 1872, 16 bands of Ute as well as some Paiute, Navajo, and Apache bands had been drawn into the conflict. All told, there were more than 150 raids, skirmishes, and battles between the Indians and Mormon militia, sometimes supported by U.S. troops.

The 1863 massacre of hundreds of Shoshone at Bear River provided fresh evidence to the Ute of the malice of whites. Something had to be done. In 1865, Black Hawk led a series of raids that captured 2,000 horses and head of cattle and resulted in the death of

32 whites in Sanpete and Sevier Counties. The Mormons retaliated, slaughtering a village of women and children in what they called the Squaw Fight, because the men had been killed and they moved in to finish off the women; some fought back with knives, and others ran away.

In 1866, Chief Sanpitch was killed and Black Hawk was left to lead the resistance by himself. That same year, at Circleville, 26 Paiutes were captured. Two were shot trying to escape and the rest were bludgeoned, then their throats were slit. Three children ran away, and a little girl who was apprehended was bludgeoned to death. The boys were never recovered.

The previously neutral Uintah band of Ute entered the conflict after being attacked by Mormon militia in 1866. In 1870, Black Hawk died from tuberculosis. In 1872, the Ute inflicted their last casualty, as the tribe reeled from dramatic population decline. Some estimates are that as many as half of the Ute population died during the Black Hawk War from disease, conflict, exposure, and starvation.

WHITE RIVER

In 1879, the White River Ute fought a major battle with the U.S. Army. In an altercation at the Indian agency, the Ute killed Nathan Meeker, the U.S. Indian agent, and nine others. Major Thomas Thornburgh led 150 soldiers into Ute land, blundering two miles ahead of his supply train onto unceded Ute land. Ute warriors occupied excellent cover from elevated positions; when it seemed obvious that Thornburgh was coming to attack rather than parley, they opened fire, pinning U.S. troops in the open, and then flanked them. In the Battle of Milk Creek, as it was later called, Thornburgh was killed, then his next in command went down, and then the next-ranking officer. All told, 13 soldiers were killed and another 44 wounded. It took a week for reinforcements to arrive so the soldiers could retreat.

In 1881, a large troop deployment led the Ute to sign a new treaty rather than fight. The Colorado Utes were relocated from White River to the Uintah Reservation in the desert. In 1882, soldiers shot and killed the remaining White River chief and moved the rest of the Ute to the reservation. ■

MORMONS More than 70,000 Mormons poured into Ute lands in the Intermountain West from 1846 to 1890, eclipsing the tribal population and pushing them off the land.

MODOC WAR
BLOOD IN THE LAVA BEDS

The Modoc, who like their Klamath cousins are a small tribe from the Penutian language family, waged a long, bitter war for survival. The outcome nearly wiped them off the map. The tribe, who were from what is now the Oregon-California border region, followed a seasonal round of gathering, fishing, and hunting. Traffic over the Oregon Trail, especially during the gold rush, overwhelmed the Modoc. They avoided contact with miners and prospectors and made adaptations for protection and prosperity, acquiring European clothing and even adopting European names. In 1852, Modoc warriors got into an altercation with a wagon train en route to California and killed several settlers. An Oregon militia retaliated, killing 41 Modoc. Amazingly, the incident did not escalate.

In 1864, the Modoc still owned a substantial 5,000-square-mile territory. They were outnumbered and disempowered, and they watched other tribes succumb either voluntarily or by force and then move to small reservations. They signed a treaty in 1864 that required them to settle on the new Klamath Reservation. Reluctantly, the last of the Modoc came to the reservation in 1869. Although the Modoc and Klamath were linguistically related, they occasionally had been at war. The move was painful for the Modoc, who had to contend not only with poverty and the loss of their beloved homeland, but also with being minorities in a larger, sometimes hostile tribal community.

The impoverishment of the Modoc at Klamath exasperated Captain Jack, a prominent Modoc chief. He led a small entourage off the reservation to hunt and sometimes to steal food from white settlements. Troops were deployed to force his band back onto the reservation.

FROM LOST RIVER TO THE RESERVATION
In November 1872, Captain James Jackson led a contingent of soldiers to round up Captain Jack at his camp. The Modoc

SCARFACED CHARLEY A Captain Jack loyalist, Scarfaced Charley led the Modoc in their victory at the Battle of Sand Butte in 1873.

agreed to return to the reservation, but looked warily on the command to surrender weapons. Nonetheless, Captain Jack reluctantly complied and his men followed his lead. A Modoc warrior named Scarfaced Charley got into an argument with an army officer, who drew a pistol. Scarfaced Charley drew his pistol in turn and they both fired, but missed. Warriors jumped for their weapons and a battle ensued. Jackson reported eight soldier casualties. Five Indians were hit.

Captain Jack fled with his people and took refuge in the Tule Lake lava beds. He had 52 warriors, plus 100 women, children, and elders. Hooker Jim, another Modoc chief, led an independent small band. They were allied with Captain Jack, although they did not always act in concert. In a short time, hundreds of infantry, cavalry, and Indian scouts were deployed against the Modoc at the lava beds.

On January 17, 1873, U.S. troops descended on Captain Jack's stronghold. With 400 men, the army troops attacked the stronghold from two sides in a pincer move. Captain Jack was ready. From concealed and well-fortified positions, his warriors opened up on the advancing soldiers, suffering no casualties of their own, but killing 35 soldiers and wounding another 25. The army retreated.

The government found the lava beds unassailable, so tried to negotiate. Captain Jack held out, engaging parleys from February through April of 1873. He demanded a full pardon for all Modoc, plus permission to select their own reservation. The government would not concede those terms, insisting that all men who killed soldiers be tried for murder and everyone else be relocated to a reservation of the government's choosing.

On April 11, 1873, General Edward Canby came to yet another peace conference but was not willing to agree to any Modoc requests. He rose to leave and Modoc warriors jumped from behind the lava rocks and shot him and another member of the delegation. The army prepared for a second assault on the stronghold, this time with 675 soldiers. The battle lasted three days. The Modoc offered stiff resistance, killing several soldiers and wounding a dozen more. Two Modoc boys died trying to pull apart a cannonball. Soldiers eventually advanced along the shore of Tule Lake, cutting off access to the water. The Modoc disappeared through a secret crevice and fled the field.

The army pursued them. Scarfaced Charley led a group of 34 warriors at the Battle of Sand Butte, engaging a 67-man patrol column. The Modoc again sustained no casualties, but killed 23 soldiers and wounded another 19. The Modoc band had yet to lose a single engagement.

Modoc fortunes changed at the Battle of Dry Lake in May 1873. Warriors attacked an army camp, but were repelled. The Modoc retreated. In exchange for amnesty for himself and his band, Hooker Jim agreed to help track down Captain Jack.

Captain Jack surrendered in June. The Modoc leaders, rather than being treated as prisoners of war, were treated as criminals, tried for murder, and hanged. Captain Jack's band was absorbed into the Quapaw Agency in Oklahoma; other Modoc were confederated with the Klamath and Yahooskin in Oregon. ■

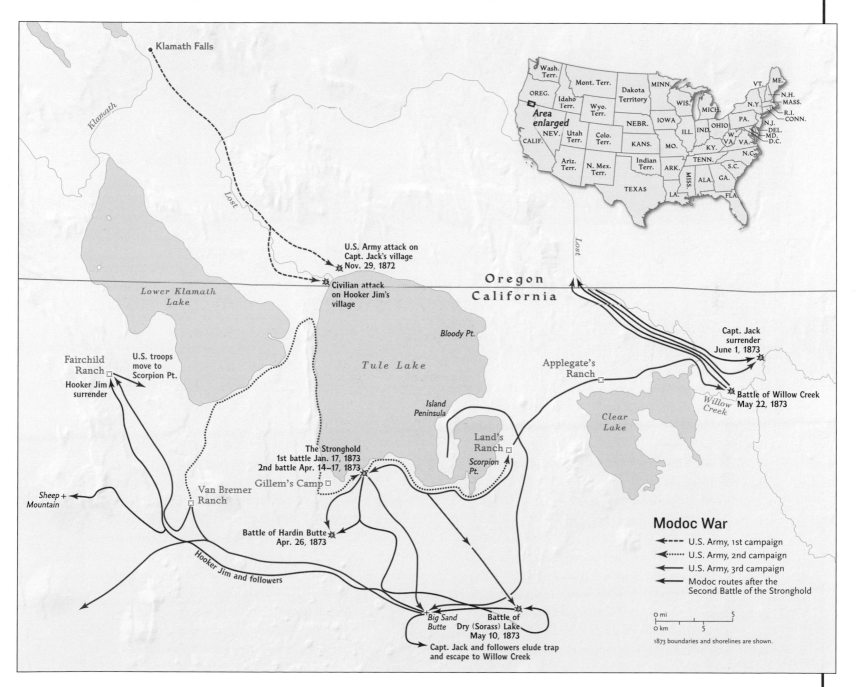

Modoc War

- - - ◄- - - U.S. Army, 1st campaign
········◄····· U.S. Army, 2nd campaign
────◄──── U.S. Army, 3rd campaign
──────◄── Modoc routes after the Second Battle of the Stronghold

1873 boundaries and shorelines are shown.

RED RIVER WAR

LAST FREE INDIANS OF THE SOUTHERN PLAINS

For many years, the tribes of the southern Plains controlled millions of unconquered acres, home to tens of thousands of people. The Comanche and Kiowa in particular had halted America's westward advance for decades. But there were millions of whites in America. They expected to own and control the land and would not tolerate free Indians. The tribes had to die, surrender, or be subjugated.

By the 1860s, the tribes were in a defensive position and their prospects looked grim. The Southern Cheyenne had suffered a terrible massacre at Sand Creek, and the Comanche were up against the Texas Rangers, who had an impressive arsenal of repeating revolvers and rifles. In 1867, the Kiowa, Comanche, Southern Cheyenne, and Arapaho signed the Medicine Lodge Treaty. It established two reservations—one for the Kiowa and Comanche and the other for Southern Cheyenne and Arapaho.

WILLIAM T. SHERMAN
Sherman and the Lakota chief Red Cloud, along with other tribal and government delegates, met to negotiate the Treaty of Fort Laramie in 1868.

The tribes did not stay put. They freely hunted the buffalo, which were becoming less numerous, but remained available. The Comanche and Kiowa still raided, attacking the Ute and Navajo, even after those tribes had been settled at Bosque Redondo.

The U.S. government had been winning the wars for the southern Plains, but to the north, things were not going well at all. Red Cloud had devastated the U.S. Army in the field, wiping out a major detachment at the Fetterman Fight and forcing the Americans to abandon the Bozeman Trail just to talk to him. Red Cloud then dictated terms at the Treaty of Fort Laramie in 1868, guaranteeing the Lakota, Northern Cheyenne, and Arapaho a vast unceded tribal territory in what are now five different states.

General William T. Sherman, a primary architect of America's Indian war policy, decided to focus on subjugating the last free Indians of the southern Plains: the Comanche, Kiowa, Southern

Cheyenne, and Arapaho. From 1870 to 1878, the American war against the buffalo reached a new intensity, with the slaughter of 60 million animals. A new tanning process enabled hunters to make even more money for their efforts. Sherman encouraged the hunting to starve the tribes into submission. It was far easier to starve Comanches than it was to kill them in a fight. The moral horror of attempting to exterminate a species of animal, starve other human beings, and take away their lands and livelihoods was all worth it to Sherman and other government and military officials. Their actions opened the southern Plains for whites.

RED RIVER CAMPAIGN

In 1874, the tribes provided just enough provocation to bring in the cavalry. At the Second Battle of Adobe Walls, Quanah Parker led a Comanche attack on buffalo hunters in the Texas Panhandle. Kiowa warriors ambushed Texas Rangers on patrol there in a separate engagement. Casualties were light in both events, but Sherman mobilized the army to end Indian depredations in the region once and for all.

Many Indians were on the reservations in Oklahoma, but 1,800 Cheyenne, 2,000 Comanche, and 1,000 Kiowa remained outside the reservations. Together they could muster 1,200 warriors. General Philip Sheridan, who was in charge of the campaign, organized five battalions of cavalry and infantry to converge on the Red River in the Texas Panhandle to subdue the tribes.

BEADED LEGGINGS Even in abject poverty on the reservations, the southern Plains tribes kept their artistic traditions alive.

The army fought at least 20 engagements with the tribes, although casualties were for the most part light. The Indians were outmatched and usually ran to avoid surrender. The army had numerous Indian scouts, adept at tracking and locating the fleeing bands. The soldiers were well supplied in rations and ammunition. Usually the army units located bands of Indians, attacked and routed the tribes, then destroyed their lodges and food. That netted few casualties, but accomplished the mission all the same. The army could operate indefinitely under those conditions, but the tribes wore out fast trying to feed their families without shelter or supplies on the cold southern Plains, which were now devoid of buffalo.

At the Battle of Palo Duro Canyon, the four tribes were camped along the Red River. Four hundred soldiers in three separate columns converged on the canyon. They first attacked and routed Lone Wolf's Kiowa camp, then displaced the other camps with sustained cavalry charges. Most of the Indians escaped by climbing the canyon walls, abandoning their horses, lodges, and food. The soldiers destroyed all tribal supplies, meticulously chopping each lodge pole and building great bonfires. They also captured 2,000 horses, most of which were slaughtered to prevent the Indians from recapturing them.

Many bands started to come to Fort Sill, Oklahoma, for placement on reservations. Most had surrendered by the fall of 1874. Lone Wolf's Kiowa held on until February 1874, and Quanah Parker's Comanche until June 1875. ■

LONE WOLF

Lone Wolf, a Kiowa chief, was born in 1820 and came of age at the height of Kiowa and Comanche power on the southern Plains. Proud but wise, Lone Wolf was selected to be a member of an elite warrior society among the Kiowa and eventually ascended to lead his band.

The Kiowa were divided on strategy during the 1860s. Lone Wolf and Dohasan scorned Kicking Bird's more accommodation-minded position. In 1867, Lone Wolf refused to sign the Medicine Lodge Treaty. In 1868, the Washita River Massacre of the Southern Cheyenne confirmed his suspicion that America wanted to wipe out the Indians. In 1872, Lone Wolf negotiated the release of two prominent Kiowa leaders held for depredations by the U.S. government. His success in diplomacy raised his status among the Kiowa and encouraged him to consider a more conciliatory view of the Americans. Then, in 1873, his son and nephew, who went on a raid in Mexico, were returning to Oklahoma when they were shot and killed by U.S. soldiers.

Lone Wolf hardened again. He was at the center of the Red River War in 1874, fighting with Quanah Parker at Adobe Walls and attacking Texas Rangers at Lost Valley. His band was one of the last to surrender. The government had no more patience or mercy for Lone Wolf. He and 26 other Kiowa were brought to Fort Marion in St. Augustine, Florida, in 1875. He was confined to a dark, dank cell. He contracted malaria in 1879, and, near death, was sent back to Oklahoma, where he passed away.

LOUIS RIEL REBELLION
MÉTIS INDEPENDENCE ON THE RED RIVER OF THE NORTH

Years of intermarriage, trade, and politics between the tribes of the Great Lakes and northern Plains and the French and English changed all nations in the region. Even today, a third of Ojibwe people have French surnames.

By the middle of the 19th century, a new people had emerged in Canada and the United States known as the Métis. Most had mixed ancestry—Ojibwe or Cree and French or Scottish. The Métis had a distinct language—Michif—which incorporated French nouns and Ojibwe verbs, widely spoken across the northern Plains, especially in Minnesota, North Dakota, and the Canadian Plains provinces. The Métis were primarily Catholic and often engaged in the fur trade and oxcart river road trade traffic between Canada and the United States. Pembina and Turtle Mountain in North Dakota, Fort Garry and Batoche in Canada, and many other Métis settlements soon dominated trade, politics, and military events. The Métis did not really identify themselves as Americans, as British subjects, or even as independent Indian tribes. They were culturally independent from all those groups, and they wanted true political independence.

The Red Lake Ojibwe in northwestern Minnesota contributed greatly to the emergence of the Métis. The Ojibwe had been moving west across the Great Lakes and into the northern Plains for generations. They populated the Ojibwe villages at Roseau River and Turtle Mountain as well as the Métis village at Pembina, North Dakota. The Red Lakers militarily protected the Métis from Dakota attacks as well. As the Métis bid for independence, the Red Lake Ojibwe remained officially neutral, but maintained their trade and cultural alliance with the Métis.

RED RIVER REBELLION, 1869–1870

In 1869, the Hudson's Bay Company sold territory known as Rupert's Land to the British government in Canada. It included much of present-day Manitoba and Saskatchewan. William McDougal was appointed governor. He came to Manitoba to assert British control over the Métis and native populations. The Métis, under the leadership of Louis Riel, rebelled. McDougal's British troops were forced across the border into the United States and sought refuge in Pembina, North Dakota. Little Rock had already led some of the Red Lake Ojibwe and Métis in raids on boats along the Red River of the North in Minnesota during the U.S.-Dakota War in 1862. Now whites throughout the region were terrified about a major Métis-Ojibwe alliance that could threaten their farms and settlements.

Riel tried diplomacy first, establishing a provisional Métis government for what is now Manitoba. The Métis occupied Fort Garry, near Winnipeg. They held court, then executed Thomas Scott, a British subject opposed to Métis independence. Manitoba became a Canadian province in 1870, with full legal protections for Catholics and French and Michif speakers. Riel's efforts seemed to have paid off, but the Anglo population in Ontario was furious about

LOUIS RIEL Riel, center front, led a major push for Métis independence along the Red River in Minnesota, North Dakota, and Manitoba between 1869 and 1870.

FORT GARRY Home to a large Métis community and trading post, Fort Garry, near Winnipeg, was a focal point of the Red River Rebellion and Métis bid for independence.

the execution of Scott. A militia was formed, called the Wolseley expedition, and marched on the Métis, intent on capturing and lynching Riel. Riel fled to the United States. He was formally exiled from Canada for five years. In a measure of his following, he was elected to Parliament every year, but was unable to take his seat.

NORTH-WEST REBELLION, 1885

In exile, Louis Riel worked on Métis independence in the Métis communities in the United States. He returned to Canada in 1885, determined to establish a lasting autonomous Métis government there. Operating out of Batoche, Saskatchewan, Riel drew numerous Métis supporters from all over Canada. The North-West Mounted Police and the Canadian Army soon deployed troops against them. Riel was by nature an idealist and a diplomat, not a fighter, but he had little choice but to lead an armed resistance. The Catholic Church denounced Riel over Métis claims that he was a prophet.

The Métis scored early victories at Duck Lake and at Fish Creek. The Battle of Fish Creek in 1885 was a remarkable military accomplishment for the untrained Métis militia.

They occupied strategic positions along creek banks and a ravine, using 20 cavalry as a diversion. The ruse worked and split the 900 British troops deployed against them into two unfortified positions. Then they used sniper fire and artillery to inflict heavy casualties, forcing the soldiers to retreat, even though they were nearly four times as numerous as the Métis.

The British then besieged Batoche. The Métis ran out of ammunition, and the British stormed the fortifications and routed the Métis. Riel surrendered and was executed. The Métis fractured. Some tried to maintain independent communities; some took refuge in Cree or Ojibwe communities. Most, though, melted into the general population. Red Lake, Minnesota, and Turtle Mountain, North Dakota, both populous Ojibwe communities, took in many Métis refugees. The large Pembina band of Ojibwe was equally populated by Métis and Ojibwe people. At the White Earth and Red Lake Reservations, where the Pembina band was settled, most tribal members today are mixed Métis and Ojibwe. Michif, the Métis language, is threatened now, but is still spoken in a few places in the United States and Canada. ∎

ASSASSINATING GREAT LEADERS

HOLE IN THE DAY (1868), CRAZY HORSE (1877), SITTING BULL (1890)

The death of a charismatic leader could doom a resistance movement, scatter armies, and lead people to surrender. It is no wonder, then, that so many great Indian leaders were assassinated.

Hole in the Day was a dynamic Ojibwe chief. He led warriors into battle against the Dakota many times and galvanized tribal resistance against the Americans at Fort Ripley in 1862. He negotiated several treaties, always with incredible effect, prompting one white trader to observe, "He was the smartest chief the Chippewa Indians ever had." In 1868, Hole in the Day was on his way to Washington, D.C., to renegotiate the White Earth removal treaty when a dozen men accosted him, then shot and stabbed him. His killing opened the floodgates of Ojibwe relocation.

Crazy Horse, the charismatic Lakota war leader of the Fetterman Fight, terrified U.S. Army officers. His presence could galvanize warriors into action no matter the odds. In 1877, the Americans worried that Crazy Horse would leave the reservation and start a new war. General George Crook ordered his arrest, even though there was no charge. Soldiers caught him at Fort Robinson, and while they forced him into a guardhouse, one of them ran him through with a bayonet. He died hours later.

Sitting Bull held the Lakota together during the Black Hills War, including the Battle of the Little Bighorn. James McLaughlin, the Indian agent at Standing Rock, feared that the chief would flee the reservation and start a major resistance. McLaughlin ordered Sitting Bull's arrest in 1890. Thirty-nine police were sent to his house to carry out the order. Sitting Bull refused to go, and many Lakota gathered around. The arresting police officer tried to manhandle the chief; another Lakota shot the officer, who in turn shot Sitting Bull in the chest. A second police officer shot Sitting Bull in the head. ■

DEATH OF SITTING BULL Sitting Bull's arrest in 1890 was a bloodbath. Six police officers were killed along with Sitting Bull and seven of his supporters.

FLIGHT OF CHIEF JOSEPH

NEZ PERCE QUEST FOR FREEDOM

During the early years of white settlement and the opening of the Oregon Trail, the Nez Perce were accommodating and diplomatic with the U.S. government. That got them reasonable terms in the 1855 Treaty of Walla Walla. They ceded a significant amount of land, but retained a large reservation in Idaho, Oregon, and Washington. The discovery of gold on the Nez Perce Reservation in 1860 transformed the tribe's world

overnight. More than 5,000 prospectors, ranchers, settlers, and soldiers flocked to the Nez Perce homeland. Most of the Nez Perce were content to ride out the storm, but government officials evaded tribal leaders who wanted a reconciliation that did not involve giving up more land. In an extremely controversial treaty in 1863, signed by only two Nez Perce leaders, the United States claimed title to all Nez Perce land and ordered all bands to relocate to a small reservation in

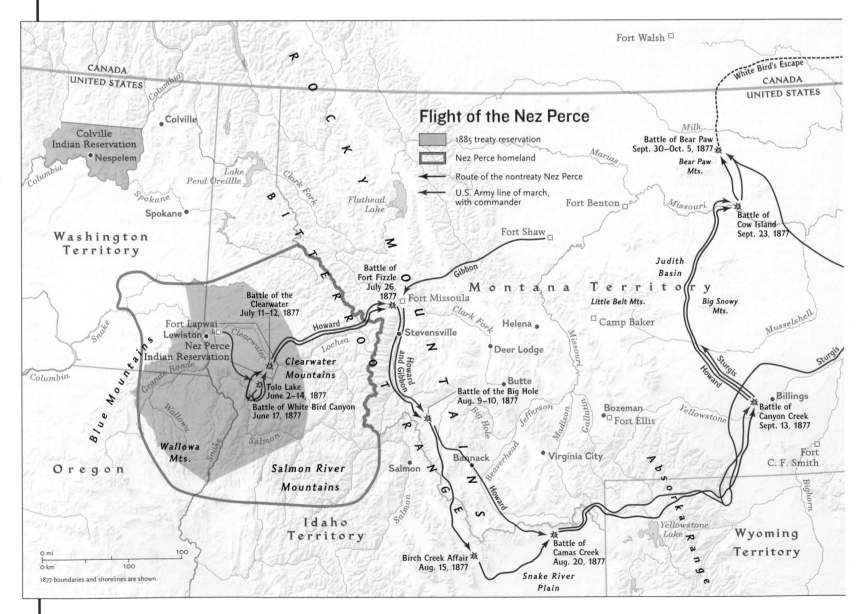

Flight of the Nez Perce

- 1885 treaty reservation
- Nez Perce homeland
- Route of the nontreaty Nez Perce
- U.S. Army line of march, with commander

1877 boundaries and shorelines are shown.

Lapwai, Idaho, even though most had not signed the treaty.

Chief Joseph, who assumed the mantle of chief from his father in 1871, advocated for peace. Through careful negotiation, he even obtained permission for the tribe to stay in the Wallowa Valley, Oregon, in 1873. The demands of the gold rushers were too much, however, and the U.S. government reversed its position, jailed a prominent chief, refused to investigate the murders of Nez Perce Indians, and sent the army to force their relocation in 1877.

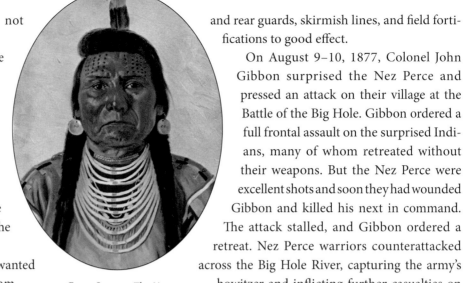

CHIEF JOSEPH The Nez Perce leader's quest for freedom captured the imagination of white Americans then and now.

Chief Joseph still wanted to work out an accommodation, but General Oliver O. Howard's arrival touched off a violent reaction by some of his young warriors, who killed four white settlers. There was no way to avoid a heavy hand from the army after that. White Bird, Joseph, and several other Nez Perce chiefs led the Nez Perce and a small band of allied Palouse (Palus) on a fighting retreat over 1,170 miles of mountains, hills, and frozen streams. They sought sanctuary first among the Crow in Montana. When they were denied a safe haven there, they continued their quest for freedom, trying to make it to join Sitting Bull and the Lakota, who had found temporary refuge in Canada.

FLIGHT OF THE NEZ PERCE

Chief Joseph left with about 800 Indians, mainly children, women, and elders, and a large herd of about 2,000 horses. Two thousand soldiers pursued them. Over the course of the Nez Perce flight, they fought 18 separate smaller engagements plus 4 major battles. In spite of having hundreds of dependents and tough weather conditions, Chief Joseph consistently amazed General Howard with clever battle tactics. He deployed advance

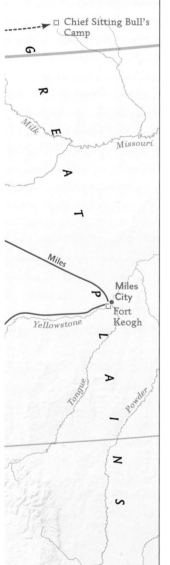

and rear guards, skirmish lines, and field fortifications to good effect.

On August 9–10, 1877, Colonel John Gibbon surprised the Nez Perce and pressed an attack on their village at the Battle of the Big Hole. Gibbon ordered a full frontal assault on the surprised Indians, many of whom retreated without their weapons. But the Nez Perce were excellent shots and soon they had wounded Gibbon and killed his next in command. The attack stalled, and Gibbon ordered a retreat. Nez Perce warriors counterattacked across the Big Hole River, capturing the army's howitzer and inflicting further casualties on the soldiers through sniper fire. While the soldiers assumed defensive positions, the Nez Perce women packed up the camp and started an organized retreat. The battle was costly for both sides. Thirty-one soldiers died, and another 40 were wounded. Gibbon's unit had a 30 percent casualty rate. The Nez Perce won the battle tactically and dictated the course of the battle and retreat, but they had suffered 90 casualties, including Chief Joseph's wife and many other women and children. Sobered by the loss, the Nez Perce pressed on, still striving for freedom. Gibbon's unit was reinforced by General Howard, and the pursuit resumed.

Chief Joseph never made it to Canada. Instead, on October 5, 1877, at the Bear Paw Mountains, only 40 miles from his objective, he surrendered with 418 of his band rather than placing the lives of his people at further risk. Joseph said, "My heart is sick and sad. From where the sun now stands, I will fight no more forever." White Bird and a group of 200 Nez Perce made it to Sitting Bull's camp in Canada. More than 150 Nez Perce were killed during the flight for freedom. The Nez Perce remaining in the United States were at the mercy of the government.

Chief Joseph's band was imprisoned at Fort Leavenworth, Kansas. After eight months in jail, they were removed to Oklahoma for seven years. In 1885, they returned to the Plateau. Most of the Nez Perce were concentrated on a reservation at Kooskia, Idaho. But the U.S. government would not allow Chief Joseph to live with the tribe. He spent the rest of his days in exile on a reservation at Colville, Washington, among 11 other confederated tribes. He died there in 1904. ∎

SHEEPEATER WAR

TURMOIL IN THE SAWTOOTH MOUNTAINS

The Shoshone are among the largest tribes from the Great Basin. About 1,000 years ago, they began to migrate west, immediately clashing with other tribes in the densely occupied Great Plains and Intermountain West. Over generations of travel, conflict, and community building they proved to be one of the most adaptable tribes in North America, occupying a wide range of territory in arid deserts, lush mountain valleys, and rugged mountains in what is now Wyoming, Idaho, Nevada, and Utah. The Shoshone venturing onto the Plains transformed most rapidly, becoming the mighty Comanche people. Because of the geographic dispersal of the Shoshone, great variations developed in lifestyle, food production, and even war.

Among the northern bands of Shoshone, those who lived along the Salmon River in Idaho's Sawtooth Mountains were often called Tukudeka, or Sheepeaters, because they depended heavily on mountain sheep as a staple food source. They were a resilient and resourceful people, well adapted to the unique water and food availability of the high reaches of the Sawtooth Mountains. Winters were harsh, and the Sheepeaters had to know a great deal about not just sheep hunting, but also every kind of food gathering and shelter construction imaginable.

The Shoshone came into conflict with the Americans in many theaters. Gold was discovered in the Boise Basin in 1862. Almost overnight, 7,000 prospectors appeared on the Panther Creek alone, in the heart of Sheepeater territory. More flooded into the Yankee Fork of the Salmon River, also in Sheepeater land. The Sheepeaters were cautious, and the odds of success in a fight were clearly overwhelmingly against them. They avoided the prospector-dense parts of their land and stuck to the higher elevations where there were no salmon, but plenty of sheep.

The Sheepeaters heard about trouble elsewhere in Shoshone country, but did their best to stay out of it. In 1863, hundreds of their cousins were brutally slaughtered in the Bear River Massacre. Some Shoshone in the nearby Snake River Valley raided white mines and settlements. The Snake War, which raged from 1864 to 1868, claimed about 1,800 lives. Tensions stayed high for many years afterward. In 1878, the Bannock War broke out, and that conflict also engulfed some of the Shoshone bands close to Sheepeater territory.

The Sheepeaters kept out of the conflicts. They were geographically isolated from the conflict zones and self-sufficient high in the mountains. The Bannock War, however, triggered a massive U.S. military response, and in 1878, the Sheepeaters saw how the U.S. Army treated Indians even if they avoided direct confrontation.

For the Americans, the distinctions between the Sheepeaters and other Shoshone meant nothing. General Oliver O. Howard, who directed much of America's military response to the Nez Perce flight for freedom in 1877 and the Bannock War in 1878, wanted to crush the Sheepeaters. He saw them as Shoshone, the same as those he fought in the Bannock War, and essentially viewed them as the last holdouts from that conflict—hiding in the mountains on the Idaho-Montana border. It didn't take much for Howard to send troops deep into the Sawtooth Mountains to hunt down the Sheepeaters.

SHEEPEATER FAMILY The Shoshone Indians living high in the Sawtooth Mountains were called Sheepeaters because mountain sheep were a primary food source.

BLOOD ON THE ROCKS

The Sheepeaters were in a tough spot from 1878 to 1879. The Bannock War, ongoing along the Snake River in 1878, had white settlers and miners in a panic. They were squatting on Sheepeater land and had never received permission to settle, mine, or camp there. The miners in particular were a lawless sort, and it was difficult to tell who was responsible when one of them showed up dead. That happened with internal squabbles often, but Indians across the Plains, Plateau, and Great Basin had done plenty of raiding, too. Soon, right or wrong, the Sheepeaters were blamed for several incidents, even though there were no eyewitnesses. In Indian Valley, someone ran off with horses from a rancher. In Cascade, Idaho, three settlers were killed as they tried to track the horse thieves. Then, in 1879, five Chinese miners were killed at Loon Creek. Two more ranchers were killed on the South Fork of the Salmon River.

Howard sent in the troops from Camp Howard, Boise, and the Umatilla Indian Agency. Twenty Umatilla and Cayuse scouts accompanied U.S. soldiers, and that made all the difference in locating the Sheepeaters and tracking them across rugged, rocky terrain. It took the army four months

SAWTOOTH RANGE **The homeland of the Sheepeaters was a labyrinth of steep slopes and rocky escarpments, evening the odds as the small band of Indians withstood a major cavalry deployment.**

of pursuit to even make contact with the tribe.

There were only 300 Sheepeaters in the entire band, and they were spread out to get easiest access to dispersed food sources. As the cavalry brought their pack train high up in the Sawtooths, one group of Sheepeaters preemptively struck. They had only 15 warriors, with 8 firearms total among them, but they put up an impressive fight. From elevated and well-concealed positions, they wounded two soldiers, and sent the column into a scampering retreat down the rocky slope. The next day, they stalked the army camp and set fire to the grass. A high wind fueled the fire, forcing the soldiers to abandon their supplies as well as 21 mules and horses, which the Sheepeaters captured.

Umatilla scouts found the Sheepeater camp soon after and attacked, exchanging gunfire but inflicting no casualties. The Sheepeaters retreated and the army destroyed their food, lodges, and supplies. The Sheepeaters agreed to surrender. There were only 51 in their party, and they were relocated to the Fort Hall Reservation. The remaining Sheepeaters stayed in the wilds of the Sawtooth Mountains for another couple of decades. ■

Chief Polk's son, Everett Hatch, also known by his Indian name, Tse-ne-gat, camped and traded with a Mexican American named Juan Chacon in 1914. Chacon was murdered soon after that, and Hatch was blamed for killing him. The Navajo Police went looking for Hatch to arrest him. When they got to Polk's home, he opened fire on the police, driving them away. Polk took his band of 85 to Navajo Mountain, planning to evade the police from a more secluded location. Chief Posey, expecting repercussions to affect his band too, joined them there. Each band had a separate camp, but stayed close enough to one another to offer mutual protection. For the next 10 months, the bands lived in peace and isolation.

BATTLE OF COTTONWOOD GULCH

Marshal Aquila Nebeker, still intent on arresting Hatch, organized a posse of 26 cowboys and 3 Colorado sheriffs to look for the "renegade" bands. He attacked Polk's camp, but Posey heard the shooting and brought his warriors. As they attacked Nebeker's force from the rear, the marshal realized he was outnumbered and in a vulnerable position, being shot at from two sides.

Nebeker sent runners to Bluff for help. About 50 armed white volunteers came to his aid. They arrived in groups over the course of a seven-hour battle with the Polk and Posey bands. Some of the reinforcement groups were isolated from the larger group and fought independent engagements. Two posse members were killed, and several were wounded. Two Indians died in the battle as well.

Nebeker retreated to Bluff, fearing an Indian siege of the town. Polk and Posey, though, moved their bands into the desert. A group of 50 Navajo police found the Ute and Paiute in the desert and attacked, but the Polk and Posey bands repelled the attack. That's when the U.S. Army was brought into the conflict.

General Hugh Scott was put in charge of handling the tense situation. On March 10, 1915, he tried a bold gamble. He left without his troops, accompanied by just a few men. Traveling deep into the desert, he made contact with the Navajo and found a Paiute translator. At Mexican Hat, he sent word to Polk and Posey that he wanted to parley. The chiefs agreed to surrender Hatch for a trial and avoid further risk to their people. Polk, Posey, Hatch, and Posey's son Jess were arrested. Hatch was tried for murder, but found not guilty. White Mormon witnesses testified to his innocence at the trial.

Polk and Posey might have felt vindicated by the trial result, but it was a short reprieve. Police systematically pursued their bands. More than 160 of their people were rounded up in small groups and brought to the Ute Mountain Reservation. In 1921, the pressure eased. Some of the Ute and Paiute stayed in the Allen and Montezuma Canyons.

For Indians living off-reservation, though, there were new challenges. Even though they had resided in their ancestral homelands since time immemorial, the U.S. government provided services to federally recognized tribes only through recognized tribal governments. Those who stayed away were without reservation or tribe. Validating land titles was difficult because white settlers had taken possession through a homesteading process or a later purchase. But the Indians had no such process. They had always just been there. Eventually, a government agency or private white landowner claimed each parcel of land, and the Indians found themselves landless in the territory they had never ceded and never left. They had to purchase the land where they had always lived or move to one of the reservations. ■

POSEY The Ute chief led the resistance during the Bluff War. He died in 1923, sometime soon after the tribe's last fight with white settlers.

YAQUI INDIANS The Yaqui, whose homeland straddles the Arizona-Mexico border,
fought the Spanish and then Mexican governments from 1533 until 1929.

BATTLE OF BEAR VALLEY

YAQUI QUEST FOR INDEPENDENCE

The Yaqui fought one of the longest resistance efforts among all the tribes in North America. From 1533, when the conquistadors first encountered them, until 1929, they fought the Spanish and then Mexican governments in Mexico. They fended off encroachment and efforts to fold their people into the *encomienda* slavery system, and fought for an independent Yaqui state in the Sonora district. Although the Yaqui lived in both the United States and Mexico in 1848, when the Southwest became part of America, they never openly fought the Americans in protracted campaigns as the Apache did. In 1918, though, a group of Yaqui were cornered by the U.S. 10th Cavalry and fought their way out.

Throughout the Yaqui Wars with Mexico, many Yaqui took refuge in the United States, even if their bands were from the Mexican side. Many worked in Tucson in the citrus groves. They often used their earnings to buy guns for relatives in Mexico, or to go fight there themselves. In the 1910s, the conflict escalated in Mexico, and American ranchers started to report armed Indians on their land, as well as some livestock depredation.

U.S.-Mexico border security was the sole responsibility of the U.S. Army. Fort Huachuca near Sierra Vista, Arizona, served as the staging ground for army work in this area, and when the reports of armed Indians on private white land surfaced, the 35th Infantry and 10th Cavalry responded. The 10th Cavalry, an all-black buffalo soldier unit, had seen a lot of action in the Indian wars, fighting the Comanche, Kiowa, Cheyenne, Arapaho, and Apache.

On January 9, 1918, Captain Frederick Ryder led the unit into the field in what would be his first live-action fighting. Ryder posted lookouts on hilltops as the detachment bivouacked at Bear Valley. Ryder was cautious and forward-thinking, having the cavalry mounts saddled and loosely buckled so they could mount up rapidly. Patrolling the border was a long, hot, monotonous task day after day. To Ryder's surprise, no sooner had his men set up base camp than a sentry reported enemies in sight. The buffalo soldiers cinched up saddles and rapidly moved toward a long line of Yaqui on horseback. The soldiers dismounted and pushed their horses into a brush bowl, then formed a skirmish line.

Ryder was just about ready to retrieve the horses and canvass the area for sign of the departing Yaqui when the Indians opened fire. The 10th Cavalry held their line in wild brush, fighting as both soldiers and Yaqui scrambled for cover behind rocks and escarpments, dodging from one boulder to the next. The Yaqui kept shooting and falling back in an organized retreat.

The soldiers fanned out and then funneled in to the Yaqui center, concentrating fire until the Yaqui held up a white flag. Ryder's soldiers advanced carefully and realized that they had captured only 10 Yaqui, left there to slow the soldiers' advance so the rest of the band could escape. One of the Yaqui was an 11-year-old boy.

The soldiers directed the captives to put up their hands. The chief still clutched his stomach. Fearing he had a knife, the soldiers forced the chief's hands up and his guts nearly spilled out onto the ground. He had been hit in the gunfire, which ignited his cartridge casings, causing a small explosion and opening a big wound. He died some hours later.

The Yaqui said they opened fire only because they thought the soldiers were Mexicans. They offered to volunteer for the U.S. Army, but the request was declined. They were tried in court and sentenced to 30 days for transporting weapons across an international border. If they had been deported, they would likely have been shot by the Mexican government as traitors.

The Yaqui never fought the Americans again, but their war continued in Mexico. In 1927, at the Battle of Cerro del Gallo, 12,000 Mexican federal troops pressed a devastating attack against the Yaqui. In 1929, the Mexican Air Force initiated a bombing campaign to subdue the tribe. ■

> "ESPECIALLY ASTONISHING WAS THE DISCOVERY THAT ONE OF THE YAQUIS WAS AN 11-YEAR-OLD BOY. THE YOUNGSTER HAD FOUGHT BRAVELY ALONGSIDE HIS ELDERS, FIRING A RIFLE THAT WAS ALMOST AS LONG AS HE WAS TALL."
>
> CAPTAIN FREDERICK RYDER

CONCLUSION

The Indian wars in America lasted nearly 400 years, from the arrival of Hernando de Soto in Florida in 1539 to the end of the Yaqui conflict in the Southwest in 1929. Hundreds of tribes fought for what they believed in—their families, their communities, their right to prosperity, and their freedom. They fought in every climate and every part of the continent, from minor skirmishes to major battles. In spite of the odds, they won some of those conflicts, and always affected their own destiny.

There were five main kinds of Indian war, and the stories here illuminate each of them: first encounters and wars of resistance, wars between empires, wars between tribes, wars of conquest, and wars for survival. In all those wars, each tribe fought for an objective rather than for the sake of conflict. They fought for freedom.

WAR ON CULTURE

As the Indian wars shifted to wars of survival, the remaining pockets of resistance were systematically overwhelmed. The U.S. government opened a new kind of war then—a war on Indian culture. It was not just the Ghost Dance that was persecuted. Indian agents were put in charge of reservations and given lists of Indian offenses—things Indian could not do. Those included dances, feasts, and traditional giveaways. Officials in Washington, D.C., would send the Indian agents circulars, or directives, about how to enforce Office of Indian Affairs rules. Some, like Circular 1665, which forbade tribal ceremonies and dances, stayed in effect until 1933, within the memory of many tribal elders today. The pressure on tribal culture persisted legally until 1978, when the American Indian Religious Freedom Act attempted to provide religious protections. The First Amendment to the U.S. Constitution was sufficient for most Americans, but insufficient for Indians. That should concern not just Indians, but also anyone who wants to mitigate the risk that the American government could ever again get in the business of suppressing religious freedom for anyone.

The war on culture spread to foster care and adoption practices as well. By World War I, roughly a third of native children were removed from their homes and placed with white families as foster children or adoptees. The rates were so high that many healthy families consistently were deprived of the right to raise their children; many children over the generations were deprived of the right to know who they are as native people. The Indian Child Welfare Act of 1978 sought to remedy that, but it has been a strained and ongoing battle to affirm the rights of tribes and tribal people in the welfare of their children.

Education was a major front in the war on culture, too. For more than a century beginning in about 1860, thousands of native children were sent to residential boarding schools run by the U.S. government. They were isolated from their home communities and families by design. When Geronimo's band of Apache were imprisoned in Florida, the children were shipped off to schools and did not see their families for years. That was typical of the experience for native children. Even though the children who were brought to these schools were monolingual speakers of tribal languages, the schools' teachers spoke English only. The young people received harsh physical discipline but no nurture. Schools at Haskell in Kansas and Carlisle in Pennsylvania kept cemeteries for students who died there. Parents had no choice but to send their children to the schools, and often they never even got a body back for burial and had no religious choice in the funeral their children received. Often three generations in a family went through the residential schools. It tore the social fabric of Indian communities. Parenting skills, family and community cohesion, and tribal cultures were all under attack. Although those who designed the residential school system thought they were doing Indians a service, that promise was never realized. Indians were told that learning English was the path to economic opportunity. Even if that had been true, the methods did more harm than good. The jobs never materialized, and the Indians, assimilated through great personal trauma, returned to the reservations. Many could no longer speak the same language as their parents. The seeds of substance abuse in Indian country were sown by the U.S. government and its war on Indian cultures. Today, most of the grandparent generation remembers this war on their tribal languages and cultures. It heightened the distrust many Native Americans have of American government and education.

PEACE DRUMS

While America transitioned from military conflict with tribes to a war on tribal culture, the tribes found many ways to reconcile with one another. The Ojibwe and Dakota, who fought for 100 years, made a ceremonial peace. The Dakota presented the Ojibwe with ceremonial peace drums, which are still a major component of contemporary Ojibwe ceremonial life. The Ojibwe sing the ceremony songs with Dakota words in them, call the drums "peace drums" or "Dakota drums," and follow the original instructions of the Dakota who gave them the drums. The intentional ownership of their Indian wars with one another and the effort to reconcile that conflict has done much to cement peace and deep friendship between the tribes. The Dakota, who are more financially prosperous in Minnesota, have been especially generous with the Ojibwe. Both tribes support one another politically and culturally.

People from many other tribes suffered together in residential boarding schools and then went on to work together

CARLISLE At the height, 20,000 Native American children attended residential boarding schools like this one, Carlisle Indian Industrial School in Pennsylvania.

in fighting on new fronts. The founding members of the National Congress of American Indians and some of the founders of the American Indian Movement went to school with one another. Despite being from different tribes, and sometimes enemy tribes, the friendships and shared struggles built bridges.

TRIBAL WARRIORS IN MODERN TIMES

For the Crow Indians, being a war chief was no simple endeavor. One had to complete four tasks—lead a successful war party, steal the enemy's horses, disarm an enemy in battle, and count coup, or touch the enemy in battle without killing him. Over the generations of conflict the Crow had with the Lakota, Blackfeet, and other tribes, many accomplished war chiefs distinguished themselves through the four acts. When the treaty period came, it was difficult to carry on such traditions. Some said the war customs of the Crow had disappeared forever.

Then along came Joseph Medicine Crow. He was the first person from his tribe to graduate from college. Then he went to graduate school, receiving an advanced degree in anthropology in 1939. Shortly after, America entered World War II. Medicine Crow was from a long line of Crow warriors, chiefs, and spiritual leaders. As accomplished as he was in academics, he answered the call and enlisted in the U.S. Army. It wasn't long before Medicine Crow was at the front lines of the European theater, fighting the Germans. In an urban fight, he waited in ambush, and to his surprise a German soldier walked right by him. Instead of killing the soldier, he knocked his rifle out of his hands and started to grapple. As he put a choke hold on the German, the man gasped, "Mama." Medicine Crow let him go. Unintentionally, Medicine Crow had just completed two of the four acts to become a Crow war chief, disarming an enemy and counting coup.

Medicine Crow's unit deployed against a German line later on and prepared for an artillery bombardment of a farm where the Germans were hiding. Medicine Crow saw that the Germans had stabled 50 horses, used for pulling artillery pieces. He asked his commanding officer if he could get the horses before the bombardment started. Casting the corral open, he jumped on the back of a beautiful stallion and stampeded the herd. To the shouts and cheers of the other men in his company, he sang the Crow praise song—saving the horses

from the bombardment, accumulating assets for the U.S. Army, and stealing the enemy's horses.

Medicine Crow was a seasoned soldier and led many missions behind enemy lines. When he returned home and told his elders about his experiences, they told him that he had completed the four deeds. They elevated him to war chief, one of the last true Plains Indian war chiefs.

Indians have fought in American military campaigns ever since America became a nation. In fact, Indians have fought for the U.S. armed forces at a higher rate per capita than any other racial group in the country. For many, military service was an economic opportunity in a world that threw up racial barriers to gainful employment for people of color. But it was also a way to continue ancient warrior traditions and earn respect from the people at home as well as others who often had little respect for Indians.

In World War II, numerous Navajo servicemen were used to develop a special code in the Navajo language for transmitting orders and military intelligence. The Japanese were never able to break the code. The code talkers provided a great service to the American nation, and earned the respect and appreciation of millions of Americans. Members from every tribe participated in numerous less publicized but no less self-sacrificing ways.

> ## "NEVER HAS AMERICA LOST A WAR . . . BUT NAME, IF YOU CAN, THE LAST PEACE THE UNITED STATES WON."
>
> VINE DELORIA, JR.

THE FIGHT FOR FREEDOM CONTINUES

The fighting spirit of native people continued to fuel the new battles in which they engaged. In 1968, Indian people in Minneapolis created an organization called the American Indian Movement (AIM). They were concerned with issues of housing, racial profiling, and economic opportunity. The activism of that time around civil rights and the Vietnam War created an opening for action on native issues as well. Indian people in the San Francisco area took over Alcatraz Island for 19 months, from 1969 to 1971. Although AIM did not organize that event, some of its members participated, and all of them saw the power of resistance.

In 1971, AIM organized a Trail of Broken Treaties march on Washington, D.C. Tribal activists marched through many tribal communities across the country and eventually took over the Bureau of Indian Affairs offices in Washington, delivering a petition to the government. For many Americans at the time, the press coverage brought the realization that

Indians were still present and their issues still unresolved.

AIM was soon involved in the takeover of the Wounded Knee Trading Post in 1972. That standoff galvanized Indians and activists on a level not previously seen. The National Guard was called out, and soon there were armored vehicles, soldiers, and snipers aiming at 300 Indians at the site of the 1890 massacre. The surreal scene eventually erupted into shoot-outs between the occupiers and the police and service units deployed against them. Two Indians were killed, and one U.S. marshal was shot and paralyzed.

Since the height of AIM activism, many Indians have been involved in social, racial, and environmental justice fights. Even though armies no longer clash with American Indians in the field, the issues of justice and freedom remain largely unresolved, and male and female warriors of every age continue the fight. That fight is with the U.S. government on political issues. It is the fight for broad social change. It is the fight with private companies building pipelines across reservations or targeting them for nuclear waste storage or for development of sacred sites. The fight is internal too, as many tribal leaders and concerned citizens engage in the war on poverty and substance abuse.

The Indian wars have given us a lot to think about. "Never has America lost a war . . . But name, if you can, the last peace the United States won," wrote Vine Deloria, Jr., a prominent author and activist from the Standing Rock Reservation. "Victory yes, but this country has never made a successful peace because peace requires exchanging ideas, concepts, thoughts, and recognizing the fact that two distinct systems of life can exist together without conflict. Consider how quickly America seems to be facing its allies of one war as new enemies." That was certainly the case with many tribes that fought along with American troops and then soon suffered as enemies of the state—the Oneida, the Cherokee, the Creek, and others. It was also true of the Russians after World War II, and remains the case for America's relations with many people in the Middle East today.

Indeed, America's military successes since its genesis have not come with comparable plans or efforts to make peace or promote reconciliation. Today, America struggles in the war against terrorism in large part because the enemy does not fit the mold that U.S. military leaders are used to fighting. There is no country to take over. There is no land to take away. There are no people to subjugate through military force, even though all of those things have been tried, even in recent years. Instead there are ideas—political and cultural

NAVAJO CODE TALKERS In World War II, Navajo servicemen used a special code in the Navajo language to communicate military intelligence, confounding the Japanese.

ideas—that inspire some to violence. By focusing on military might instead of strategies for peace, we have no solution. Leadership is influence, and influence is not earned on the field of battle, but in relationships. Of all the lessons to be learned from the Indian wars, this seems to be one of the most important. America needs to learn how to make and keep a peace, how to build relationships across racial and religious divides—how to tolerate instead of subjugate.

In spite of all the injustices and the length, depth, and breadth of the Indian wars, America's first people have endured. What is most amazing about their story of resistance is not what has been lost but what has been preserved. Native nations still maintain their sovereignty, languages, and cultures. Through their actions, they have changed everyone and transformed themselves in the process. The tribes have shown the meaning of resilience and preserved a warrior spirit that serves and should guide us all. Bravery is nothing without the wisdom to know how it should be applied. ∎

ACKNOWLEDGMENTS

Writing and publishing *Indian Wars* was only possible through the assistance of many people. Thank you to Susan Straight for keeping us on track and for editorial expertise and leadership. Thank you to Maryann Haggerty for text fitting and lots of editing work. Thank you to Jane A. Martin for help with photographic layout and permissions. Thank you to Linda Makarov for layout support.

Special thanks for support to Dora, Tony, and Brooke Ammann; Bill Blackwell, Jr.; Dustin Burnette; Alfred Bush; Barb and Brad Caspers; Collette Dahlke; Vivian Delgado; Heid Erdrich, Louise Erdrich; Sean Fahrlander; Henry Flocken; Anna Gibbs; Thomas Goldtooth; John Gonzalez; Charles Grolla; Renee Gurneau; Deb and Matt Hawthorne; Daniel and Dennis Jones; Richard and Penny Kagigebi; Lisa LaRonge; Cary Miller; Leonard and Mary Moose; Mark, Mike, Melonee, Midge, and Frank Montano; Misty and John Morrow; Keller Paap; John Patrick; Monique Paulson; Mark Pero; George and Lisa Perry; Tessa Reed; Skip and Babette Sandman; Thomas Saros; Robert Saxton; and Krysten and Michael Sullivan.

I am also always forever indebted to my family—my parents, Robert and Margaret Treuer; my siblings David, Derek, Megan, Micah, Paul, and Smith Treuer; my children Jordan, Robert, Madeline, Caleb, Isaac, Elias, Evan, Mia, and Luella; and my wife, Blair. You all sacrificed a lot of time with me to make this book possible. Thank you.

RECONCILIATION

There are two parts of the black experience in America that get at least a little attention in the curriculum of public schools—the Emancipation Proclamation and the civil rights movement. I believe that these two important pieces of history get that attention because they are the two parts of the black narrative that give white people a sense of resolution. We feel like we can talk about the bad things that happened—slavery and Jim Crow in this case—because those are the two things we eventually got right. And in America we like to believe that we always get it right. Focusing on those two stories and paying too little attention to everything else in the black narrative buys a lot of complacency about what is currently wrong in America's treatment of black people today, so it is a problem in and of itself. But it is the need to feel resolution that inhibits true learning about our country's ugliest chapters.

In the Native American narrative there is no resolution. There is nothing that we got right. That encourages people to avoid the stories and never to own them. Nobody wants to get beat up for the sins of their ancestors. Looking at the Indian wars conjures strong feelings. For native people, the feeling conjured is often anger; for white people it is often guilt. Those emotions can eat like a cancer. Instead, we need to turn those emotions into positive action. There is no way around this history. There is only a way through it. We cannot forget about what happened in the past. We have to learn from it.

If I moved to Germany, I would expect someone to speak to me in German. I would take it upon myself to learn about the history of Germany and the little part of Germany where I happened to live in particular, and I would consider myself rude if I did not. Here in America, there are thousands of years of human history and we only teach about what happened after the first white men showed up. We are afraid to lean in. That keeps us ignorant about the Indian experience. And when we do not know about someone or something, it is a lot easier to be ambivalent about its destruction or even (knowingly or unconsciously) participate in it. That's what we are doing to the natural world. And that's what drives the persistent racial divide in our land.

America needs to reconcile its diverse people, and that starts with a reconciliation of our history. I think the United States should do what about 20 other nations have done around the world in struggling to grapple with an oppressive past. We need a truth and reconciliation effort. We need a national commission charged with empowering all people of all backgrounds to do some truth telling and some deep listening. We need to infuse that effort into the way we educate our citizenry. We need to require our citizens to learn about native narratives. Montana's K–12 education standards require all students to learn about Indian history and contemporary governments. The curriculum scaffolds one year after the next and should help raise the profile and understanding of indigenous people for all Montanans. It does not take anything away from the teaching of history to do this. On the contrary, it gives it more meaning. And it provides long-overdue engagement for Montana's native children. That should be done nationally. That's what it means to own our history. It won't tear anyone down; it will build everyone up. Of course there will be push-back with any such endeavor. That's the nature of oppression. Let's call up that warrior spirit for a worthy cause. Frederick Douglass was right: "Power concedes nothing without a demand."

ILLUSTRATIONS CREDITS

Front Cover (UP), Smithsonian American Art Museum, Washington, D.C./Art Resource, NY; (LO), Photos.com/Getty Images; back cover (LE), "Joseph Brant, Chief of the Mohawks," 1742–1807, Romney, George (1734–1802)/National Gallery of Canada, Ottawa, Ontario, Canada/Bridgeman Images; (CTR LE), "Attack of Seventh Cavalry Commanded by General Custer at Cheyenne Camp on Washita River at Dawn, November 27, 1868," painting by Charles Schreyvogel (1861–1912), Native American Wars, United States, 19th century/De Agostini Picture Library/Bridgeman Images; (CTR RT), Library of Congress Prints and Photographs Division; (RT), "The French Help the Indians in Battle," from *Brevis Narratio*, engraved by Theodore de Bry (1528–98) published in Frankfurt, 1591, Le Moyne, Jacques (de Morgues) (1533–88) (after)/Service Historique de la Marine, Vincennes, France/Bridgeman Images; 1, "Indian Telegraph," 1860 (oil on canvas), Stanley, John Mix (1814–72)/Detroit Institute of Arts, U.S.A./Detroit Museum of Art Purchase and Popular Subscription Fund/Bridgeman Images; 2–3, "Comanche Feats of Martial Horsemanship," 1834 (oil on canvas), Catlin, George (1796–1872)/Private Collection/Peter Newark American Pictures/Bridgeman Images; 4, Curley, Crow Scout, 1880s (black-and-white photo), Barry, David Frances (1854–1934)/Denver Public Library, Western History Collection/Bridgeman Images; 9, "Charging Indians on Horseback" (gouache on paper), Eyles, Derek Charles (1902–74)/Private Collection/Look and Learn/Bridgeman Images; 10, Edward S. Curtis; 11, "Captain Meriweather Lewis and William Clark Encountering Native American Indians," 1920 (oil on canvas), Berninghaus, Oscar Edward (1874–1952)/Private Collection/Bridgeman Images; 12–3, "Landing of Menendez at the Miami River in 1565," 1973 (oil on canvas), Hughes, Ken (fl.1973)/HistoryMiami, Florida, U.S.A./HistoryMiami/Bridgeman Images; 15, "The Landing of de Soto at Tampa Bay in 1539," 1853 (color litho), Eastman, Captain Seth (1808–75) (after)/Newberry Library, Chicago, Illinois, U.S.A./Bridgeman Images; 18–9, "The French Help the Indians in Battle," from *Brevis Narratio*, engraved by Theodore de Bry (1528–98) published in Frankfurt, 1591 (colored engraving), Le Moyne, Jacques (de Morgues) (1533–88) (after)/Service Historique de la Marine, Vincennes, France/Bridgeman Images; 19, "Hernando de Soto" (1496/1497–1542). Spanish explorer and conquistador. Engraving. Colored/Private Collection/Photo Tarker/Bridgeman Images; 20, North Wind Picture Archives; 21, Granger, NYC—All rights reserved; 22, North Wind Picture Archives; 23, George H. H. Huey/Alamy Stock Photo; 24, "Spanish Conquistadors" (gouache on paper), Coton, Graham (1926–2003)/Private Collection/Look and Learn/Bridgeman Images; 26–7, "The Pueblo of Acoma, New Mexico" (oil on canvas), Moran, Thomas (1837–1926)/Private Collection/Peter Newark American Pictures/Bridgeman Images; 28, "Pomeiooc Elder in a Winter Garment," from *Admiranda Narratio*, published by Theodore de Bry (colored engraving) (1528–98), after White, John (d. 1593)/Service Historique de la Marine, Vincennes, France/Bridgeman Images; 29, "The Massacre of the Settlers in 1622," plate VII, from *America, Part XIII*, German edition, 1628 (colored engraving), Merian, Matthaus, the Elder (1593–1650)/Virginia Historical Society, Richmond, Virginia, U.S.A./Bridgeman Images; 30, Geographicus Rare Antique Maps/Wikimedia Commons/PD-1926; 31, Robert Clark; 32–3, North Wind Picture Archives; 34, North Wind Picture Archives; 35, North Wind Picture Archives; 36, Stock Montage/Getty Images; 37, MPI/Getty Images; 38, From the collection of the York County Heritage Trust,

York, PA; 39, Granger, NYC—All rights reserved; 40, Title page from a book about King Philip's War in 1675–76, published in Boston, 1716 (litho), American School (18th century)/Private Collection/Peter Newark Pictures/Bridgeman Images; 40–41, Wikimedia Commons/PD-US; 42, North Wind Picture Archives; 43, Granger, NYC—All rights reserved; 44, "The Pueblo Indian Revolt of 1680" (colored engraving), Dixon, Maynard (1875–1946)/Private Collection/Peter Newark American Pictures/Bridgeman Images; 45, "Palace of the Governors," Santa Fe (oil on canvas), Sloan, John (1871–1951)/Private Collection/Christie's Images/Bridgeman Images; 46–7, LACMA—Los Angeles County Museum of Art; 48, Francis Back; 49, MPI/Stringer/Getty Images; 50, Granger, NYC—All rights reserved; 51, Granger, NYC—All rights reserved; 52, Colonial Carolina (lithograph), Moll, Hermann (fl.1678–1732) (after)/Private Collection/Peter Newark American Pictures/Bridgeman Images; 53, Granger, NYC—All rights reserved; 54, Map of Fort Rosalie des Natchez, Louisiana (gouache on paper), French School (18th century)/Bibliotheque Nationale de Cartes et Plans, Paris, France/Archives Charmet/Bridgeman Images; 56, Library and Archives Canada; 57, Musée McCord—McCord Museum, Montréal/Art Resource, NY; 58, Granger, NYC—All rights reserved; 59, Library of Congress Prints and Photographs Division; 60–61, Laguna Art Museum; 63, "The Shooting of General Braddock at Fort Duquesne, Pittsburgh," 1755 (oil on canvas), Deming, Edwin Willard (1860–1942)/State Historical Society of Wisconsin, Madison, U.S.A./Bridgeman Images; 66–7, North Wind Picture Archives; 67, The first page of the official account of the Portola Expedition of 1769–70 (printed paper)/Museo Naval, Madrid, Spain/Bridgeman Images; 68, Fray Junipero Serra Postcard. ca 1915–1925/Lake County Discovery Museum/UIG/Bridgeman Images; 69, W. Langdon Kihn/National Geographic Creative/Corbis; 70, Wisconsin Historical Society; 71, Library of Congress, Geography and Map Division; 72–3, "War Dance of the Sauks and Foxes," illustration from *The Indian Tribes of North America*, vol. 1, by Thomas L. McKenney and James Hall, pub. by John Grant (color litho), American School (19th century)/Private Collection/Bridgeman Images; 74, "Portrait of Queen Anne," ca 1705 (oil on canvas), Kneller, Sir Godfrey (1646–1723)/Private Collection/Photo Philip Mould Ltd., London/Bridgeman Images; 75, Junius Brutus Stearns, "Hannah Duston Killing the Indians," 1847, oil on canvas, 36¼ x 42¼ in. Colby College Museum of Art. Gift of R. Chase Lasbury and Sally Nan Lasbury, 1992.001; 76, "The Indian Chief Paugus Is Killed by an English Militiaman" (litho), English School (20th century)/Private Collection/Ken Welsh/Bridgeman Images; 77, Collections of Maine Historical Society, A83-5; 78–9, National Army Museum/The Art Archive at Art Resource, NY; 80, The Trustees of the British Museum/Art Resource, NY; 81, adoc-photos/Corbis; 82, Granger, NYC—All rights reserved; 83, "Brigadier General Charles Lawrence" (engraving), English School (18th century)/Private Collection/Look and Learn/Elgar Collection/Bridgeman Images; 84–5, Don Troiani/Corbis; 85, "Pontiac" (1720–69) 1763 (oil on canvas), Stanley, John Mix (1814–72)/Private Collection/Peter Newark American Pictures/Bridgeman Images; 86, Mackinac State Historic Parks Collection; 87, Smithsonian American Art Museum, Washington, D.C./Art Resource, NY; 88–9, Gerry Embleton/North Wind Picture Archives; 89, "Yoholo-Micco, a Creek Chief," 1825, illustration from *The Indian Tribes of North America*, vol. 2, by Thomas L. McKenney and James Hall, pub. by John Grant (color litho), King, Charles Bird (1785–1862) (after)/Private Collection/Bridgeman Images; 90, Pipe Tomahawk, ca 1770 (wood steel and lead), American School (18th century)/Peabody Essex Museum, Salem,

Massachusetts, U.S.A./Bridgeman Images; 91, Harvey Meston/Getty Images; 92, "The Death of General Montgomery in the Attack on Quebec," December 31, 1775, 1786 (oil on canvas), Trumbull, John (1756–1843)/Yale University Art Gallery, New Haven, CT, U.S.A./Bridgeman Images; 94, "General Anthony Wayne" (1745–96) (oil on linen), Savage, Edward (1761–1817)/Collection of the New-York Historical Society, U.S.A./Bridgeman Images; 95, Granger, NYC—All rights reserved; 96–7, "Washington Crossing the Delaware River, 25th December 1776," 1851 (oil on canvas) (copy of an original painted in 1848), Leutze, Emanuel Gottlieb (1816–68)/Metropolitan Museum of Art, New York, U.S.A./Bridgeman Images; 97, Iroquois Pipe, ca 1725 (wood), American School (18th century)/Private Collection/Photo Boltin Picture Library/Bridgeman Images; 99, "Red Jacket" (ca 1756–1830) (w/c on paper), Catlin, George (1796–1872)/Private Collection/Peter Newark American Pictures/Bridgeman Images; 100, Library of Congress Prints and Photographs Division; 101, "Tecumseh" (1768–1813) (oil on canvas), American School (19th century)/Private Collection/Peter Newark American Pictures/Bridgeman Images; 102, "Death of Tecumseh" (1768–1913) (colored engraving), American School (19th century)/Private Collection/Peter Newark American Pictures/Bridgeman Images; 103, RF Corbis Value/Alamy Stock Photo; 105, "The Creek Indians Massacring the Inhabitants of Fort Mims, Alabama," 1813 (engraving), American School (19th century)/Private Collection/Peter Newark American Pictures/Bridgeman Images; 106, MPI/Stringer/Getty Images; 106–7, "Seminole Indians Ambush a U.S. Marines Supply Wagon," September 11, 1812 (color litho), Waterhouse, C.H. (fl.1812)/Private Collection/Peter Newark American Pictures/Bridgeman Images; 108, Granger, NYC; 109, Minnesota Historical Society; 110, Library of Congress Prints and Photographs Division; 112–3, "Scalp Dance of Hidatsa Indians," engraving by Karl Bodmer (1809–93), North America, 1839/De Agostini Picture Library/Bridgeman Images; 115, Library of Congress Prints and Photographs Division; 118, "Death of Hiawatha," back cover illustration from Le Petit Journal, supplement illustre, July 27, 1913 (color litho), French School (20th century)/Private Collection/Bridgeman Images; 119, "Joseph Brant, Chief of the Mohawks," (1742–1807), Romney, George (1734–1802)/National Gallery of Canada, Ottawa, Ontario, Canada/Bridgeman Images; 120, Library of Congress Prints and Photographs Division; 121, Flintlock rifle (wood and metal), French School (16th century)/Musee de l'Armee, Paris, France/Bridgeman Images; 122, Fur trade contract between Francois Francoeur and four voyageurs for transport of goods and purchase of beaver pelts in Michilimackinac and Chicago, 1692 (pen and ink on paper), French School (17th century)/Newberry Library, Chicago, Illinois, U.S.A./Bridgeman Images; 123, "The French Jesuit Missionary Brebeuf Among the Algonquins" (color litho), American School (19th century)/Private Collection/Peter Newark American Pictures/Bridgeman Images; 124, National Park Service; 125, North Wind Picture Archives; 126–7, "View of Fort Snelling," ca 1850 (oil on canvas), Thomas, Edward K. (1817–1906)/Minneapolis Institute of Arts, MN, U.S.A./The Julia B. Bigelow Fund/Bridgeman Images; 127, Scalping knife and sheath, Eastern Sioux, from Fort Snelling, Minnesota (mixed media), American School (19th century)/Brooklyn Museum of Art, New York, U.S.A./Henry L. Batterman Fund and the Frank Sherman Benson Fund/Bridgeman Images; 129, Corbis; 130, Library of Congress Prints and Photographs Division; 131, Library of Congress Prints and Photographs Division; 133, "North American Indians" (color litho), Catlin, George (1796–1872)/Private Collection/Peter Newark Western Americana/Bridgeman Images; 134, "Meeting Between the Expedition Party of Otto von Kotzebue (1788–1846) and King Kamehameha I (1740/52–1819) Ovayhi Island" (color litho), Choris, Ludwig (Louis) (1795–1828) (after)/Bibliotheque Nationale, Paris, France/Bridgeman Images; 135, Copyright Herbert K. Kane, LLC; 136, Tarker/Corbis; 138, Granger, NYC—All rights reserved; 139, Library of Congress, Geography and Map Division; 140, "Osage Settlement Near Missouri River," from Le Costume Ancien et Moderne, vol. 1 or 2, plate 3, by Jules Ferrario, published ca 1820s–30s (color litho), Campi, Felice (1764–1817)/Private Collection/The Stapleton Collection/Bridgeman Images; 141, Smithsonian American Art Museum, Washington, D.C./Art Resource, NY; 142, Pawnees, 1874–75 (pen, ink, and w/c on ledger paper), "Howling Wolf" (1849–1927)/Allen Memorial Art Museum, Oberlin College, Ohio, U.S.A./Gift of Mrs. Jacob D. Cox/Bridgeman Images; 143, Library of Congress Prints and Photographs Division; 144, Library of Congress Prints and Photographs Division; 145, Mingei International Museum/Art Resource, NY; 147, Library of Congress Prints and Photographs Division; 148–9, "The Battle of the Washita, November 1868," from Life on the Plains (engraving) (black-and-white photo), Kappes, Alfred (1850–94) (after)/Private Collection/Bridgeman Images; 151, Medford Historical Society Collection/Corbis; 153, "Geronimo and His Band Returning From a Raid Into Mexico" (oil on canvas), Remington, Frederic (1861–1909)/Private Collection/Photo © Christie's Images/Bridgeman Images; 154, North Wind Picture Archives; 155, Hopi man with a hoe, Arizona, 1902 (black-and-white photo)/Underwood Archives/UIG/Bridgeman Images; 156–7, Granger, NYC—All rights reserved; 159, Library of Congress Prints and Photographs Division; 163, "Scalping" (oil on canvas), Rindisbacher, Peter (1806–34)/West Point Military Academy, U.S.A./Bridgeman Images; 164, "The Death of Captain James Cook, 14th February 1779" (oil on canvas), Zoffany, Johann (1733–1810)/National Maritime Museum, London, UK/Bridgeman Images; 165, The Trustees of the British Museum/Art Resource, NY; 166, Library of Congress Prints and Photographs Division; 167, "View of the Honolulu Fort Interior" (oil on canvas), Paul Emert (1826–67), ca 1853/Pictures From History/Woodbury & Page/Bridgeman Images; 168–9, DEA Picture Library/Getty Images; 169, Library of Congress Prints and Photographs Division; 170, Library of Congress Prints and Photographs Division; 171, Haida "Thunderbird" statue (painted wood)/Private Collection/Peter Newark Western Americana/Bridgeman Images; 172, "The Fort Dearborn Massacre on the 15th August, 1812" (oil on canvas), Page, Samuel (19th century)/© Chicago History Museum, U.S.A./Bridgeman Images; 173, Michael Maslan Historic Photographs/Corbis; 174, North Wind Picture Archives; 175, The White House/Public Domain; 176, Library of Congress Prints and Photographs Division; 177, Library of Congress Prints and Photographs Division; 179, Library of Congress Prints and Photographs Division; 180, NativeStock/North Wind Picture Archives; 181, Smithsonian American Art Museum, Washington, D.C./Art Resource, NY; 182, Buffalo Bill Center of the West/The Art Archive at Art Resource, NY; 183, Library of Congress Prints and Photographs Division; 185, Library of Congress Prints and Photographs Division; 186, Science & Society Picture Library/Getty Images; 187, Granger, NYC—All rights reserved; 188, North Wind Picture Archives; 190, Indian Campaign of 1832: Map of the Country, 1832 (pen and ink on paper), American School (19th century)/Newberry Library, Chicago, Illinois, U.S.A./Bridgeman Images; 191, Library of Congress Prints and Photographs Division; 192, "Comanche Warrior With a Shield, Lance and Bow and Arrows" (ca 1835) (color litho), Catlin, George (1796–1872)/Private Collection/Peter Newark American Pictures/Bridgeman Images; 194–5, "Delaying Action: The Battle of Plum Creek, 1978" (oil on panel), Lee Herring/Image Courtesy of William Adams and the Texas Ranger Hall of Fame and Museum; 196, Library of Congress Prints and Photographs Division; 197, "Battle of Adobe Walls" Nick Eggenhofer, FOUN 8549, in the collection of Fort Union National Monument, Watrous, NM. Courtesy of the National Park Service; 198, "The Siege of New Ulm, Minnesota, 19 August 1862. Attack by Sioux Tribesmen From Nearby Reservation on Town of 900 Settlers," after painting by Heinrich Augustus Schwabe (1843–1916). Dakota War Native American Battle U.S.A./Universal History Archive/ UIG/Bridgeman Images; 201, Granger, NYC—All rights reserved; 202, Denver Public Library, Western History Collection; 204, "Attack of Seventh Cavalry Commanded by General Custer at Cheyenne Camp on Washita River at Dawn, November 27, 1868," painting by Charles Schreyvogel (1861–1912), Native American Wars, United States, 19th century/De Agostini Picture Library/Bridgeman Images; 206–7, DEA Picture Library/Granger, NYC—All rights reserved; 208, Granger, NYC— All rights reserved; 209, Library of Congress Prints and Photographs Division; 210, Granger, NYC—All rights reserved; 211, Chief Red Cloud of the Fetterman massacre and Ft. Phil Kearny wagon box-fight, 1872 (black-and-white photo), Gardner, Alexander (1821–82)/Denver Public Library, Western History Collection/Bridgeman Images; 212, "Discovery of Skeletons of the Bodies of American Soldiers Slain by Indians During the Kidder Massacre in July 1867" (colored engraving), American School (19th century)/Private Collection/Peter Newark Western Americana/ Bridgeman Images; 214–5, Tarker/Corbis; 216, Corbis; 217, Le general Custer/Photo © PVDE/Bridgeman Images; 218, HIP/Art Resource, NY; 219, Library of Congress Prints and Photographs Division; 220, North Wind Picture Archives; 221, Denver Public Library, Western History Collection; 222–3, Mary Evans Picture Library/Alamy; 225, Library of Congress Prints and Photographs Division; 228, Library of Congress Prints and Photographs Division; 230, Granger, NYC—All rights reserved; 230–31, HIP/Art Resource, NY; 232, "Pomo Indians Gather Acorns for Winter Storage in Hivelike Granaries" (color litho), Kihn, William Langdon (1898–1957)/National Geographic Creative/Bridgeman Images; 233, Copyright Phoebe A. Hearst Museum of Anthropology and the Regents of the University of California (Catalog No. 1-216892); 234, Ron Koeberer/Corbis; 235, Library of Congress Prints and Photographs Division; 236, The New York Public Library, Astor, Lenox, and Tilden Foundations; 237, Beinecke Rare Book and Manuscript Library/Public Domain; 238, Oregon Historical Society, #ba018083; 239, W.W. Bretherton photo, Oregon Historical Society, #CN003842; 240, "The Defiance of Whist-alks" by Nona Hengen; 241, Edward S. Curtis/Library of Congress Prints and Photographs Division; 242, Washington State Historical Society; 243, University of Washington Libraries, Special Collections, Neg. UW4101; 244, Time Life Pictures/Getty Images; 245, Library of Congress Prints and Photographs Division; 246, Library of Congress Prints and Photographs Division; 247, Ansel Adams, Owens Valley from Sawmill Pass, Kings River Canyon (proposed as a national park), California, 1936. National Archives and Records Administration/Public Domain; 248, Corbis; 249, Oregon Historical Society bb004551; 250, "Hush-Low" (1899) (oil on canvas), Burbank, Elbridge Ayer (1858–1949)/ Butler Institute of American Art, Youngstown, OH, U.S.A./Museum Purchase 1912/Bridgeman Images; 251, Washington State Historical Society; 252, Library of Congress Prints and Photographs Division; 253,

Photo courtesy of Sharlot Hall Museum Library and Archives, Prescott, Arizona, SHM Photographs Collection; 254, Utah Division of State History; 255, Library of Congress Prints and Photographs Division; 256–7, "Snake Indians" (oil on canvas), Miller, Alfred Jacob (1810–74)/Private Collection/Photo © Christie's Images/Bridgeman Images; 258, Oregon Historical Society bb004555; 259, Denver Public Library, Western History Collection; 260–61, The Museum of the Southeast American Indian; 262, AS400 DB/Corbis; 263, Library of Congress Prints and Photographs Division; 264, Granger, NYC—All rights reserved; 265, United States Geological Survey/Public Domain; 266–7, The Art Archive at Art Resource, NY; 268, National Museum of Health and Medicine, https:// www.flickr.com/photos/medicalmuseum/310540601/CC license at https://creativecommons.org/licenses/by/2.0/legalcode; 269, Corbis; 270–71, Wilson44691/Wikimedia Commons; 271, bpk, Berlin/Ethnologisches Museum, Staatliche Museen, Berlin, Germany/Art Resource, NY; 272, Granger, NYC—All rights reserved; 274, Richard H. Kern/Wikimedia Commons; 276–7, Granger, NYC—All rights reserved; 278, Buffalo Bill Center of the West/The Art Archive at Art Resource, NY; 279, Library of Congress Prints and Photographs Division; 280, 917 Collection/Alamy Stock Photo; 282, NARA/Public Domain; 283, Buffalo Bill Center of the West/The Art Archive at Art Resource, NY; 284, Library and Archives Canada PA-012854; 285, Library and Archives Canada PA-011337; 286–7, Library of Congress Prints and Photographs Division; 289, Library of Congress Prints and Photographs Division; 290, Jackson Hole Historical Society Museum; 291, Fredlyfish4, https://commons.wikimedia.org/wiki/ File:Sawtooths _and_Toxaway_Lake.JPG, CC license at https://creative-commons.org/licenses/by-sa/3.0/legalcode; 293, Library of Congress Prints and Photographs Division; 295, Minnesota Historical Society; 296, Courtesy Oklahoma Historical Society; 297, Library of Congress Prints and Photographs Division; 298, Nevada Historical Society; 299, Buffalo Bill Center of the West/The Art Archive at Art Resource, NY; 300, Utah Division of State History; 301, Utah Division of State History; 302, Library of Congress Prints and Photographs Division; 305, Library of Congress Prints and Photographs Division; 307, Corbis.

NATIONAL GEOGRAPHIC
THE INDIAN WARS

Since 1888, the National Geographic Society has funded more than 12,000 research, exploration, and preservation projects around the world. National Geographic Partners distributes a portion of the funds it receives from your purchase to National Geographic Society to support programs including the conservation of animals and their habitats.

National Geographic Partners
1145 17th Street NW
Washington, DC 20036-4688 USA

Become a member of National Geographic and activate your benefits today at natgeo.com/jointoday.

For information about special discounts for bulk purchases, please contact National Geographic Books Special Sales: specialsales@natgeo.com

For rights or permissions inquiries, please contact National Geographic Books Subsidiary Rights: bookrights@natgeo.com

ISBN: 978-1-4262-1743-2
ISBN: 978-1-4262-1744-9 (deluxe)

Library of Congress Cataloging-in-Publication Data

Names: Treuer, Anton, author.
Title: The Indian Wars : Battles, Bloodshed, and the Fight for Freedom on the American Frontier / Anton Treuer.
Other titles: At head of title: National Geographic
Description: Washington, D.C. : National Geographic, 2017. | Includes index.
Identifiers: LCCN 2016054831 | ISBN 9781426217432 (hardcover : alk. paper)
Subjects: LCSH: Indians of North America--Wars. | Indians of North America--Wars--1815-1875. | United States--Territorial expansion. | Frontier and pioneer life--United States.
Classification: LCC E81 .T74 2017 | DDC 970.004/97--dc23
LC record available at: https://lccn.loc.gov/2016054831

Printed in China

17/PPS/1